MW00487966

PLEROMA

PLEROMA

MERIDIAN

Crossing Aesthetics

Werner Hamacher
& David E. Wellbery
Editors

Translated by
Nicholas Walker
and Simon Jarvis

*Stanford
University
Press*

———

*Stanford
California
1998*

PLEROMA
— Reading in Hegel

Werner Hamacher

Stanford University Press
Stanford, California

Originally published in *Hegel / Der Geist des Christentums*

© 1978 Werner Hamacher

English translation © 1998 The Athlone Press
Originating publisher of English Edition:
The Athlone Press, London

First published in the U.S.A. by
Stanford University Press, 1998

Printed in Great Britain

Cloth ISBN 0-8047-2183-1
Paper ISBN 0-8047-2185-8
LC 92-85548

This book is printed on acid-free paper

Table of
Contents

mother a hindrance – ontology can be misconceived –
the All in All, and its fall – as – Logos, and self-
excommunication

Kant's moral revolution – the law as transgression –
fate – parricide and reconciliation – beauty as mimosis
– self-castration –capitalism in ethics –self-consciousness, guilt-consciousness – reading as exculpation –
pouring, tearing – a Christian socio-ontology – pleroma
and addendum – material of the text – being, a fetish –
revolution miscarried, ontology miscarried –
Systemfragment 1800 – philosophical unity in place
of political unity – sacrifice: purposeless destruction –
philosophy as sacrificial meal – tragedy of ethical life,
disfigured, delayed – a history of eating – the mouse –
reformation of partaking – revolution of reading –
reading: a political act – the concept within the
tabernacle – the dissonant note within philosophy – revolution without conclusion

the absolute and the time of reading – hic et nunc –
truth inscribed – the double now – reading as
equivalation – retention – movement of inscription
as condition of time – concentric temporality – the
language of time: alteration, iteration – this system
in decay – time eats – corporeal schema – sucking,
drawing, withdrawing, delaying – reading, a fissure
in the absolute – metaphorology – incarnations of the
idea – the active sense of hearing: animal time – logos,
orality – superfluous digestion – blood and nous –
nausea – retching: consolidating the schema – the
disfigured mouth, the distorted analogy – a nauseous
reading – legible–illegible – a mother's milk – Nietzsche
reads – the leech – the eternal return – ruminating
return – Hegel, a woman – process of the genus
as process of disease – vomitives – dialectic of
homeopathy – scene of healing, scene of reading –
feminine cunning, an absolute

PLEROMA

Hegel – once more – wants to conclude and to close.

A philosophy like his, closed as it is in order to round out the circle of the encyclopaedic system, one which has supposedly arched its way back to the very beginning of all philosophy, cannot possibly exclude its future either, must, like a maelstrom, draw every other conceivable theory, every critique which contests it, every new reading which addresses it, back into its own circle, must suck everything back in. . . .

What is supposed to be closed, once and for all, can never cease to close.

And thus every new reading of Hegel's writings finds itself confronted by the dilemma of inevitably figuring at a place already appointed for it within the text it seeks critically to locate, of already being grasped by what it struggles to grasp, of already belonging in advance to what it would appropriate understandingly for itself. It finds itself already read by what it seeks to read. And every new attempt to understand the structure of the speculative-dialectical system, every attempt to analyse it critically, even every attempt to ignore it and turn to something more important, must be prepared to recognize – if indeed the object of understanding, of analysis, of marginalization in general is specifically determined as a system of dialectic – that in searching to identify this determinate object, it has already been discovered by the system, already been caught up within its circling coils. To recognize that it is itself the instrument for closing once again the circle of the system, that in this very reading philosophy and its entire history – once more – contracts.

'The last philosophy includes (. . .) the preceding ones, grasps all previous stages within itself, is the product and result of all preceding ones' (20: TWA, *Hist. Philosophy*, III, 461). But since this *ultima philosophia* claims to be not merely a result but also an act, not merely the product but also the production of what has preceded it, the interpretation of the same must represent more than a purely passive consequence or result of previously inscribed trains of thought, must be its re-production, one in which this philosophy, as if for the first time, produces itself. Thus, after the last philosophy and the end of history, the last philosophy and the history it has completed, once again, return. Thus, according to Hegel, whose philosophy is supposed to grasp every other philosophy, and to grasp this grasping as well, every reading which does it justice and participates in absolute spirit would have to relate to itself as if it were identical with that philosophy and the world-history implied in it, and thereby implicating its 'self' as an act of absolute self-consciousness would have to 'sublate' its object and itself, would have to draw the same teleological conclusion which the last philosophy has drawn before it. Every further stage would belong to the already completed ladder of history, every additional step from which knowledge might relate to itself and to the ladder as a whole would constitute, as it were, the H with which Hegel occasionally signed himself.

The dilemma of interpretation that arises in the case of the last philosophy is an inversion of the hermeneutic circle. Not that the true sense of the text would be rendered inaccessible or somehow distorted by prejudgements that already inevitably deviate from it. Rather that the dialectic of cognitive processes also obeyed by the exposition and critique of this philosophy threatens to become the very same dialectic which is articulated by the texts themselves. That the absolute philosophy and its philosopher, therefore, cannot be disturbed in its 'circle of circles' because every disturbance would already be an element of the circle, or, at the very least, one of its tangents.

This dialectical-hermeneutic circle, not so much an aporia for the speculative process itself as the very form of its self-presentation, can be recognized as a dilemma for the dialectic too only if we ask the question: what defines the transition between the totality of the last philosophy and what comes afterwards in such a way that this synthesis exercises its power even over what seems implicitly to escape its sway? For the speculative theory of philosophy and of history there is, in the strict sense of the word, nothing which can come *after* the last philosophy, nothing which can come *after* the history which is completed, at least abstractly, by that philosophy. There is no 'after' that is not already and still remains a 'before', no 'further' [*fort*] that is not a 'here' [*da*]. Whatever follows the text of this philosophy, even as a reading of the same, is already inscribed within that text, and as the totality of philosophy, internally divided within itself, it must precede itself as its determinate reproduction or as its determinate critique. This structure of prior supplementarity, in which this last philosophy and its reading alike must constitute a feast if they are to arrive upon the scene *post festum*, posits a double demand: that the dialectical unity of before and after, of conclusion and inauguration, must be realized and yet, at the same time, nevertheless remain suspended. For even before the reading reproduces the sense of absolute knowing, whether affirmatively or *ex negativo*, through its supplementary interpretive addition to the text, the reading in question has already entered the circle of the text, already become an immanent moment of its movement. Since in relating to its object it is related to its own structure, the act of reading culminates in self-reflection and thereby becomes itself another variant of the theory of absolute self-consciousness. And even before the reading becomes what it already is, even before it enters the dialectical circle of cognition, even before the active consciousness grasps itself at work there, this reading is still not yet what it already is, still halts before the threshold of its origin and falls short of its destination, arrives too early – and too late – for itself and its consciousness, and thereby opens out its hermeneutic-dialectical circle into a parabola. Although the reading does not approach its text in an external fashion, it is not yet the immanent movement of self-reproduction which it already is. The reading – that of the 'last philosophy' more decisively perhaps than any other – must commence from the not yet in the unity of the not yet and the already present: at a remove from that unity of arche and telos which would constitute the finally successful reading itself as identical with the system of absolute self-consciousness. For the dialectical logos the reading remains an endless foreword, one which transforms the logos into an anticipation of itself and without which that logos could not exist; a supplementary addition which reveals the final conclusion always already drawn by the system to be open after all. The reading introduces its 'self' into the circle of synthesis as a difference that cannot be synthesized.

This difference, which has both logical and phenomenological, structural and temporal determinants, is the condition for the reproduction of the text in its reading, and through those traits of delay, of remainder, of anticipation which it introduces into every act of interpretation, this difference presents the dialectical operation of reading with an insuperable obstacle at the very entrance to the dialectical circle: an incorrigible deviation from meaning's path and process of meaning towards itself. Insofar as this difference makes possible both the self-reflection of the text of the last philosophy in its reading, and the self-reflection of this reading in the text read, opens up, as it were, entry to the path of this reading, it simultaneously excludes itself from its conclusion and renders the speculative self-implication of consciousness impossible within its very 'self'. Through this minimal disruption the categories of self and consciousness, meaning and its reproduction, subject and object are displaced in such a way as no longer to fit into their dialectically defined relations without at the same time exposing these shifts and displacements, without at the same time exposing the impossibility of such relations.

A prior delay is needed to prepare the way between the circular totality of the last philosophy and its determinate reproduction, in order to facilitate their dialectical transition into one another and into themselves; dialectical mediation cannot do without this delay; yet insofar as this difference is not an ontological quantity, cut according to the measure of the concept, it must decentre the absolute centre or middle term which dialectical mediation is intended to establish. The path which difference clears undermines the edifice of the speculative-dialectical system. But this difference, one which corrodes the categories of self and being, of consciousness and meaning, cannot preserve any substantial identity of its own; difference cannot persist, because it 'is' not, and consequently disappears, an apparently subordinate function, within the movement of the dialectical process. The reading which is at work in the text of absolute knowing itself, as its condition, is devoured by that text and, in the double sense which Hegel established for this word, sublated [*aufgehoben*]. Thus only traces or displaced remains of difference can be seen in this text of the last philosophy, which is obliged ever and again to present itself as a reading of all the philosophies which have preceded it, obliged ever and again to formulate the problem of how this text itself comes to be read, and to anticipate its own reading. A reading which wishes to elude the suction of the dialectical circle as far as possible, in order to put itself in a position to descry the structure and dynamic of this circle, must begin precisely from these remnants of its own activity in the text, from that which it is not yet itself, or which it no longer itself is. It must begin, therefore, not merely from the logical structure and the systematic implications of such remnants, but also from the metaphoricity of the text and the phantasmic dimension which is at work in it, from the as it were literary character which determines the self-presentation of the absolute, and from the genesis of the system, which cannot be thought solely on the basis of the completed system's own genealogical model. A philological task, then, which necessarily complements the philosophical task and indicates its limits.

Reading – once more – repeats the conclusion of the last philosophy. But insofar as it repeats this conclusion and turns itself into a moment of a completed history and the thought which thinks it, it opens the circle which it has itself closed and allows the last philosophy, of its own accord, to step out of its own circle.

In the Preface to the *Phenomenology of Spirit*, in the context of his now celebrated analysis of the speculative proposition, Hegel dedicated an admittedly rather incidental discussion to the problem of reading and its repetition. In order to clarify the difference between the formal-grammatical and the dialectical structure of propositions, he explains, using the example of the proposition 'God is Being', how its grammatical subject, 'God', 'dissolves' into its predicate, 'Being', because the subject here encounters its own substance, rather than something merely accidental. A thinking which is orientated towards the grammatical schema of propositions, along with the metaphysics of a fixed subjectivity and an external attribution of accidents, makes no progress in its path from subject to predicate, but instead feels 'much rather restricted and thrown back on to the subject's thinking, because it lacks the same', since the propositional subject 'gets lost' in the predicate that constitutes its substance. Thinking has thereby arrived where it started out; but it has arrived, not at what was originally laid down as a basis, but at what has rightly been lost. The subject can no longer appear as the bearer of accidents, but instead combines and closes with its predicates, insofar as every accident now presents a case of essential predication and therefore reveals itself as cosubstantial with essence. In the speculative proposition the subject ceases to be an independently subsisting objective quantity; instead it unites itself with itself, in the substance which is expressed in its predicate as a moment of itself. The subject, 'God', 'falls' into the universal and is lost, but in its fall into being, which is its essence, it is 'sublated' and finds itself unified with its whole speculative movement of fall and sublation: it becomes the concept. Thus it is no longer the grammatical, objectively underlying subject which is the subject of the speculative proposition, nor is it any longer the predicate which serves to present the substance. Instead the speculative proposition in its totality is subject and substance in one, a circular process of interfusion. In the speculative proposition, in this paradigm of the whole speculative movement of spirit, in which 'the true' is grasped 'not merely as *substance* but just as much as *subject*' (3: TWA, *Phen.*, 23), the grammatical logic of subsumption characteristic of 'representational thinking' [*vorstellendes Denken*] is replaced by the circular logic of dialectical thinking.

This 'dialectical movement, this self-generating, self-developing path which returns into itself' (3: TWA, *Phen.*, 61) of the proposition must provoke an equally dialectical reading, if it is not to be exposed to the rationalistic misapprehensions of 'representational thinking'. As so often, Hegel introduces the model for such a reading in the course of a digression – on the familiar lament concerning the 'incomprehensibility of philosophical writings': 'It is upon this unfamiliar obstacle' of the transition from subject to predicate 'that most of the laments concerning the unintelligibility of philosophical writings are based, even if the individual actually possesses the usual cultural preconditions for understanding them. In what has already been said we can see the reasons for that quite specific objection which is often raised to such writings; namely that much in them must be read repeatedly before it can properly be understood' (3: TWA, *Phen.*, 60). Reading, like thinking, starts out from a static and linear relationship between subject and predicate and finds itself confronted, in the speculative proposition, with the destruction of its presuppositions, the loss of its mere 'opinion', and, as a result, with the loss of what makes its whole activity possible. Just as in the dialectical process of knowing the hypostasis of the securely presupposed subject of knowing collapses, so in the process of reading the subject of reading, which has likewise been represented as a substantial subject, must collapse together with the reified subject of the grammatical proposition (3: TWA, *Phen.*, 61). But just as knowing repeats its reading and returns to the proposition which it could not comprehend by virtue of a restricted concept of propositional structure, just so the reader, the subject of reading who was also himself determined by this restricted concept of propositional structure, is forced to see his own status shattered through his incomprehension, forced to emerge as a subject now 'differently constituted' from the repetition of his reading. The dialectical movement between subject and predicate which is inaugurated by the speculative proposition must therefore be repeated in the relationship between the reader and his text. Only in this way is it possible for the proposition to become more to the reader than an external object which the reader could take into secure possession, while remaining firm, unmoved and at rest within himself; only thus can the proposition become more than a table on which familiar or new items of cognition would be served up. Insofar as he attempts to regain the fixed ground, which he is nonetheless obliged to relinquish, and repeats his reading in this altered situation, he encounters, instead of the fixed substantialized subject, another different subject, one which is bound up with its text as its substance, which has sublated the experience of its loss into itself, and now knows itself to be the result of this loss and of the movement of the text. This is how the speculative proposition draws the subject of reading into its circle. The subject of reading, the reader, and more precisely the act of reading, like the text of the last philosophy, becomes the subject of absolute knowing. Reading becomes absolute reading, a speculative dialexis.

Philosophical writings, then, require unintelligibility as one of their necessary means of presentation. When reading them, not only must the reader (as Hegel's introductory lecture to the *Encyclopaedia* demands) (10: TWA, *Enc.*, III, 415) relinquish his sight and hearing; his understanding along with all its grammatically pre-constituted forms of knowledge must also disappear. The less he understands, the more he comprehends. The more his 'opinion' is given over to destruction by writing, the more securely the system of knowing erects itself within him. Yet speculative reading, like the speculative proposition, can operate according to this model only if it holds fast to its own beginning, to its – false – presupposition, and precisely as a presupposition which has been relinquished. Speculative reading must always be able to return to this beginning, in order to rediscover it as altered. The expressions which Hegel uses to expound the dialectical course of reading and of knowing – to 'go back', to 'come back', 'return' and 'repetition' [*zurückgehen, zurückkommen, Rückkehr, Wiederholung*] – all mark the sameness, if not of the matter, then certainly of the site to which reading returns after the subject of reading, its particular actuality, everything which appeared to it to be a secure possession, has been lost. Something of what is external, restrictive and false must remain, if its loss is to be converted into the gain of immanent truth for the whole. A double relationship, then, prevails here. Only if formal and exoteric understanding disappears can the speculative rise in its place and bring the process of understanding to a close in dialectical unity; yet only if this empty, formal reading migrates into the speculative, fulfilled reading can the dialectical movement of the constitution of truth be the 'path which *returns into itself*'.

Only if an undialectical remnant persists can dialectic enter upon its course and combine what is true with what is untrue as a moment of the true itself. This difference, however minimal, which the speculative act of reading is obliged to leave open in its circle, if it is to close it, is the catalyst of its dialectic. Speculative reading operates with this difference, but can never allow this formal, empty and speechless moment to hold sway except as subordinate to, or as the sheer refuse of, its own eloquent and richly substantive process. It is by virtue of this remnant inhering in dialectic – that something of what has been sublated, and which the course of dialectic seeks to erase until only a trace is left, must still remain – that the reading of the dialectical text, even when it enters into this text and follows its course, can never be wholly dissolved into it without a residue, can never wholly correspond to it without some falsification. Precisely because this reading seeks to be dialectical, it can no more remain immanent to the dialectical process than it can remain external to it. It hovers, uncertain, unfixable, between that inside and the outside, between the subject and its essence, between the actual and the universal, between the particular and the totality, between the same and the same, without reaching what mediates them, their middle. Dialectical reading is a step by means of which the Absolute does not ascend, an inducting ladder which is not speculative dialectic's introduction to itself.

"The last philosophy . . . includes all other stages within itself.' Almost all.

Reading repeats Hegel and repeats, once again – in order to dissolve its own presuppositions – itself. It must repeat itself, because it could not avoid originally losing itself. But what it retrieves is in part distinct from what was given up and lost. Reading returns to 'itself', to Hegel's text, only through this partition, through this internal splitting within its own presupposition, within what is repeated; and in such a way that reading itself still remains afflicted by this split. In such a way that, together with this split, precisely what was separated off also persists within reading. Formal reading, which operates according to grammatically fixed categories of the understanding, must continue, accordingly, to contribute to that speculative reading, which becomes involved in the predication of essence. The inert and object-like, the conceptless subject, the 'name as name' (3: TWA, *Phen.*, 62) – Hegel's name, 'for example' – must continue its work within the purely self-relating concept, within the Absolute. And if the empirical subject of the last philosophy is also to be liquidated in the 'presentation' of that philosophy, like the grammatical subject in its predication of essence, it must continue to exercise its effect within the text of the last philosophy, precisely as something negated. Hegel's philosophy is also Hegel's death. He lies in his text as though in his sarcophagus. Interpretation of Hegel, consequently, must encounter him not merely as a surviving spirit, but also as a corpse. In expounding his spiritual presence, interpretation must also be Hegel's necrologue, a necro-philological operation.

> *There are two versions of an anecdote in which the problem of a hermeneutic adequate to Hegel's philosophy is connected*

> *with the scene of Hegel's death: one provided by Heine,*
> *the other by Kierkegaard: 'I allude here above all to the*
> *comic aspect of our philosophers. They continually*
> *lament that they are not understood. When Hegel was*
> *lying on his deathbed, he said: "Only one person has ever*
> *understood me", but at once added morosely, "and even*
> *he did not understand me".' (42:* Zur Geschichte der
> Religion und Philosophie in Deutschland *[Leipzig:*
> *1970], 152)*
> *'Thus even Hegel apparently died saying that nobody had*
> *understood him apart from one man, who had misunder-*
> *stood him, even if Hegel himself misunderstood himself.'*
> *(56:* Concluding Unscientific Postscript to the
> Philosophical Fragments, *tr. David F. Swenson and*
> *Walter Lowrie [Princeton: Princeton University Press,*
> *1941], 65n.)*

If translated from humour back into deadly seriousness, Hegel's lament
about not being understood – even if he did not understand himself –
would refer to the fact that those elements of his philosophy which are
merely formal, external and mortal, and which therefore are always
already dead, have not yet been subjected to the work of negation; that
he himself, as the empirical subject of his philosophy, has not yet died,
has not yet been resurrected as the speculative subject of his philosophy
in the understanding of its meaning. Only as something which is
essentially past can his 'name as name', his object-like persona, emerge
into the present tense of the concept. From any reading that would
understand him Hegel demands that it take his life. But in this murder
– since there can be no death from natural causes if the death of nature
is a deed and fact of spirit – his body and the corpus of his doctrine
must rise again, transfigured. The life of which reading robs him and
which must also be preserved by this reading is now in immortal form.
The reading must keep at one remove from the corpse, the inorganic
remnant of the organism, just as the corpse itself must be removed
from its tomb of incomprehension.

But Hegel's philosophy itself is already a permanent attempt to
anticipate its own reading by another, to anticipate its own murder. If

Hegel's characterization of the struggle for recognition, which is also a struggle for cognition and the immanent struggle of self-consciouness, is applicable to the act of reading, then every sentence which the philosopher writes, and which, simply as something written, is already aimed at the negation of the immediate present of the reader, exposes the philosopher in his turn to negation, to death through the other. But: 'To him as a consciousness it appears that it is a question of the death of another; but it is a question of his own death; (it is) suicide, in that it exposes itself to danger' (24: *Hegels Jenaer Realphilosophie* [*JR*], ed. J. Hoffmeister [Hamburg: 1967], 211). The self-exposition of the philosopher in his writing is, since he exposes himself to the danger of murder, of the misunderstanding of his intended meanings, suicide. If, however, he succeeds, as his own other, in understanding his own text, then this murder of his constricted subjectivity, consciousness's self-murder, also proves to be the genesis of an indestructible self-consciousness in which the philosopher is securely preserved from the power of the merely empirically other. Yet even factical death at the hands of this empirical other, which for Hegel counts only as an abstract negation, even the understanding of speculative philosophy by an 'other' reader than Hegel 'himself', follows the same economy of self-appropriation. For the other is the power of the self to the extent that the former loses only its object-like character, and, thereby, its limit, through the act of the latter; and thereby lives on unlimited within the one who robbed it of immediate life. The other would not be the murderer, the reader, if the text which he destroys or even simply injures did not survive in him. A reading would operate according to the very strategy of the struggle for recognition and knowledge deployed by Hegel's texts only if it were indeed to act murderously towards its object, but also to know the corpse as its own doing and to know itself as the product of this deed and, in that respect, as also the product of the murdered victim. In such a reading, according to the law of reading laid down by Hegel, the destroyed self, now fortified by the power of the other and protectively clad in the armour of spirit, would be resurrected. The murder glorifies the victim. His text dies and is transfigured in the reader. Hegel's observations on the economy of the demise or survival of philosophical works in his Jena Wastebook are spun around two biblical aphorisms:

> 'Our posterity lasts only until the next mass is said. *Just as everything comes together in the perspective of Reason, so the torrent comes into view from the mountains.* Pedes eorum, qui efferent te, sunt ante januam.'

> '*Science. An individual can only assure himself and others that he really possesses science. Whether it is true will be decided by his immediate environment, the people about him, and then posterity, if indeed the former have already given their approval. Yet consciousness has been developed so greatly through education, the barbaric exertions of comprehension have become so much more rapid and fluid, that posterity arrives in only a few years. Kant's philosophy has long since come to judgement, whilst the Wolffian philosophy lasted for more than fifty years. The standing of Fichte's philosophy has been determined even more rapidly. It will not take long before the essential quality of Schelling's philosophy is revealed. Judgement on this stands, as it were, at the very door, since many already understand it. Yet these philosophies succumbed less to refutation than to the empirical experience of how far one could get with them. Their adherents blindly develop them, but the fabric becomes ever thinner, and they are at last surprised by how transparent the cobweb has become. It has melted away like ice and run through their fingers like quicksilver, without their knowing how this has happened. They no longer possess what they had, and whoever looks into the hand with which they offer their wisdom sees nothing but the empty hand and scornfully continues on his way. Whilst the disciples, feeling the cold, still cry up their wares, the latter think they have fathomed the matter, since they perceive only the nothingness of this philosophy, and not what it once was. Both parties are alike deceived. The truth, meanwhile, is that it is just that which has disappeared which has brought them thus far.*

*The text of scripture is brought to pass: "If we are silent,
the stones cry out."' (73: Ros., 544)*

From reason's perspective, and also from that of reason's medium,
philosophical science, death is what is closest at hand. If the text of the
philosophical work is a web which spreads over the eyes of its adherents, it is the understanding of this text which erodes this web, which
turns this blinding veil to gossamer transparency and thereby causes it
to disappear. Reading raises [*hebt auf*] the curtain on the text. Yet the
empty stage which it exposes to view is no less a ruse than was the curtain which previously concealed it. The scene of the history of philosophy does not present an empty waste of falsified theories, but offers
an ensemble of raised curtains, of incidents and stories which are
themselves the work and property of the gaze trained upon this *the-
atrum philosophicum*. A theory which is not to succumb to the delusion of such an empty waste, such a false transparency, which is not
blindly to excise its own genesis or its own actions, must keep the curtain raised, that is, sublated; its perspective upon the text is the perspective determined by the very text which has been dissolved.
Between blindness and insight, identical with neither blindness nor
insight and yet with both at once, this theory stands upon the
forestage. The corpse which posterity's reading is preparing to carry
from the now empty room remains on the threshold of its exit and
remains *as* the petrified threshold. The feet of those who remove the
corpse are the door and, in their haste, understand themselves as such:
the door of truth.

> *The reader has entered the scene and become an actor in a
> play which he simultaneously watches as a spectator. The
> scene, the interior opened by the reading, is a room with
> a deathbed in it. Yet the identification with the dead
> man practiced by the reader must be represented in such
> a way that the reader survives himself in the corpse and
> beholds himself as a dead man.*
>
> *Two perspectives intersect: the reader's perspective on
> Hegel's corpse, and Hegel's perspective on the reader's
> corpse. Where they cut across each other, however, as their
> divergent intentions meet, penetrate each other and are*

interchanged, the gaze which falls upon the corpse is always also the blind gaze which the corpse – le mort saisit le vif – casts upon the posterity which commemorates it. Two corpses and two masses – four scenes, which from the first sentence of the reading interlock and intervene in one another. For the mass, the double mass of Hegel and his other, the 'Introibo ad altare dei' has always already been sung 'in and for itself'. Yet even if it has faded away, the overture is not over yet. It remains – the threshold.

Hegel, then, once again, is reading. He reads in advance the readings of those whose object is his text and who would like to see in him nothing but an empty hand, a dead dog,[1] whose cadaver is fit only for the knacker's yard. Every reading of Hegel's writings must proceed as though Hegel himself has already read it, as though it were not simply encountering, always arriving on the scene too late, the stiff body of speculative idealism laid out in state, but also coming upon the cadaver of its own form. As though it were coming upon this residue of an organic totality, a residue which, preserved and elevated, nevertheless cannot be smoothly accommodated into the schema of speculative sublation. If both readings, Hegel's proleptic reading and that of his reader, are entangled, mutually implicated in this way, the mass which posterity attempts to read over Hegel's philosophy proves also to be read by Hegel himself over posterity and its masses. The liturgy which both Hegel and his reader observe is not the positivistic liturgy, for which the text merely presents itself as a brute fact, nor the rationalistic liturgy, which reduces all moments of the text to the universally valid continuum of the abstract laws of the understanding, nor the historicist liturgy, which treats the past as something dead and done with for all time, whatever the future may bring; nor indeed its sociological variant. It is the speculative and distortedly speculative liturgy, which receives into its own structure its collapse at the hands of its readers, its petrifaction in the high mass of those who celebrate it, the derision it suffers in the black masses of travesty. In this way, the speculative

---

[1] 'In his own time Lessing remarked that people treat Spinoza as if he were a dead dog; one can hardly say that speculative philosophy is treated any better in more recent times' (8: TWA, Enc., I, Preface to 2nd edn, 22).

liturgy averts its own demise, and yet thereby miscarries in these other liturgies which it also is.

This liturgy and this reading can, therefore, no more be grasped by the concepts of a binary logic than by those of speculative synthesis. The reading does not follow the path of a cultic re-collection [*Er-Innerung*], as urged by hermeneutics, and does not dedicate itself to that external devotion, which imagines that it can treat its text purely historically and control its dynamics. It exercises neither Hegel's mastery nor mastery over Hegel, over his system, his language and its meaning, over meaning *tout court*: otherwise it would be Hegel's slave. And just as identical concepts collapse for such a reading, so likewise the identity of the text, Hegel's status as an author who realizes his intentions, and only his intentions, in the text, the abstract fixing of Hegel's name, and even the identity of the reader and the truth-claim of his reading, also collapse. Even this reading, perhaps, as something which is both more and less than itself, cannot be retained either, cannot be securely preserved and maintained against objections.

Perhaps the mass cannot be celebrated.

> '*Memory is the gallows on which the Greek gods hang, strangled to death. It is often called 'poetry' when one is able to display a gallery of such hanged figures, to drive them around in a circle with the wind of wit, to make them tease each other, and to blow them around into all kinds of groups and bizarre combinations. Memory is the grave, the receptacle of the dead. Everything dead rests in memory as something dead. It is exhibited like a collection of stones. Putting the collection in order, going through it, dusting it, all this bustle has indeed some relation to what is dead, yet is independent of it. – But to mouth incomprehensible prayers, to read masses, to recite rosaries, to perform meaningless ceremonial services, this is the very activity of deadness. Man here attempts to become a sheer object, to allow himself to be altogether governed entirely by something alien. And such service is called devotion. Pharisees!*' (73: Ros., 518–19)

Hegel, strangled, in a gallery of criminals hanged on the gallows; Hegel, hanged himself, driven round in a circle by the wind of wit: this is a fantasy in the style of Callot. But every exegesis of Hegel's writings which tries to catch hold of him and keep him risks gripping his neck and closing around him like a rope. Hegel's reader becomes his gallows, his sarcophagus: his reading becomes a sepulchre of stone on Hegel's name. But the belief that we have thereby grasped and retained something substantial is as illusory as the belief in the mastery of the grammatically determined subject over its predicates. The attempt to mortify the content of the text and its author, setting a stone [*Stein*] in place of this being [*Sein*] can successfully be accomplished only by those who allow themselves to be governed by this content as by something 'alien', who make themselves into its object, who become dead and stony themselves. With the symmetry of a mirror, the hangman is the hanged man, and the apparent independence of reading is only the mirror-image of its absolute dependence on the gallows of the text. 'To read masses', 'to carry out meaningless ceremonial services' – this is the hermeneutics of the dead, the sclerotic circle of interpretation, in which subject and object are petrified and silenced. A dead circle of meaninglessness, in which nothing appears to remain of the life of the spirit, and in which spirit's meaning, itself circular, escapes precisely because it was supposed to be captured.

But in the centre of the mass the altar-stone is erected as a privileged place, without which the mass cannot be celebrated. If this one stone falls outside the context of life and meaning, into which a hermeneutic of non-mechanical reproduction should be able to insert it, then this other stone will be sublated: it will raise its voice. 'The saying of scripture is brought to pass: if we are silent, the stones cry out.' And: 'But God does not remain petrified and dead, since even the stones cry out and raise themselves to spirit' (9: TWA, Enc., II, §247, Addition). As witnesses of death the stones point to the life which is past and are themselves, to this extent, moments of the present knowledge of it. The dead circle of meaninglessness turns into the circle of living meaning. In this way Hegel escapes from the noose of a restrictive hermeneutic, even as he puts his neck inside it and allows it to provoke a cry from him. He turns the mortifying hermeneutic into an affirmation of the true life of his own texts and makes it work to produce his own immortality. But despite this sublation of murder through its meaning, of the stone through its cry, the other stone of which Hegel speaks here, the other gallows which inaugurates no new life, remains behind as a *corpus delicti*: the stone and gallows of the one for whom the mass is not the Christian practice of an identification with a God resurrected from his death, but the pharisaical, Jewish identification with the dead God. Memory, which for Hegel represents a transition into the activity of thinking, remains in this case a thoughtless fixation of what is dead, a gallows, which is supposedly unable to grasp itself, a stone, which is supposedly incapable of crying out.

The deadly silence of reading; a ceremonial standstill of the speculative process before the ghostly scene of the dead burying their dead.

If there is such a hermeneutic of mortification, of the kind which Hegel denounces in the literary and philosophical works of his time, and one which could still be invoked against his own writings, a hermeneutic which does not understand the meaning of that to which it refers, but simply repeats what has been destroyed through its own praxis – how can the stone of this a-hermeneutic practice be transformed into the other stone, which can be made to cry out? What liturgical system would facilitate the sublation of this stone into the Being of the spirit? What liturgical system, what theory of religious practice, would allow the deathly standstill to become a moment in the progress of divine life? Is there such a system, such a theory? Is there a semiotic which can demonstrate that memory is capable of dissolving its merely mechanical reproduction without remainder into the pure production of meaning? For so long as a residue of the merely formal relationship to the text remains, then the totality of meaning sedimented in this text will be unable to return to itself, and the circle of the speculative reading of the absolute, itself still trapped in the circle of a mechanical reading, will remain open.

How are the principles of reason, the laws of the understanding and the demands of sensibility to be related to each other if the open system of a 'popular religion' is to be possible? The theoretical project of such a religion would be directed against the prevailing religious dogmatism and political despotism of the time, and the (still awaited) praxis of this religion would have to be the form in which a politically and religiously self-emancipating and emancipated society would express itself. The problems of an emancipatory hermeneutic and the social generalization of such a hermeneutic, which are the object of Hegel's first efforts as an author, face him in this Kantianizing form.

The theory of religion demanded privileged attention, because it marked the point of intersection between the ideological power of the state apparatus and an ethical reason which had declared itself autonomous. Hegel's questions, inspired by Rousseau and Kant alike, were these: how could dogmatism and heteronomous moral decision have arisen in societies supposedly legitimated on moral grounds; and by what theoretical and political interventions could petrified orthodoxies be dissolved? For Hegel these questions could be answered only by recognizing their necessarily mutual (if only partial) interpenetration. However rigorously Hegel distinguishes the religious system which he contests from those to which he aspires, he emphasizes equally strongly the way in which they are bound up with each other. Hegel emphasizes the distinction between objective, or positive, religion, and subjective religion:

> '*Objective religion is* fides quae creditur *[the faith that is believed], memory and understanding are the forces which are effective here, which examine, elaborate, retain or even believe items of knowledge – instances of practical knowledge can also belong to objective religion, but then they represent only dead or inert capital – objective religion can be tabulated in the mind, can be made into a system, presented in book form and communicated to others through speech; subjective religion only expresses itself in sentiments and deed – subjective religion is a living thing, it is effective in our inner being and in our outward actions. Subjective religion is something individual, objective religion is an abstraction, the former the living book of nature – the latter the display cabinet of the natural scientist who has killed the insects, withered the plants, stuffed the animals or preserved them in spirit.' (21: Nohl, 6–7; 39:*

H. S. Harris, Hegel's Development: Towards the
Sunlight 1770–1801 *[Oxford: Clarendon, 1972], 484)*

Two books, a living book of nature and a dead book of science; a living, circulating capital and a dead, inert capital. Yet there must be some
exchange between the two: the dead account must be entered into the
living one. Each has to be read in the other; one must have commerce
with both. As far as the objective or dead side is concerned, only a
'small and rather ineffective part' of it is 'bound up with subjective religion' (21: Nohl, 7; 39: Harris, 484). The remainder is assimilated into
the living part of religion and modified according to the constitution of
the subjective element. Just as the page of the dead book can be divided
into a redeemable part and a non-redeemable part, so too the living
page of religious inwardness is also divided within its very constitution.
For insofar as it is religion, it must by definition transcend mere morality and the principles prescribed to morality by practical reason, if it is
to satisfy the demands of sensuousness and to make the abstract laws of
ethical life effective in the realm of the sensuous. Religion, even subjective religion, is practical reason's defence mechanism or reinforcement-
mechanism against 'the might of sensuous impulses' (21: Nohl, 5).
Religion is a 'dam'. In order to withstand the sea of sensuousness and
to be capable of exerting an effect upon it, reason must concede a part
of its abstract immovability to the sensuous and unite with it in 'beautiful phantasy' and 'pictorial images'. What reason thereby loses in dignity, it regains as power. The two mutually opposed systems are
reciprocally reduplicated into a four-fold ground plan upon which the
altar-stone for the absolute mass is to be erected. This reduplication
seems unproblematically to stand in the service of the unity and consolidation of the beautiful life of ethical reason. The exchange between
ethical reason's living capital and the dead capital of a sensuousness regulated by rational principles appears to operate for the sake of producing and expanding pure ethical life, of amortizing any loss to a
dangerous sensuousness and an unproductive understanding. The
economy of the living book and of its directly practical reading, is
supposed to master the other, an-economic book by reducing it to a
mere moment of itself, to a sign in the service of sense, a meaning in
the service of being.

All reduction, however, leaves a residue. If religion, by definition, 'cannot possibly be built upon reason alone', but must, for the sake of realizing its own moral principle, enter into an alliance with the sensuous and with the understanding which governs the sensuous, then the theory behind the critical renewal of religion must take account of the logic of these moments which are originally alien to it; and thus also of the logic of the residue, the logic of the surplus of sensuousness and the understanding. 'Sensuousness and phantasy are the sources of prejudices' and 'errors' (21: Nohl, 13) and as such remain an obstacle to ethical truth on its path to self-realization. The understanding, likewise, instead of influencing practical life, merely inhibits that life through its rules. Instead of making it easier for the individual to take possession of his common property in the work 'of knowing God and knowing human duties and nature', the understanding only turns this common property into a bad copy for the sake of realizing narrow private interests. Like sensuousness and phantasy, then, the understanding remains a source of obstruction and deterioration within the system of ethical life. One who follows the dictates of the understanding and 'copies its general structure' cannot be said to live in his own house, 'where even if he has not quarried each stone himself he has at least handled each stone and laid it correctly – he is a dead letter of a man – who has not lived his own life and woven his own character' (39: Harris, 494). The understanding lays down the letter of the law. The law which governs the household of practical reason, its economy, can never lead to the universal appropriation of what is one's own, so long as it promotes a mere copy of this appropriation. Without the spirit of virtue which has disappeared from the written record, from a life which has been literally 'written to death' (21: Nohl, 16), there remains, according to a remark from Lessing's *Nathan der Weise* which Hegel quotes on several occasions, only 'cold booklearning, which is merely imprinted on the brain in dead signs' (44: *Dok.*, 169).

Hegel reads the imprint of the dead sign throughout the whole history of Christianity. Originally a religion of virtue, Christianity has become an objective religion through precisely the means of sensuousness and the understanding which were necessary to its expansion and consolidation, has enthroned the means over the end, the letter over the spirit. The course of history has followed the imprint of the dead sign, beneath whose pressure its meaning threatens to expire. That is why the fatal imprint of sensuousness must be repressed and marginalized. The stone which remains alien, the letter without the spirit, the mechanical gesture devoid of reason: everything which Hegel calls the *fetish* must be superseded – but not without leaving a residue.

> '. . . *it is quite crucial for mankind, that it be led up ever closer to rational religion and that fetish faith should be suppressed; and since a universal Church of the spirit is only an ideal of reason, and it is not really possible that a public religion should be established which removed every possibility of reviving a fetish faith from it; the question arises as to how a folk-religion has to be set up in order (a) negatively, to give as little occasion as possible for cleaving to the letter and the ceremonial observance, and (b) positively – that the people may be led to rational religion and become receptive to it.'* (21: Nohl, 17; 39: Harris, 495)

Yet even suppressed, placed in the service of the idea and sublimated, even so the sublated fetish reduced to a residue retains its destructive power – where it fails to become the purest of ideal means, 'the least susceptible of abuse', to become that 'holy music and the song of an entire people', which Rousseau in his *Letter to D'Alembert* (74: *Oeuvres*, XI [Paris: 1820]) had presented as the pure self-enjoyment of society. Every fetish weakens the presence of what it serves, and leads to the loss of its power. Every fetish, even the most sublimated one – and no system of morality can get by without a fetish, as Hegel concedes – remains a dangerous detour.

> '*This detour to morality via the miracles and authority of an individual, together with the numerous places* en route *where stops are necessary, has the defect of any detour, because it makes the destination farther off than it really is, and it may readily induce the traveller to lose sight of the road altogether in the course of his deviations and his distracting way-stations. But this is not its only defect; in addition, it does injury to the dignity of morality, which is*

> *independent, spurns any foundation outside itself, and insists on being self-sufficient and self-grounded.' (21: Nohl, 161; Knox, 79)*

Ever ambiguous, serving both morality and its antagonists, the fetish introduces a foundation beneath an ethical life already autonomously grounded in itself, one which is alien to that ethical life. This foundation undermines its law, occludes its self-presence and seduces it into seeing the final goal not in itself but in one of the 'distracting way-stations' that lie along the way. The detour via the fetish is supposed to seduce sensuousness into morality; but this detour leads sensuousness astray.

In order to explicate the relationship between the concepts of fetish and writing, so closely connected with Hegel, we must ourselves take a detour. Along with some of the writings of Kant, Rousseau and Schiller, Fichte's *Critique of All Revelation* and Schelling's earliest publications, Moses Mendelssohn's *Jerusalem oder über religiöse Macht und Judentum* (63 [*J*]) must be recognized as a key point of reference for Hegel's first philosophical sketches. In seeking an explanation for the degeneration of an original Judaism with its 'ceremonial law' Mendelssohn discovers – inscription itself. The decline of a living and meaningful religion of law began with its inscription and commentary. 'The dissemination of writings and books, which, through the invention of printing, have infinitely increased in number in our age, has utterly transformed humanity. The mighty upheaval in the whole system of human knowledge and sentiments which it produced' (63: *J*, II, 60–1), this 'revolution' (ibid., 64), did indeed ensure the survival of the law, but it has also had the result that 'one human being has almost entirely lost his value for another' (ibid., 62). 'We do not need a man of experience, we need only his writings. In a word, we have become *litterati, men of the letter.* Our entire being hangs on the letter' (ibid., 63). The anthropological devaluation produced by the letter is redoubled by the degradation of the hidden, invisible Godhead to a concept bound to a sensuous sign. Mendelssohn's semiotics, which is to embrace the whole range of intellectual and cultural practices –

*'In order to show more clearly what influence this has
exerted upon religion and customs, I must once again permit myself a digression from my path, but one from which,
however, I shall shortly return.' (63: J, 63–4)*

– takes its point of departure, like the most advanced eighteenth-
century theories of history and signification, those of Rousseau and
Condillac, from the question of the origin of language. This digression
to the origin leads Mendelssohn to a 'spur' impressed by 'wise
Providence' upon each soul, a spur inciting the soul to form concepts
through the abstraction and classification of striking characteristics of
the sensuous worls, and to fix those concepts in 'sensuous signs' allow-
ing them to be remembered and communicated. Language and writing
are pricked by one and the same spur and originate from the same
process. In just that process by which they sustain the faculty of knowledge, social relations and historical progress, language and writing also
bring about the mortification of cognition, society and history.
Language and writing are cells in which, bee-like, reason collects her
honey and 'stores it for her own enjoyment and that of others' (63: *J*,
77); yet they are also the 'dead corpse' from which all spirit and meaning appear to have fled (ibid., 90). To read these signs is at once to sup
nectar and to devour the flesh of the dead.

The 'mighty transformation', this 'revolution' of social and cultic
relations, which has become an all-encompassing reality with the dis-
covery of printing, is, then, already structurally inscribed in the origin
of language and writing. And that is why even the most recent, alphabetical form of writing, which makes man 'too speculative' and mis-
leads him into confusing a virtuous life with mechanical ritual, is in no
way more dangerous to morality than its original form, in which signs
were 'the things themselves' from which the concepts, like the proud
beauty of the peacock, were then removed. To see in signs – and therefore in things – not merely signs but the things themselves, to see in
animals not a reference to their quality but that quality itself, to see in
images not the representation of a divinity but that divinity itself, to
see in laws not the pointer to morality but the form of its reality – this
inversion, this revolution and perversion, is the work of writing.
Writing is a substitute for the concept which displaces it and usurps its

truth, a truth the idea of which arises in the same process as does writing itself.

> *'And we have seen how such an innocent thing, a mere manner of writing, can soon degenerate in the hands of men and pass over into idolatry.' (63: J, 83)*
>
> *We can be sure 'that the need for written signs offered the original occasion for idolatry.' (63: J, 84)*

'The black marks on a white background' – this 'innocent thing', which, itself inscribed by the 'spur' of providence, rebels against providence and puffs itself up into a providence and into a divinity – is at the same time the most culpable thing. It is a gigantic travesty of the moral law which it preserves; it is a monstrous distortion of the countenance of God which was to shine through it. It is a fetish.

The deterioration of practical reason corresponds to the destabilization of the powers of the theoretical understanding through the fetish of writing. For unless the reader has been initiated into, and thereby already blinded by, the sorcery of the letter, he is unable to decide, on Mendelssohn's account, whether cultic objects are really idols or simply written signs that point towards the true God.

The reader is unable to see where the fetish ends and where the concept of the matter itself begins. It cannot be decided what is corpse and what honey, what is truth and what deception. These terms – for the concept itself is also structured like writing – are too alike.

This is the summit of the fetish: not merely to displace the essence for which it was to serve as a sign, but also to displace itself and consequently to elide the dichotomously conceived difference between sign and signified, between concept and thing, between presence and representation, in such a way that neither term in these oppositional pairs can preserve its validity. What gets lost sight of in this detour is not simply the destination but the detour itself *as* a detour, the categorial possibility of the 'as', and with it any possibility of selfhood and identity.

Like Mendelssohn, Kant in his theory of the fetish – yet another detour – also fails to draw the systematic consequences for his own conceptual framework arising from an analysis of the fetish's function. Both authors describe the fetish, but instead of recognizing the suspension of the system of identity which is marked by the fetish, they attempt to re-establish this system, to fix the fetish *as* fetish in the appropriate place in their respective ontologies and thereby at once to ensure the untruth of the fetish and to redeem the truth of their own discourse.

Kant's analysis operates with means related to, and yet distinct from, Mendelssohn's. Kant's critique traverses a series of 'complements'. Just as – according to the formulation of the *Critique of Practical Reason* – the moral law as a causality through freedom serves as a 'complement' to the possibility of freedom which is merely feigned by theoretical reason (and in which an 'empty place' is as it were kept free for freedom [53: *CPrR*, A 83/85]); just as, furthermore, 'our incapacity' to think the possibility of the highest good or of happiness according to the simple law of moral self-determination is 'complemented' by Christian ethical teaching and the symbol of a 'kingdom of God' (ibid., A 215, A 231) – so too our 'incapacity' for a virtuous life according to the principles of ethical law is 'complemented' by 'conventions' which are to make us worthy of 'supernatural assistance', and therefore of a supernatural complement (55: *Religion* . . . , A 257). The logic of the supplement does not lead to a totality closed in on itself. Insofar as the system culminates at its highest point in 'conventions' which are always susceptible to misinterpretation it remains incomplete, in need of a further complement which cannot be provided. The necessity of a sensuous 'representation' of the ethical collides, in the methods it employs, with a danger of the destruction of the ethical, a danger which can be averted only by empirical and technical means.

> 'Yet for man the invisible needs to be represented through the visible (the sensuous); yea, what is more, it needs to be accompanied by the visible in the interest of practicability and, though it is intellectual, must be made, as it were (according to a certain analogy), perceptual. This is a means of simply picturing to ourselves our duty in the service of God, a means which, although really indispensable, is extremely liable to the danger of misconstruction; for, through a delusion which steals over us, it is easily held to

> *be* the service of God itself, *and is, indeed, commonly*
> *thus spoken of.' (55:* Religion . . . *, A 282; Greene and*
> *Hudson, 180)*

The 'delusion which steals over us' uses the capacity inherent in the human faculty of knowledge to intuit objects even in their absence in order to suggest that the supersensuous is present in its sensuous representation. 'Delusion is the deception of regarding the mere representation of a thing as equivalent to the thing itself . . . even *madness* is so named because it commonly takes a mere representation (of the imagination) for the presence of the thing itself and values it accordingly' (55: *Religion* . . . , A 242; Greene and Hudson, 156). 'Religious delusion' is an excess on the part of the faculty of moral knowledge, which has not ascertained its own rules and cannot ascertain them even by means of theoretical reason. The ground of ethical self-determination, realizable only in an infinite practical approximation, marks the limit of self-knowledge; it opens up before self-knowledge as an absolute lack, as the 'abyss of a mystery' (55: *Religion* . . . , A 199). The hypostasis of the fetish – and in Kant's view not only all religious but all philosophical systems before his own 'critique' have proceeded fetishistically – erects itself as a defence against the maw of this abyss, against that place where the faculty of knowledge lacks an object and threatens to fall and fail.

The difference of knowledge from itself – a difference between the various faculties of knowledge, which is opened by the structure of the imagination – the difference between representation and ideal, requires (as Kant concedes), in order to be bearable, a series of supplements, including the supplement of sensuous perceptibility. The abyss requires a bridge, to whose construction the whole of the *Critique of Judgement* is devoted. Yet the fetish's attempt to make good this lack throws no bridge from the firm rule of knowledge to the mystery of the unknowable, but rather denies their absolute difference and insinuates the unification of the visible and the invisible in the visible, the unity of practical reason and intuition in intuition itself. 'To dream according to principles (to rave with reason)' (52: *CJ*, 125B) like the religious fetishist and like every other fetishist, therefore, *de facto* leaves open the difference which has been denied.

If the Kantian system of complements is not at every point to fall into the danger of a transcendental subreption and a consequent lack of self-determinedness, a lack no longer mastered by any identical determination, even a negative one, then no complement must be allowed to overstep its proper status as a complement. In the system of ethical concepts this is first of all to be demanded of the concept of God, and then of the doctrine of divine blessedness, the equivalent of religion, and in particular of revealed and ecclesiastical religion and their cultic forms. Each of these is to be understood 'as complementary causes of our incapacity in respect of the final moral end' (55: *Religion* . . . , A 267). To wish to influence God is already to have overstepped the limits of the concept of complementary causes of our incapacity in respect of the final moral end (ibid.). To wish to influence God is already to have overstepped the limits of the concept of complement which alone God represents. It is to treat God no longer as a means of moral self-understanding and virtuous practice, but as an object; and to treat that object according to the rules of rational knowledge even though it is beyond such knowledge. It is to make God into a fetish.

> '*Now the man who does make use of actions, as means, which in themselves contain nothing pleasing to God (i.e. nothing moral) in order to earn thereby immediate divine approval of himself and therewith the attainment of his desires, labours under the delusion that he possesses an art of bringing about a supernatural effect through wholly natural means. Such attempts we are wont to entitle* sorcery. *But (since this term carries with it the attendant common concept of commerce with the evil principle, whereas the abovementioned attempt can be conceived to be undertaken, through misunderstanding, with good moral intent) we desire to use in place of it the word* fetishism, *familiar in other connections. A supernatural effect induced by a man would be one whose possibility would rest, as he conceives the matter, upon a supposition that he works on God and uses Him as a means to bring about a result in the world for which his own powers, yea,*

> *even his insight into whether this result may be well-pleas-*
> *ing to God, would, of themselves, not avail. But this*
> *involves an absurdity even in his own conception of it.' (55:*
> Religion . . . , A 256–7; Greene and Hudson, 165–6)

Kant registers, like Mendelssohn, like almost every later theoretician of fetishism, a perversion. The inversion of means and ends, of representation and Idea, of symbolic action and thing, appears with all the more complexity in Kant's system because the substitution occurs in Kant's case within the construction of the hierarchy of supplements. In this detour the inversion for the first time threatens to shatter the system of the ethical. The moral goal, absolute self-determination and freedom, is spirited away: its transcendental complement, God, is regarded as an object knowable by reason and, thus inverted to become a means in the service of the despotism of sensuousness and theoretical reason, can no longer serve as a means of realizing the concept of freedom. The production of the fetish inasmuch as it perverts in this way what for Kant was its original intention, moral praxis, represents a 'filthy superstition (*cultus spurius*)' (55: *Religion* . . . , A 215): it besmirches and spits upon the holy thing it claims to consecrate, the holy mystery of the abyss. The sacrilegious perversion of the maker of fetishes lies in his belief that he has stopped up the yawning abyss of the unknowable, that he has grasped the thing which he has in fact erected there himself.

But the fetishist is groping in a void; in the void of the creations of his imagination, of what his delusion suggests to him as real. From the subjective necessity of his fiction the fetishist concludes that the predicates of the object of that fiction are real; consequently he comes to a conclusion only within the system of his theoretical faculty of knowledge and cannot successfully close his own difference from himself as a subject of freedom. The fetishist closes the argument badly, because he *closes* it. To infer the supersensuous from the sensuous is to graft sensuous forms on the former without critically setting their limits. The *'schematism of analogy'*, from the abuse of which fetishism arises, is, as a footnote to *Religion within the Limits of Reason Alone* explains, indispensable (55: *Religion* . . . , A 75). But what is a schema must remain a schema, and may not (as in the 'cultus spurius') function as a conclusion.

'At this point let me remark incidentally that while, in the ascent from the sensuous to the supersensuous, it is indeed allowable to schematize *(that is, to render a concept intelligible by the help of an analogy to something sensuous), it is on no account permitted us to* infer *(and thus to* extend *our concept), by this analogy, that what holds of the former must also be attributed to the latter. Such a conclusion is impossible, for the simple reason that it would run directly counter to all analogy to conclude that, because we absolutely need a schema to render a concept intelligible to ourselves (to support it with an example), it therefore follows that this schema must necessarily belong to the object itself as its predicate. . . . On the contrary, between the relation of a schema to its concept and the relation of this same schema of a concept to the objective fact itself there is no analogy, but rather a mighty chasm, the overleaping of which [metabasis eis allo genos] leads at once into anthropomorphism, as I have proved elsewhere.' (55: Religion . . . , A 76; Greene and Hudson, 59)*

Only an act of knowledge which opens up the gulf of difference within its own conclusion and keeps that gulf open can bring itself to a close and complete itself as the self-experience of the subject of pure practical reason. If the maker of fetishes cannot comprehend his own nature and limit his own practice; if he remains, autistically, subject to that very power of the other which he has denied; then the subject of morality subjects itself to the law of difference and, in the 'eternal check' which is imposed upon it as a result, understands itself as absolute (53: *CPrR*, A 131). This conclusion, the element in which the whole *Critique of Practical Reason* moves, is – perhaps – unique and valid once and for all. It is a conclusion of pain – arising from that feeling in which sensuousness, curtailed by pure reason, recognizes *a priori* both pure reason and itself, recognizes *a priori* the connection of pure self-determination of the will with empirical heteronomy: 'Here we have the first and perhaps the only case wherein we can determine from *a priori* concepts the relation of a cognition (here a cognition of pure practical reason) to the feeling of pleasure or displeasure' (53: *CPrR*, A

129; Beck, 75). In the moral feeling of respect which arises from pain – once again 'the only one which we can know completely a priori and the necessity of which we can discern' (ibid., A 130; Beck, 76) – the subjugation of the subject to the law of freedom is a subjugation to the law of its own reason and thereby an 'elevation' (ibid., A 143; Beck, 83), self-sublation. The more bowed one's back, the higher one holds one's head; the fuller the conjunction of phenomenon and noumenon, the surer the bridge across the abyss of the rupture: this is the Kantian transition to speculative dialectic.

The pain of the negative within the action of the absolutely autonomous subject, whose Kantian back is bent double, is the pain of the 'comparison' between the subject's 'sensuous propensity' and its moral law, the pain of a collision (53: *CPrR*, A 129; Beck, 75). This pain is the labour of the negative, to which has been prescribed, as its telos, self-appropriation and self-sublation according to the 'schema (if this word is suitable here) of a law' (53: *CPrR*, A 121; Beck, 71). The analogy which was discredited by Kant with respect to the cultivation of the fetish therefore recurs in the only comparison which can be accomplished a priori between the causality of freedom and the causality of nature. The fetishizing schema which institutes a connection between representation and the matter itself is recapitulated in the schema of the law and in the typic of practical judgement, which are themselves indispensable to the knowledge and the realization of morality.

Both Kant, the critic of fetishism, and the criticized maker of fetishes each in their own way throws a bridge across the threatening gulf in self-consciousness; the former through a 'monstrous leap', which leads into anthropomorphism, the latter by determining the abyss of difference as a difference within himself, and by reducing this abyss in such a way that the phenomenal subject can reunite with itself as the noumenal subject – even if only *modo negativo*. Both systems are theo-anthropologies, both systems are fetishisms in that they restrict the immanent split (and necessarily so as far as Kant's bridge is concerned) and place it under the guardianship of the unity of consciousness, a unity which is felt as subjectively realized. The bridge of the fetish-maker, however, is regarded as bad and as a bridge to what is bad, while the bridge of the moral subject is regarded as good and as the bridge to the good. The bridge of the fetish is a substitute, a misinterpreted complement, a surrogate; the bridge of practical reason is the only authentic, original, complementing bridge, the true path of ethical consciousness to its own sensuous actualization. The critique of the fetish, and to a certain extent even the analysis of the fetish, is – as in Mendelssohn, so in Kant – bound to the position of the true, the authentic and the original. But it is also – as a theory *of* the fetish – also bound to the position of a complement which can be misinterpreted, of the delusion of imagination, of the schematizing eradication of infinite difference, of the 'abyss of a mystery'. In order to be able to occupy his anti-fetishistic position, the critic of fetishism must himself reproduce the fetishistic operation of a compact which closes the difference between sensuousness and reason.

And once again – in Kant as in Mendelssohn and, later, in Hegel – the aporia of the critique of fetishism is repeated in the critique of writing and its literalness. For the a priori self-cognition of the moral subject must indeed exclude the untruth of the heteronomous cognition of the understanding, and its fixation upon fetishistic practices, since it is in this cognition that the moral subject grasps itself as a will which freely wills itself. Yet as a cognition which can only be subjective, and which can secure its own ground only with the addition of a regulative complement, a complement which is indeed necessary, albeit subjectively valid, it must expose itself to the risk of fetishism in the subjectively demanded attempt to universalize itself, in the objectification which is postulated by the subjective law. That which is excluded by the fact that the ground, or the abyssal un-ground, of practical reason can indeed be known a priori in the schematism of pain, yet cannot be grounded and therefore cannot be 'publicly communicated' (55: *Religion* ... , A 122), what is therefore excluded as the distorting, fetishizing objectification, must itself be drawn into those forms of objectivation required by the moral law's demand for universality. The pure religion of reason must take a detour through the institutions of church and state, a detour through writing, in order to realize itself in a social association, an 'ethically common substance' (ibid.), and in order to counteract the objective dominance of the fetish which has been made possible by the subjectivity of moral cognition. But following Paul's dictum, which Kant often quotes, that it is the spirit which brings life, whereas the letter kills, the religion of reason risks its own death, by entrusting itself to the letter of a 'statutory ecclesiastical faith' as the 'vehicle and means of public unity'. Yet the life of reason can profit from its death in the letter. This is the place of its 'immutable conservation [and] universal uniform dissemination' (ibid., A 144), which cannot be demolished or interrupted by 'devastating revolutions in the state'. In the writing of 'languages now dead' an immortal remnant of a 'supersensuous origin' remains: objectified, immutable, indestructible. Dead, the corpus of writing is the surest protection against the death of reason. A fetish, writing is the surest monument against the threat of reason's disappearance. The letter is forked in two. If its dead and fatal part, which is supposed to protect, uphold and disseminate its living, supersensuous and original part, is not to invade the latter and destroy it; if the living remnant of an 'aptitude for moral religion' is not to be fetishistically perverted by the act of writing; the letter must be subjected to a comprehensive interpretation in terms of a meaning 'which concurs with the universal practical rules of a pure religion of reason' (ibid., A 150). The 'literal', monumental, fetishistic, sensuous meaning of writing must be brought to reason by interpreting it, the monument of 'immutable conservation and dissemination' must be smashed, literal writing must be returned to that writing inscribed within the heart of moral subjectivity. Yet if the expansion of the reappropriation of reason through the hermeneutic of morality is not to be undone in the letter, it must take place in a medium which allows those heteronomous external authorities which such a hermeneutic contests, in critical fashion, to enter into its circle. The repressed threat of writing to the objectively incomplete autonomy of pure reason, a threat which had supposedly been vanquished, returns unsublatably and *ad infinitum* in the shape of 'particular interpreters' and shatters the boundaries of this autonomy. Even when, as Kant recommends, scripture is not read literally, or, still better, not read at all (ibid., A 144), its interpretation according to principles of practical reason remains bound to the occasion of interpretation, the letter, or, if not to this, to the ecclesiastical or political status of its 'depositories'. The heteronomy of the letter and of its administered reading does not erase but transfixes the autonomy of moral reason and compels moral reason to work away its own marked difference from these heteronomous elements on the way to its objective realization. Through the condition of the possibility of its objective realization, through writing and exegesis, moral self-cognition is deferred *ad infinitum* and the realization of moral meaning becomes, *strictu sensu*, impossible.

Whether interpreted or read literally, writing becomes a fetish, the abyssal un-ground of the mystery runs aground, finds itself condemned to become the ground of writing. In writing, in scripture, dead as it is, the abyss of the mystery has erected for itself a monument of its own life, one which constitutes the condition of the possibility for the objectification of autonomy. In writing as a heteronomous material, one which can never be reduced unproblematically or completely to the required moral-rational sense, the mystery (of the abyss) simultaneously encounters the condition of the impossibility of all such objectification. The infinite progression in the history of political and religious societies finds its structural limit in this aporia of the fetish, which is as necessary as it is destructive to moral self-knowledge.

In his earliest texts, for which, in any case, the boundaries of the Kantian system were never binding, Hegel had already turned the denunciations directed against 'men of the letter' and the fixation upon moral prescriptions, denunciations then current amongst liberal apostles of the enlightenment, in a historicizing direction which prepares for his later critique of Kant. Kant's critique of fetishism, of mere literalness in symbolizing the cognitions of reason, of the dead element in objectivity – a critique which was made possibleonly by presupposing the absolute subjectivity of moral life – was bound to run up against the aporias of its own foundations as soon as it attempted to construe theoretically the conditions for securing and expanding ethical self-consciousness socially. Hegel, then, whose own procedure is no less aimed at a reduction of writing and of the fetish, attempts to link the realization of practical reason neither to subjective inwardness, nor to the 'private religion' of Christianity, but instead to a constitution which would be immediately social, both political and cultic. Freedom, which was for Kant the ground and residue of the self-relating subject of moral cognition *against* the claims of its own sensuousness, is understood in Hegel's work as sensuous, objective, political.

Different grounds, different origins, different parents. Kant's clerics – 'that label which indicates only the appearance of a spiritual father (παπα)' (55: *Religion* . . . , B 269) are despotic fathers of fetishism, who usurp the place of the real father of pure morality, the *summum ens* which is never present and never knowable, and merely conceal his sublime absence with the illusion of his presence. No mother comes to the aid of these children. Hegel's Greece – which, following after Winckelmann, Lessing and Forster, he constructs as a positive counter-image to the Christian West – is a Greece of nurturing mothers, and of a father who reveals himself in his sons:

> 'The father of this Genius is Time, on which he remains
> dependent in a way all his life (the circumstances of the
> time) – his mother, the πολιτεια, the constitution – his
> midwife, his wetnurse, Religion . . . – an aetherial essence
> – that is drawn down to the earth and held fast by a light
> bond which resists through a magic spell all attempts to
> break it, for it is completely intertwined in his essence.
> This bond, whose main foundations are our needs, is
> woven together from the manifold threads of nature.' (21:
> Nohl, 27–8; 39: Harris, 506)

'Garlanded with roses', the Greek genius recognizes this bond as something completely intertwined with his essence; he recognizes in this bond his own work, a part of himself. The fabric woven from the flowers of nature and imagination, the fabric into which he himself has been woven, is not threatened by any 'spectre of darkness'. For even the 'impenetrable veil which withdraws divinity from our view', even this veil, which might, as an obstacle to cognition, endanger the self-identity and the social coherence of a free people, is decorated by the wetnurse, religion, with the flowers of a free and beautiful imagination, and behind this veil the genius of the people conjures up 'living images, to which the grand ideas of its own heart, together with all the fullness of higher and more beautiful sentiments' are attached (21:

Nohl, 28). The social fabric woven out of imagination and nature is interwoven with the veil of Isis, which is a fetish removing from sight the potentially fatal truth of the divinity hidden behind it. But what withdraws, procures. The veil, which conceals the truth of the mother – for Kant an incomprehensible 'abyss of a mystery' – simultaneously opens the possibility of securing the homogeneity of the social fabric by means of imagination, even beyond the bounds of pure reason. The aesthetic self-knowledge of society, which is grounded in Greek popular religion in this way, thus also takes advantage of a fetishistic subreption, which grasps the fiction, but not the actual nature of this mystery.

The fetishistic rejection of the beyond, a beyond which could signify death, is the falling of a veil. Only 'copies' remain of the genius of Greece, copies in which it also resembles that other genius which the West has 'cooked up', resembles the son of a father 'bent double', joylessly and myopically fixated upon 'petty objects' (21: Nohl, 29). It is the kingdom of readers, a kingdom without a maternal *politeia* and without the comforting nurse of popular religion, the kingdom of Kant and of the castrated father. If popular religion nourished its children with the 'uncontaminated and healthy milk of pure sentiments', the children of Christian private religion are terrified of being 'infected by drinking from the fraternal communion chalice cup immediately after someone suffering from venereal disease' (ibid., 27). The politico-religious problem of the fetish, the semiotic problem of writing and of memory, the economic problem of dead, unemployed capital, are all – according to a logic and a metaphoricity whose mechanism remains to be examined – bound up with the organic problem of nourishment. The anti-Kantian affect, upon substantially Kantian premises, remains evident on all levels of Hegel's work:

> *'the man who is always throwing around such terms as 'enlightenment', 'knowledge of men', 'history of mankind', 'happiness', 'perfection', is nothing else but a gossip of the Enlightenment, a market huckster crying stale panaceas for sale – these folk feed one another on barren words, and overlook the holy, delicate web of human feeling – . . . If one or another learns through life itself to understand better something that previously lay in his soul like dead and*

> *unemployed capital, yet still in every stomach there*
> *remains a clutter of undigested book learning – and since*
> *this gives the stomach quite enough to do, it gets in the way*
> *of any more healthy nourishment – it will not let any*
> *nourishing sap flow to the rest of the body – the bloated*
> *appearance gives the illusion perhaps of health, but in*
> *every limb a sapless phlegm cripples free movement.' (21:*
> *Nohl, 16; 39: Harris, 47)*

For the organism of sensuous life, which Hegel's theoretical intervention wishes to unify with the organism of rational life, the meal served up by the moralizing private religion of Christianity in its writings and practices remains indigestible – even and indeed especially where it follows the recipes of enlightenment philosophy. The writing of the fetish, a 'sourdough' compounded of mystical and rationalistic ingredients which is crammed into society's memory and conscience, thereby remains an 'undigested heap of words', which cannot be assimilated in any way into the organism of practical and rational life, which cannot successfully be sublated in it. Hegel develops the dialectic of the private and public spheres, of institution and society, in investigating the process by which the Church, originally operating against fetishism, has grown from a sect to a *status in statu* and then to a state, and thereby dominates the entire market of the social exchange process with its cookery. The Church is the dead capital which trafficks in the secretions of the life process. The 'regiment of clerics' of the Christian state fabricates a negative image of the Greek polis, whose nurse nourished it with the pure milk of sentiment and of the ideal of universal freedom. In this Christian state unfreedom has degenerated into a universal ideal, and truth into a matter of memory, of money, into a 'dead sign', the refuse of real wealth – into a cesspool. If the polis was the kingdom of lactophagy, the state is the kingdom of coprophagy. Truth, aware of itself as life there, has become a ware, a commodity here.

> *'Every church gives out that its own faith is the* non plus
> ultra *of truth, it starts from this principle and assumes that*
> *its faith can be pocketed in the brain like money. The faith*
> *really is treated like this. . . . For the churches it is false to say:*

> " 'Tis the earnestness that flinches from no toil,
> That alone can catch the gurgle of truth's deep-hid spring."
> The Church offers truth in the open market; the stream of
> ecclesiastical truth gurgles noisily in every street, and any
> wayfarer may cram his mind with it.' (21: Nohl, 204;
> Knox, 134)

The polemical opposition between good and bad, freedom and unfreedom, separation and unification, bad and good unification, continues. If pre-Christian peoples could 'fill their souls with great resolutions on the occasion of public festivals' (21: Nohl, 215; Knox, 146), which strengthened their social self-consciousness, Christian doctrine, with its mechanical psychologism of the believer deprived of all 'political imagination', allows only the private self-reflection of

> 'sufferers who can no longer tolerate healthy air and fresh
> water, and who have come to live on insipid broths and
> pharmaceutical concoctions; every wind that presses on
> their innards, every sneeze, every clearing of the throat is
> entered in their diary. Preoccupied as they are with no one
> more than themselves, the most they will do for a fellow
> suppliant is to offer one of their home remedies and com-
> mend him to God's care.' (21: Nohl, 43; G. W. F. Hegel,
> Three Essays, tr. J. Dobbins and P. Fuss [Notre Dame,
> IN: 1984], 73–4)

Hegel wants to introduce a different cuisine, one in which self-conscious spirit would blend sensuousness and reason together. He wants to replace the contagious meal, which sustains commonality only through sickness and which perverts the sacraments into secret mysteries, with another, which would distribute political community to the children from the breasts of a kindly nurse or through her cooking-pots. Hegel's texts wish to be an omnipresent, omnipotent, reconciling nurse – and, finally, to be the mother herself, for whom the nurse is only a stand-in and a helper, a complement. They wish to offer a breastwork against the abyss which opens up under the regime of a stooped and strengthless father – to offer a breast. Every reader would be Hegel's child, reading would be suckling and eating. Yet in order to bring his text closer to the distant Greek nurse, the midwife and wet-nurse (Hegel points repeatedly to Socrates's midwifery as a contrast to Christ's manner of teaching), in order to bring in a better cuisine, to provide a healing medicine against the poisoning ideologies of the Christian state and an aid to digestion for its indigestible excremental writing, a more precise diagnosis and an aetiology of the reigning sickness are required. In order to inaugurate a different mass, the liturgy of the false mass and the ideological and historical grounds of its lasting dominance must be exposed.

The historical moment, the 'now' in which Hegel attempts to intervene, is double, split into two parts – and this is the condition of possibility for any intervention, as well as for Hegel's text as a whole. 'Today those masses of humanity who no longer possess public virtue and have been contemptuously relegated to an oppressed condition need other props'; 'When we have only a private existence, our highest interest has to be our love of [our own individual] life. . . . But now that moral ideas can play a role in the lives of human beings, such blessings sink in value' (21: Nohl, 70–1; Dobbins and Fuss, 102). In the Now of Hegel's texts historical time itself is comprehended in transition. The immanent discontinuity between the Now of Christian oppression and the Now of republican emancipation, between the Now of private property in life and goods and the Now of property in the idea of one's own self and one's social freedom: this rupture in the Now, this difference, however slender, which here opens up, is what makes possible both the theoretical analysis of the form of its past, and, at the same time, the theoretical and practical construction of its future shape.

The rupture opens for the sake of closure. Whereas now,

> *'since the interest in the purely individual character (*Christ as the personal representative of God*) is disappearing . . . and what formerly made the individual interesting to us little by little emerges as the Idea itself in all its beauty, is thought by us as such and becomes our property again, now we can reclaim what is beautiful in human nature, which we formerly projected upon an alien individual, reserving for ourselves only everything nauseating of which 'human nature is capable*

– and it is a question of nausea here –

*can joyfully recognize this beauty as our own work once
again, appropriate it for ourselves once again, and thereby
learn to feel self-esteem for ourselves, whereas we formerly
believed that only what was worthy of contempt could
really belong to us.' (21: Nohl, 71)*

This now, which 'little by little' has begun to overcome its difference
from itself, from its authentic self, would be the fullness of time, the
absolute present, the parousia of the Idea in its beauty. How can the
text which introduces the advent of this parousia wholly become its
arena and, furthermore, how can the society which this text seeks to
construct also do likewise? How can the text actually secure its rights
in, and take possession of, the beauty which has been made over to an
'alien individual', the idea which it has projected on to a divinity, the
treasures which it sees squandered upon heaven, rather than merely
vindicating these in theory (21: Nohl, 225)? How can the existing
alienation be sublated through the construction of a general social
practice?

In order to be able to intervene on terrain ruled by a foreign power,
one requires a pact or tactical accord with that terrain's ruler. The
attack conducted by Hegel is organized according to the strategy learnt
from Socrates, Jesus and Kant, and attempts to destroy the opponent,
not by a frontal assault, but on the flanks and from within.

'Kant abandoned polemic, arguments ad hominem, *he
establishes his principles quietly without drawing attention
to their consequences. . . . – Thus Jesus established the
principle of virtue, although he incidentally also thereby
directly attacked the statutes of the Jews which were
destructive of morality. . . . Socrates, likewise did not
directly contest the mythology of his people' – direct attacks
overturn one positive religion, but lead* eo ipso *to another.'
(21: Nohl, 363)*

Hegelian negation is lateral. It is conducted according to this strategy for the first time in the only text amongst the writings of his youth
which gives the impression of being finished, the *Life of Jesus.* Once he

has, in his previous studies, analysed the historically determined strategic mistake in the introduction of Christianity – to have erected, against the fetish of the religion of law, another fetish, one of miracles, names and observances; to have erected, against the fetish of a hating God, that of a fatherly God – Hegel then attempts to write a gospel of pure reason, to the end of a deliverance from the Judaism epitomized by the ruling ecclesiastical forms of belief. This gospel is still, indeed, fixed upon Christ as an individual, but it is divested of all other fetishisms. Yet even this attempt to bring Christianity to reason and at the same time to legitimate, in its beauty, Christianity's connection with the sensuous domain – as with Kant and Fichte, who wished to bring religion back within the bounds of a pure religion of virtue, and would tolerate religion itself only as an ancillary support for autonomous subjective morality – is quickly pushed aside by Hegel, on his path to a principle of unification which could also constitute a principle of republican society on the model of the Greek polis.

If the *Life of Jesus* was still prefaced by an introduction to John's gospel which was at once Kantianizing and reductive of Kant, 'Pure reason, which cannot in any way be limited, is divinity itself' [21: Nohl, 75], it was followed a year later, in about the beginning of 1796, by Hegel's first great calculated attempt to carry out a critique of Kant by Kantian means, a critique of the concept of duty, of the doctrine of blessedness, and even of the concept of God which Kant had held to be indispensable. Reason is no longer itself the divinity, but rather, where it is 'amalgamated' with sensuousness, something which produces divinity as an 'auxiliary' heterogeneous to reason itself. The divinity is a substitute for a lack in reason opened up by sensuousness, a complement which has become a fetish through its hypostatization. The divinity itself is a fetish. But the lack which this fetish conceals is not, as Kant had asserted, reason's structural inability to grasp itself, but an external deficiency first induced by a historically determined sensuousness, a 'lack of awareness that reason is absolute and perfect in itself – its own infinite idea must be self-created, free from any foreign admixture, that this idea can be perfected only by a removal of just this obtrusive foreign element – not by incorporating this element' (21: Nohl, 238). Hegel the republican defends himself as an atheist against the 'obtrusive foreign element', against the idea of God and its 'foreign admixture' with respect to pure reason, not, as in earlier versions, because he wishes to make the claims of sensuousness and imagination in the social fabric universally valid against the unknowability of the Idea, but because reason itself is for him the absolute, and the idea of a free society is the infinite which must be brought to completion absolutely autonomously, without any heteronomous representation. Atheistic republicanism, as Hegel sketches it in this fragment, is absolute transcendental idealism, freed from Kant's compromises with the reigning political and moral systems.

This Hegelian critique of the Kantian 'complement' which, as an 'auxiliary' of reason, itself opens the gap which it attempts to fill, and thereby brings about the downfall of what it is supposed to shore up, this critique of the fetishism of Kant's critique of fetishes must first and foremost address the amalgam of sensuousness, and thereby oppose a category which appeared indispensable to the project of a popular religion and to the reconstruction of Greek republicanism. The lost unity which Hegel attempts to vindicate here can therefore be no other than the unity of reason with itself, a self-sustaining reason, which needs the mediation of a sensuous nurse as little as it needs a barrier against sensuousness, or the objectification of sensuousness in an image, even a beautiful one.

The purification of practical reason into a principle for a republican constitution free of sensuousness, however, does not lead simply to a conflict with the historical fact that the Greek republic adhered to a 'religion of imagination', but arrives also at a conflict with Hegel's own attempt to protect as intelligible a universal connection between the aspirations of sensuousness and the claims of reason. Instead of leaping over the hyper-Kantian rigorism which has led him into these contradictions, Hegel becomes completely absorbed in it, pushes it to the point where its aporias emerge, and shatters it upon its own immanent contradictions – an example of eristic dialectic, which takes up the position of the opponent in order to defeat it all the more surely; a lateral strategy, deployed now no longer against the Christian gospel, but against the Kantian gospel of pure reason (with the help, it may be added of Schellingian arguments). In the notes of the late Basel and early Frankfurt periods, unity figures as the directly subjective 'unity itself', as the activity of practical reason free of all mediation, from which must be excluded not only the concepts of theoretical knowledge and the manifold of the empirically objective, but also moral laws and their 'infinite object', God, as positive fixations of the pure activity of reason and, consequently, as non-identical with such activity. 'Practical unity is *asserted* by the fact that what opposes it' – and this includes its own concept insofar as it is not one with this practical unity – 'is entirely sublated.' Everything that is object – the infinite, the sensuously finite, the conceptuality of one's own self – is annihilated by the I of practical unity. Ethical subjectivism, freed from the Kantian qualification that its unity is necessarily fictional, conquers the summit, reaches its topmost peak. It *asserts* [*behauptet*] itself and entitles itself to stand at the head [*Haupt*] of all.

A head which – cut off by another head, another title: 'Religion, to found a religion', another text – falls.

Subjectivism proved, when absolutized with Kantian means so as to go beyond Kant, to be an 'extreme'. It proved to be a limit against something other, from which subjectivism must preserve itself and, as Hegel formulates it, from which it must *'save'* itself (21: Nohl, 374), in order not to succumb to its dominant tendencies. But its ruling principle of unity is vulnerable to the contradiction that this unity can 'only' assert itself as the opposite of negated sensuous mutiplicity. The threat which has been warded off returns within subjectivism itself. Since its own principle collides with itself in this way, since its boundary with other things is also its own internal boundary, this unity must absolve itself of its own absolutization. A transition to a different unity, a unity which is no longer liable to the restrictions imposed by subjective reason, must result from the imminent movement of the self-constitution of a pure unity of reason. Whilst the 'highest subjectivity' 'fears objects, and flies before them', its unity arising from a 'fear of unification' with that which would mean the death of its principle (21: Nohl, 376), this highest subjectivity and its ethics prove to be a further figure of its fetishism. An inverse fetish, as it were; for if Kant, in order to safeguard for practical reason the freedom guaranteed by unity, linked his concept of the fetish to the rule of objects and the hypostasis of theoretical reason, Hegel demonstrates, by radicalizing the principle of subjectively practical reason itself, its own (negative) dependence on the world of objects, the fetishism of the practical unity of reason itself. This dependence is positively reproduced in Kant's epistemological reduction of the ideal of pure reason to a mere representation, so that the realization of its freedom and infinity must always remain only a representation or unification with a representation; the status of true reality, the fullness of being, is never attained:

> 'to say that "I believe that it [the existent, unification] is" means "I believe in the representation, I believe that I am representing something to myself, I believe in something believed" (Kant; divinity); Kant[ian]. Philosophy – positive religion. (Divinity is holy will, humanity absolute negation; is united in the representation, representations are united – representation is a thought, but what is thought is nothing existent.' (21: Nohl, 385)

The representation of subjectivity is a fetish. It imagines a unity with objects and thereby imagines the unity of subject and object, which it must itself assert to be possible. This is the consequence of Kant's doctrine: that each of the highest concepts towards which moral action is directed has only the character of a complement and a regulative fiction. These moral fictions, representations and fetishes are to compensate for the absence of reason, in order to facilitate the installation of reason as a measure of conduct. To the extent that these subjectively necessary fetishes exclude the objectivity at which they themselves are aimed, they negate the principle of their own formation. The affirmation and the negation of unity, of being, come together in the hypostasis of the pure unity of reason, in the fetish. The fetish of pure subjectivity, the conceptless measure of action, the head which seeks to affirm itself, hesitates, sways, turns around and falls headlong into the fetish.

> The child has 'retained his faith' in the 'phallus of the woman (the mother)' but has also 'given it up. . . . In very subtle instances both the disavowal and the affirmation of this castration have found their way into the construction

> *of the fetish itself'. (36: Freud, 'Fetishism', in* On
> Sexuality *[Harmondsworth: 1977], 353, 356)*

Both the assertion and the decapitation [*Enthauptung*] of the unity of
pure practical reason are implied in the fetish of Kantian subjectivism.
Hegel makes himself the executor and executioner of these implications, especially of self-affirmation and self-negation, which for him
indicate the ground-plan of the Kantian system. He allows the veil to
be lifted and discloses to the gaze the idea of a more complete unity,
the scene of love:

> *'only in love are we one with the object; it does not domi-
> nate, nor is it dominated. . . . Every unification can be
> called a unification of subject and object, of freedom and
> nature, of the actual and the possible. . . . Love can only
> occur over against the same, over against the mirror, over
> against the echo of our own substance.' (21: Nohl, 376–7)*

The main interest of recent research into the genesis of German
Idealism has centred on the text cited here, entitled 'Morality, Love,
Religion' by Nohl. This research regards this text as evidence of an
unmediated revision of foundations on Hegel's part, and believes that
it cannot be explained as following on from any previously existing text
of Hegel's. In its first half this sketch still argues from Kantian premisses, whilst in the second half, 'almost as if through an incomprehensible rupture', an 'entirely different' theoretical orientation appears, an
orientation which can be conclusively explained only by the influence
of Hölderlin's earlier doctrine of unification to which Hegel was
exposed in Frankfurt.[1] So Dieter Henrich, who first discovered the
connection between Hölderlin's philosophical sketches and the development of Hegelian philosophy, formulates the matter. Yet the
'incomprehensible rupture' is the rupture of the concept of abstract
subjectivity. In the first half of the text Hegel elaborates its negatively

[1] 43: D. Henrich, *Hegel im Kontext* (Frankfurt am Main: Suhrkamp, 1971),
63 ff., 24 ff. Henrich suggests that the second half, headed 'Religion, to found
a religion', be treated as a self-sufficient text. On the grounds of the argument
set out here it cannot claim such self-sufficiency. The possibility that the two
halves of the text might have been written at a distance of several days or perhaps even weeks from each other has by no means yet been excluded. The state
of the manuscript makes such an assumption probable.

determined character with great rigour ("Unity itself, which only saves
itself against . . . is asserted through the fact that what is opposed to it
is entirely sublated') and demonstrates with the same rigour, especially
in the last three sections of this part, the necessity of immanent contradictions in an ethics gounded upon pure reason, which is here discussed within the categorial framework which Schelling took over from
Fichte. The argumentative use of a Kantian systematics serves the
intention, more radically here than in earlier texts, of destroying this
same systematics from the inside. The self-negation of Kantian theory
which Hegel's texts carry out mimetically, as it were, proceeds rigorously – not with linear rigour, indeed, but with dialectical rigour – to a
unification which, in contradistinction to the unity of practical reason,
appears to be able to remain true to its concept: the unification of love.
Here Hegel can fall back – as he also does in other contexts in his previous writings – upon a very early conception of love, whose synthesizing anti-Kantian potential first vigorously asserts itself in this context.
In a Tübingen fragment on popular religion he constructs an apparently 'empirical' character, whose basic principle, love, an analogue of
reason, is supposed to ground 'moral feeling' or, in Kantian terminology, the a priori moral self-knowledge of pure reason:

> *'To this empirical character, enclosed within the circle of*
> *the inclinations, the moral feeling also belongs, which must*
> *send out its delicate threads through the whole web; the*
> *fundamental principle of the empirical character is love –*
> *which has something analogous to Reason in it, thus far –*
> *just as love finds itself in other human beings, or rather by*
> *forgetting itself – goes beyond its own existence, and, so to*
> *speak, lives, feels and acts in others – even so Reason as the*
> *principle of universally valid laws recognizes itself again in*
> *every rational being, as a fellow citizen of an intelligible*
> *world.' (21: Nohl, 18; 39: Harris, 496)*

Hegel indeed qualifies his argument with the reservation that it
refers only to the empirical sphere and suffices as a principle only in
respect to the foundation of a popular religion; yet whilst he conceives
the latter in its turn as an instrument of, and a form of articulation for,
a universal free unification, love, as the analogue of reason and the

foundation of reason's experience, attains a rank which enables it to solve the dispute between reason and sensuousness in a different way from that allowed by the Kantian schema. That Hegel could take up this concept again in Frankfurt does not mean, of course, that this would have been possible without Hölderlin's influence. The confrontation with Hölderlin's theorems must have had an extraordinary effect upon Hegel, just as the confrontation with Schelling's dialectic had done earlier. But this effect was not a rupture of, but rather a catalyst to, the Kant-critique which Hegel had long been continually radicalizing, and to his attempts to construct a connection between sensuousness and reason which had been developing in the earliest sketches. None of Hölderlin's arguments enters Hegel's text in an unmediated form; each of them, even the account of the immemorial unity of pure being, which can never be an object of consciousness, and which cannot be restored in any identity, is won anew by passing through reflections which in each case are linked to particular passages from Kant. Hölderlin's influence on Hegel, then, however great it might have been, is reworked to such an extent in Hegel's Frankfurt texts that it no longer represents the incursion of an 'entirely different' theoretical conception, but a dialectical rupture with positions whose fragility had already been intimated.

The reasons for the lasting sway of positive religion (so Hegel can now answer his old question from the basis achieved in Frankfurt) lie not only in the way the ideology of this religion has become objectified in material relations of domination, but also in the radical critique of these relations, which, under cover of opposing them, makes common cause with them: 'Kant. Philosophy – positive religion'. If Kant's rigoristic moral philosophy is in solidarity with the fetishism which he criticizes – if this ethics is in solidarity with the fetish – then Hegel's own attempt to secure anew the principles of Christianity on the basis of practical reason must be seen as a failure and, once again, must be undertaken on the basis of love. For love is henceforth the grounding principle of unification which can sublate the incoherence of a fetish-ethics understood as a contradiction, which can bring together in a totality the concepts of subject and object that such an ethics opposes to each other, and so can for the first time accomplish what Hegel requires of religion, that it be able to unify the characteristics of sensuousness with the claims of imagination and the laws of the understanding. Only a religion capable of providing this unity can inaugurate a republican social constitution and serve as its ideological buttress; only such a religion arises from ontological premisses which are free from contradiction – free from contradiction, in that it is destined to dissolve all contradictions, oppositions, and to disclose logical as well as political relations of domination – and forestalls its own degradation to a fetishistic means employed by a society, since it represents itself the principle of socialization. True 'religion is one with love' (21: Nohl, 377).

Whilst Hegel seeks to found such a religion and, since he finds the principle of such a religion present in Christian doctrine, prepares to restore Christianity as a religion of love, he does not merely *read* the history of the emergence and development of Christianity, but also *writes* the gospel of a new Christianity, the gospel of speculative idealism, and describes its forms of objectivation and its necessary collapse. In reading Christ and in restoring his religion, Hegel identifies himself with Christ, the first founder of a religion of love. And just as Christ erects his doctrine against the empty formalism of a belief in fetishes, against the letter of the Jewish law, and demands that the spirit of the law should be satisfied; so Hegel turns against the Judaism into which Christianity itself has ossified, and against the puritan moral law of Christianity's critics. Kant is the Jew; Hegel, Christ. But insofar as he writes his own work, his own philosophical foundation of a religion, as an allegory of the gospel of Christ, he has also already given up the identification with Christ, and is able, as a different figure from the finite Christ, resurrected only in finite form, to describe the collapse of the gospel as conceived by speculative idealism, and the collapse of its historical objectivations, as though he were a spectator independent from the course of its history.

In this way Hegel's speculative idealism, which finds in 'The spirit of Christianity and its fate' its first, still sketch-like elaboration, is exhibited or allegorized, not merely as a theory, but always also as a metatheory. Hegel reads himself writing. The difference between writing and reading which is at work here, and which determines both, must, however, displace, or, as Hegel puts it, sublate, any position as soon as it has been adopted. Transcribing himself from his own future, the Hegel allegorized in Christ becomes more than the mortal and dead Christ, more even than the merely allegorically resurrected Christ who still survives, in a limited way only, in his congregation: he becomes the Christ who has become one with the father, the speculative Christ, who can always already localize the shape in which he has historically come to be – his corpse, his scripture, his fetish – in a historical space which he himself produces and exceeds. A writing which, in erasing itself, spiritualizes itself. A feast of love, in which everything death-like is consumed and transformed into the substance of spiritual life. A politics of religion, whose moments of domination are eroded by mutual collision, in order to make room for concrete freedom. Yet this transubstantiation is open to a reading other than this circular one, a reading of this reading, in which its unity – once again – collapses, and in such a way that unity is not restored as the unity of the self; a reading in which difference, which this reading has freed from the deformations of allegorical form, opens up like a tear in this allegorical figure, out of which authentic, speculative meaning is to speak.

If it is a question of the genesis of a speculative Christianity, of a religion of the fulfilled unity of being, how is the defectiveness of the moral law exhibited in the historical allegory of the cultic and political constitution of Judaism, on the basis of which Christian doctrine can emerge? On the basis of which of those arguments, which have, as it were, become history, is anathema pronounced upon idolizing a deity which has become a representation [*Vorstellung*] and an object-like [*gegenständliches*] image? And what new insights into the structure of a fetishism condemned yet universalized by both Kant and the Jews are brought to light in the philosophical allegory of its genesis? Why – once again [*noch einmal*] – the feast [*Mahl*] of writing? And if the gap in the letter, in the fetish and in fetishistic ethics is to be susceptible of being closed, how did it open up?

The diremption from nature, from which the split beween the law of nature and the law of freedom results, the split between subject and

object, between reason and its ground and, beyond this, the domination of cultic regulations, is the consequence of a diremption *within*
nature. A diremption within the giver [*die Geberin*], within the one
who gives birth [*die Gebärerin*], within Mother Nature (21: Nohl,
355), who here appears cold and there was mild, who once appeared
in her nourishing form and now appears in her devouring form, at
first a unity and later a figure of division. It is 'Noah's flood', a deluge
which 'spared nothing for the sake of any distinction made by love'
and thereby effected a complete tear in nature's image and in the relationship of her children to her (ibid., 368, 243–4). This tear within
the mother is repeated on every level of Jewish experience. Abraham
tore himself free, first from his homeland and then from his whole
family, and the first act 'through which he becomes the ancestral
father of a nation is a separation which tears apart the bonds of love
and communal life, which tears apart the totality of the relationships
in which he had previously lived with nature and other human beings'
(ibid., 245–6). He owes his fatherhood itself to the repetition of this
tear, as it has been experienced in the shape of the mother. The tear at
the origin of the whole Jewish nation, which separates itself from all
other nations, serves at the same time, through repetition, to ward off
the tear which opened up in nature. For that which posits itself as different from something other to it – as different from nature, from
other peoples, from the family, from its own deity – gains, in losing its
unity with these, the security of not losing its own life in this unity.
The tear protects against this tear and masters it through identification. The ideal of this domination is not posited by Abraham as something actual that is subject to the dominion of nature, but rather as
something thought, which in its strict opposition to the whole nevertheless guarantees unity with it. Not the unity of a loving unification
into the form of a beautiful nation, such as the Greeks could create,
but rather a unity under the abstract principle of an all-ruling idea.
Abraham, who conceived this idea of an absolute authority following
Noah, certainly found his own separation (from mother, family, the
rest of humanity) repeated in it, and saw the power granted him
through this tear infinitely intensified; yet since in this defence against
the threat of the mother, her power, the power of what has been sepa-

rated off, also makes itself something infinite, he must himself depend upon his own positing. The dialectic of defence – that it recapitulates once again the very danger which is to be defended against – is the dialectic of parting, the dialectic of the mother. This tearing off from the mother is supposed to be banished, the abyss is supposed to be bridged, by the fact that something infinitely different from her is set opposite her, according to the principle of separation which is laid down in the mother herself. But in this infinitely different element the mother's duplication, her tear, her parting, is repeated and reduplicated. With the hypostasis of the Jewish principle of the unity of an imageless God, the tear in material nature is transcendentalized to just the extent that it is warded off. That which can alone be present in imageless presence is excluded from any present whatsoever. Parting is the Absolute.

But if it is absolute, how can it give evidence of itself? Where the pure tear holds sway in its double form as both threat and protection, there is no longer any space for the knowledge and objectivation of its transcendence. And yet the minimal condition for just this mastery over the world of the finite, the world of particularization, of separation, is that something finite and distinct from pure separation survives. Since the totality of the Jewish deity is not the unity of separation and unity, as is the god which emerges from the play of the Greek national spirit with nature (21: Nohl, 369), but rather a particularized moment hypostatized into the whole, everything which is distinct from it, that which is separate from a totalized separation, must be reducible to it. As something reducible, however, it must *remain* and therefore remain as something different from the transcendental. What is separate from separation, the movement of the self-appropriation of separation, remains, therefore, suspended and set against its own truth. The mirror-relationship between the transcendental and what is thematized under this term, a relationship upon which Hegel emphatically insists in his exposition of the Jewish religion (ibid., 369, 372, 373), can reveal itself only in the possibility of rupture, through the necessity of a difference between pure separation and separation as it is manifested in the social and cultic constitution of Judaism. A mark must interrupt the empty, imageless mirror.

In his exposition of the unity of the Jewish race, Hegel (albeit cautiously) emphasizes, as he had already done in his reading of the biblical allegories of 'Noah's flood' and the tower of Babel, the sexual traits which are at work in its constitution. The being and the unity which Abraham attempts to guarantee in the idea of God is, with mirror-like symmetry, at once the unity and the being of Abraham's race. Since, however, the idea of the unity (of separation) excludes a unity with what has been separated, the empirical race must live as a heterogeneous element, disturbing pure unity, in a state of sacrificial victimhood, in a state of castration. Where the race becomes actual, in the form of Abraham's son, and begins to differ from the ideal unity of being, it appears as 'something heterogeneous, as disturbing pure unity, as unfaithful to this unity through love of the same' (21: Nohl, 372). In order to protect the transcendental unity of the race in God, the condition of its possibility, the empirical race in its individuality, must be sacrificed; for the sake of Being the actuality of the race must collapse, even though Being was set up as a measure of that actuality. Or rather, the actuality of the race must be capable of collapsing. For if the destruction of the empirical race for the sake of the purity of the ideal race were to be completed, the unity and the mastery which the latter itself demands would be destroyed likewise. The castration through which pure unity is realized as pure separation would be reduced to a circumcision. Abraham 'cleaves to his isolation, which he also made conspicuous by a bodily peculiarity imposed upon himself and on his posterity' (ibid., 246). Abraham's race is not castrated, but it carries the mark of castration.

Between pure difference and empirical difference, the difference of the mark inscribes itself as the condition of the possibility of both the former and the latter. The tear of the mother still holds sway in the relationship between the transcendental and the empirical forms of the defence against this tear. Absolutization, the mirror's pure speculation, castration, sacrifice, are interrupted; henceforth Abraham's race lives as the mark of this rupture between the transcendental and its objects, between pure meaning and its sign. The rupture within the mother also denotes itself with this mark: it is neither the opening of pure lack, nor pure presence, which declares itself in its absence, neither castration nor the phallus in its negativity, neither sensible nor intelligible, but between and identical with both: the fiction of castration which wards off its impossible actuality.

The mark of circumcision, which feigns the pure cut, is a fetish, which infinitely postpones and distorts the pure cut, and through its infinite delay first makes this cut possible as ideal or material. A fiction without which there could be no truth. A compromise between the claims of the transcendental and the empirical domain of its rule, a sign of the covenant, a covenant in which the rigorous bond of identity is cut through, precisely in order to preserve the parties to this covenant.

The kingdom of the Jews is the kingdom of the universal fiction of castration. In order 'to realize their idea of unity ... they rule' – as Mother Nature does in pouring forth her flood – 'mercilessly, with the most outrageous, harshest, tyranny, exterminating all life; for unity hovers only above death' (21: Nohl, 248). Whatever enters the isolated domain of this unity of death is, 'with satanic abomination', levelled down to this fictive homogeneity. Hegel comments thus upon a passage from the first book of the Pentateuch, chapter 34, in which circumcision is connected with death:

> '*Outside the infinite unity in which none but they, the favorites, can share, everything is matter (the Gorgon's head turned everything to stone), a stuff, lifeless, with no rights, something accursed which, as soon as they have power enough, they treat as accursed and then assign to its proper place if it attempts to stir.*' (21: Nohl, 248; Knox, 188)

The Medusa allegory returns in Hegel's essay on the 'relation of scepticism to philosophy', against those who, like the Jews, contest the possibility of reason's self-knowing. They thus make it easy for themselves

> '*to remain quite ignorant of reason and its self-knowledge and instead, hiding behind a Gorgon-shield, immediately, not through any malicious twisting or artifice, not as though they had once seen otherwise, but in the gaze itself, they transform reason subjectively into the abstract intellect, and*

> *objectively into stone, and call whatever they think goes*
> *beyond the abstract intellect, beyond petrifaction, "ravings"*
> *or "phantasies".' (2: TWA, 235)*

The 'infinite unity' against whose destructive power the people whom it has elected protects itself, by making themselves identical to this 'unity', is something which has been split off, something distinct from the organic unity of natural and rational life. Once cut off, this unity is the Medusa's head, the material fiction of its lack of unity and totality, which must make that upon which its gaze falls like itself in order not to become like it. Thus at its glance everything turns to stone, to understanding, on the spot; it becomes inorganic matter and statutory law, which stops the breath and brings to a standstill the freely flowing life of reason. The erection of the stone is the reverse image to that of the fiction which, as 'castration', has become the principal object of psychoanalytic research.

> 'We have seldom attempted to interpret individual mytho-
> *logical figures. Yet it is natural to do so in the case of the*
> *terrifying cut-off head of the Medusa. Cutting off the*
> *head = castration. Horror at the Medusa is also horror at*
> *castration, which is also connected to a gaze.*
> *The Medusa's gaze turns us rigid with horror, turns the*
> *onlooker into stone. It has the same lineage as the castra-*
> *tion-complex and results in the same transformation of*
> *affect! For rigidification signifies erection, that is, in the*
> *original situation, the compensation for the onlooker. He*
> *still has a penis and is assured of this by becoming stiff.'*
> (37: Freud, Das Medusenhaupt, in Gesammelte Werke,
> XVII [1922], 47–8)

Hegel's use of the 'mythological creation' of the Medusa emphasizes, more decidedly than Freud's interpretation, that the subject of understanding's self-protection against what it is not, the petrification of the race in the face of the threat to its existence, the self-assertion of the head against the cut-off head, themselves repeat the cut against which they defend themselves. Like the exhibition of the cut-off head, the exhibition of the vulva, according to Freud, represents an 'apotropaic action'; just as, therefore, the exhibition of the cut protects against the cut, so the erection of the stone against the cut, which the Medusa's apotropaeon uses as a threat, itself sets up the cut. The erection of the stone, of 'loveless and lawless matter', is a mimesis of the 'infinite unity' of death, of which the Medusa's head, the circumcised Jewish race, set themselves up as the image. One apotrope is set up against another: one sign of the cut against another. The difference which is exhibited by both, is not a substantial defect, an essential Nothing; rather, it is a fiction, which is intended to show the border of another fiction, the border with its 'self'. Thus neither death nor an authentic life, neither castration nor the complete phallus, neither the free flow of reason nor the stasis of the understanding, are possible except by differing from what they 'are'.

> *There is no apotrope that would not also be a castration; no castration that would not also be an apotrope. No apotrope, no castration. No dividing cut can be made between the two. Both are fictions, which make their own truth impossible. Not even the gaze of the reader, paralysed by the Medusa's mark, by the letter of its law, a gaze which is itself part of the scene it surveys, can restore its substantial truth. At once stone and Medusa's head, even this gaze remains merely the threshold of the truth of its object and of its own truth. Allegorism – allegory.*

The difference from living unity in the 'infinite unity' of death opens an infinite series of compensations. Since there only ever is a unity as something different and split off, then a relation to the material which is immediately at hand, to matter, is possible only as a relation to something indifferent, the loss of which can in any given case be compensated for by something equally indifferent. 'Matter is in this way absolute for human beings' (21: Nohl, 378). Precisely because matter is not absolute in itself, not something unconditional, it remains, posited by human beings by means of theoretical reason, something opposed to humanity, something which is endlessly different. Since it no more contains 'the root of its essence in itself' than does humanity, there is, as with human beings, no connection between its potential infinity and the finite form of its appearance. The 'alien power' which could provide such a self-relation of matter is itself thinkable only as posited in opposition and is equally incapable of producing a connection between its own infinity and any finite appearance: divinity is itself modelled on the structure of matter.

The system of Jewish – and Kantian – ethics is, according to Hegel's critique, a transcendental materialism. Its divinity is a matrix from which, restricted to its own infinity, everything finite is of itself excluded, leaving only a husk behind as its substitute, a husk which separates divinity from its children. The transcendental mother withdraws herself and her love. What remains is a 'holy mystery'.

> *'The infinite subject has to be invisible, since everything visible is something restricted. Before Moses has his tabernacle, he showed to the Israelites only fire and clouds which kept the eye busy on a vague play of continually changing shapes without fixing it on a [specific] form. An image of God was just stone or wood to them; "it sees not, it hears not," etc. Though there was no concrete shape to be an object of religious feeling, devotion and reverence for an invisible object had nonetheless to be given direction and a boundary inclusive of the object. This, Moses provided in the Holy of Holies of the tabernacle and the subsequent temple.' (21: Nohl, 250; Knox, 192)*

Divinity, in order not to be limited, is indeed invisible, and yet is an 'enclosing boundary', and, in the temple, a cut-out quadrature is set around divinity itself, not merely as a place for its adoration. The unlimitedness of divinity is a curtailed unlimitedness, and where a foreigner seeks the 'root of the national spirit' at the 'centre of worship' he is 'disappointed' to find this mysterious secret 'in an empty space' (21: Nohl, 251) – not indeed within an empty space, but precisely as this empty space. The dialectic of infinite negation: what makes the chosen people into nothing is itself a nothing; what turns other things to stone is itself the pure form of the stone; what 'castrates' is itself 'castrated'. Hegel notes, not in his text but in a marginal note cut off from his text, that

> *'The priests of Cybele, the sublime godhead which is all that is, was, and is to be, whose veil no mortal has ever lifted – her priests were castrated, unmanned in body and spirit.' (21: Nohl, 250; Knox, 191n.)*

Hegel is noting an analogy. He links the name of Yahweh handed
down by Moses – I am that I am and that I will be – with the trait of
unknowability and sublimity and implicitly cites a marginal note from
the *Critique of Judgement*: 'Perhaps nothing more sublime has ever been
said, nothing more sublime has ever been thought, than in that inscription over the temple of *Isis* (Mother *Nature*): "I am all that is, that was,
and that will be, and no mortal has ever lifted my veil"' (52: *CJ*, A 195).
The differences are obvious. What all named and unnamed divinities –
Cybele, Isis, Kant's sublime divinity and that of the Jews – have in
common, however, is that they hide like a pudendum behind the veil
of invisibility; that divinity is a female who deprives her priests of the
possibility of 'knowing' her – sexually or intellectually. She enthralls
them, according to Hegel's exposition, in the form of the 'empty space'.
Space, the matrix, the condition of the possibility of empirical knowledge, at the same time exhibits the condition of the impossibility of
any knowledge in itself. For just as the mystery of the 'empty space' can
never become an object, since, in Kantian terms, it only ever constitutes the subjective *condition* of objectivity, if the limitedness of subjectivity is hypothetically sublated, empty space means 'nothing at all' (54:
Kant, *CPR*, A 26). Space itself, therefore, is the most durable, irremov-
able veil, the pure form of sensuousness which is imposed together
with mortality, which only death, the absolute negation of sensuousness, will tear away. For mortals the veil, the curtain, the fetish cannot
be lifted, cannot be sublated. To sublate it, or to preserve it – both
mean death.

The priestly apparatus of the Jews, their temple and their tabernacle,
form the scene of death. In an early text treating of the difference
between the Christian and the Greek ideas of death, Hegel compares
dying both with a feast and with the theatrical self-presentation of an
orator, events for which the Christian prepares himself as for a 'terrible
catastrophe', whilst the Greek 'goes directly and uninhibitedly to meet
it as though he were at home with it'. The metaphorical concern of the
fragment is an explication of the Greek word σκηνή, which figures in
the fragment's title and signifies protection, shadow, tent, hut, stage, a
cultivated space, dwelling and feast (cf. 44: *Dok.*, 51). Just as the stage
of the Jews is imageless, their tabernacle empty, and just as they only

find a place to dwell, which preserves their separateness and protects them from contamination by anything heterogeneous, after long wanderings, so their feast is also insubstantial and empty. 'The possession of a land rich in milk and honey, the assurance of eating, drinking and reproducing children' are indeed, like everything else, a gift from the deity and its way of manifesting itself to the faithful: for without a 'gift', without an 'exception' from infinite difference, neither difference itself, nor infinity and unity, nor the limitedness of the finite could be asserted. Yet this present, a gift and an exception, is in the event withdrawn, insofar as nothing ideal, nor anything significantly symbolic which could furnish a connection between the ideal and sensuousness, is given in this gift, but only the means of reproduction of their 'animal existence', their nothing. The exception sets up the rule of 'infinite separation'. There is indeed something given – but there is no gift.

With the reproduction of their sensuous existence they likewise weave the veil which separates them from the absolute riches of the divinity; as they devour the meal of milk and honey, they reproduce the rupture which separates them from the engulfing mother, and, as they receive her gift which is withdrawn, relinquish the capacity to know more of her than the indication of the impossibility of knowing her. The meal [*Mahl*] of milk and honey repeats the mark [*Mal*] of castration. In that 'an assurance of being able to eat, drink and reproduce' opposes the terror of the physical power of lack and death; in that they ward off the rupture [*den Riß*], the bite [*den Biß*] of the mother, when they eat the meal vouchsafed them by their divinity, their eating is directed as an apotrope against the threat of castration. The apotropaic feast is the castrational feast once again. Both cling to the limit, to the law, to the veil – to the fetish; the fetish is served up at both feasts.

The logic of the fetish-feast is the logic of transcendental materialism: every mouthful of knowledge indeed prolongs sensuous enjoyment, but at the same time separates this enjoyment from substantive knowing. A poor meal of leavings which have fallen from the sumptuous feast of truth at the table of the divinity. Unphilosophical fragments. They feed on refuse, and this – refuse, withering leaves, excrements – is what they are:

> *'The Jewish multitude was bound to wreck Jesus's attempts to give them the consciousness of something divine, for faith in something divine, something great, cannot make its home in a dunghill . . . the whole of life* has no room *in a withering leaf . . .* [the Jewish relationship to God is] *a child's relation in which a man might put himself with the rich overlord of the world whose life he feels wholly alien to him and with whom his only connection lies in the gifts showered upon him, only through the crumbs falling from the rich man's table.' (21: Nohl, 312; Knox, 265)*

But the Jews, contrary to what the implicit quotation of the parable of Lazarus suggests, are starving people who are not received into the nourishing lap of the father; they are refuse that is not picked up [*aufgehoben*]. They do not sit at the table where the father and son share the meal of reconciliation, but sit at the fetish which divides them from any possible reconciliation and exposes them to the compulsions of a merely fictive unification, to a hunger for a merely fictive food. Yet fetishism, which is supposed to be incapable of any ontological relation, is nevertheless related *to* the ontological; the empty fetish is still a derivative of the plenitude of being. What falls – whether withered leaves, scraps, stone, or excrement – falls as an unvalued superflux from the full table of a feast of love which life sets before itself; a bare, dead remnant, which is not preserved within the totality of plenitude. The fetish itself, accordingly, would be refuse, superflux and remnant, incapable of sustaining the ontological relationship in which the whole and its parts come together in the speculative movement of totality. It would be the fiction which is not dissolved in the truth of the absolute, the meal which totality itself must exclude in order to be the *whole* meal. This partition carried out by the absolute is an obstacle to the material concretization of the absolute in history and in the cultic and political constitution of society, a moment which dismantles the truth of the absolute. Hegel's whole exertion must therefore consist in the attempt to show that the remnant is an integral part of the whole, to incorporate the scraps into the feast of the absolute, to admit the fetish on to the universal scene of truth and – once again – to make the stones cry out.

But how can the fall of Judaism be prevented? How can it even be sublated? How can the letter of its law be read other than as affirmation of the fictive character of truth? How can a stone be turned into bread, how can the scraps of the fetish be set out at the feast of the concept? Is there a whole without a remnant – a meal [*Mahl*] without a mark [*Mal*]?

Hegel leaves us in no doubt that the system of transcendental materialism is incapable of sublating itself into a whole; that it remains a mere fragment. The mouthful which is never the whole must always take another bite; the hunger which is never satisfied by the meal of the fetish must surrender itself to the hunger for another kind of food, in order to be satisfied. If, that is, the 'bestial existence' (21: Nohl, 258) to which the Jews find themselves reduced through the hypostatization of their divinity, is restricted by the boundaries of finite life, these boundaries can be crossed only through free submission to them for the sake of the ideal. In the movement of a late Jewish sect, the Essenes, Hegel notices the first step towards such a transgression.

> *'Unlike later enthusiasts,* [the Jews] *could not give themselves up to the axe or to death by starvation, because they adhered not to an Idea, but to an animal existence.' (21: Nohl, 258)*

The Essenes were the first who were able to free themselves in this way from the dependence on eating and drinking, which for the Jews represents the only dependence. As they give themselves up to the axe or to death by starvation, they do not claim the means to their sensuous existence, but they do claim the right to them. If the Jewish system of self-preservation was built on an economy of symmetrical exchange, it is the Essenes who, like the Greeks, break through the circle of fictive equivalence and give up actual life for the idea of their life; who sacrifice one thing which is heterogeneous to another.

> *'It is contradictory to stake this property and this existence for property and existence as such; if one thing is sacrificed for another, both must be heterogeneous – property and existence only for honor, for freedom or beauty, or for something eternal. But the Jews had no share in anything eternal.' (21: Nohl, 253; Knox, 195)*

The greater the loss, the greater the gain. The more unreserved the relinquishment of property, the more secure is ownership of its idea. Yet even the Essenes did not succeed in satisfying this core proposition of dialectical theory – which Hegel, incidentally, could have read in Schelling's interpretations of tragedy in the *Letters on Dogmatism and Criticism.* Hegel characterizes them, using a Kantian formula, as 'enthusiasts', because their sacrifice remains a flight from actuality into the idea of a unity without multiplicity, and therefore remains empty. The pang of transcendental hunger, to which they surrender themselves, is unable to satisfy the idea of reason in its actuality. The hunger pang of the difference between unity and difference remains unsatisfied. Even the developed economy of the abolition [*Aufhebung*] of property pauses before the threshold of the concept. The rupture remains open, although its closure is announced with the Essenes.

The status which the Jews assume in Hegel's early texts is comparable with that ascribed to the Negroes in his later system. But if Hegel absolutely denies to the Jewish religion of the fetish the possibility of sublation, he already attempts both in the lectures on the philosophy of history and in those on the philosophy of religion to emphasize those moments in the very structure of Negro fetishism which are determined by the movement of the concept and which can therefore be admitted into the fully developed form of the concept. Nevertheless, African religion is not discussed in the lectures proper on the philosophy of history, but only in the general introduction, where it is expounded under the rubric of the geographical basis of world history. This place in the exposition of history befits it because Africa 'is the compacted land of gold, the land of children which is veiled in the black hue of night beyond the daylight of self-conscious history' (12: TWA, *Phil. History,* 120) – because it keeps itself 'closed' against any connection with the historical world and, historyless, unopened, merely tarries 'on the threshold of world history', before the 'actual theatre of world history'. Its cultus does not realize the true concept of religion and is, as its 'lowest, untruest stage' (16: TWA, *Phil. Rel.,* 272), not even 'worthy of the name of religion' (ibid., 275). Nameless in this way, invisible as night, and closed off, this untruest and remotest stage of spiritual life resists the participation of 'our' feeling – for 'we' can indeed understand a dog, as Hegel frames the comparison, but cannot empathize with it (ibid., 276) – but the concept, on the contrary, does not shrink before it. In this its blackest, most spiritless shape the concept still sees its own light revealing itself. The spiritual in the dog. History in the historyless. The theatre in its forestage. For the 'first form of religion, for which we have the name of sorcery, is this' – and in this it is already a prelude to the highest form of religion – 'that *the spiritual is power over nature*' (ibid., 278).

Mastery over natural forces, which the apotropaic religion of law of the Jews also serves, is expressed in what Hegel calls natural religion through the fact that everything natural is supposed to be effected by the self-consciousness of humanity. Thus the Mongolian shaman or the African sorcerer, decked out with costume, jewellery and mask, rails against hostile storms, chews roots, spits into the wind, stabs with a knife at the clouds and 'inscribes circles and figures in the sand' (16: TWA, *Phil. Rel.*, 283). Whilst the individual consciousness objectifies itself in spitting (once again – a *cultus spurius*), in stabbing and inscribing, it opens itself up to the objective moment in material nature, recognizes its own power, now universalized, in material nature, and 'unites itself with itself as essence'. In fetish-worship, this speculative syllogism takes place not in a spiritual element but in what 'remains external', in a significant thing which is discovered or made; yet in a thing which by the fact that it changes and destroys the other thing represented by the menacing power of nature, goes beyond its mere materiality and posits itself as ideality.

The fetish-object, then, is not merely an instrument for mastering nature and for the accomplishment of sensuous desires (to which the fetishism of the Jews seemed to be restricted); it is, beyond this, a mediation between the desire of sensuous consciousness, which is objectified in the fetish-object, and the self-consciousness which emerges from the destruction of the fetish-object's mere materiality. Consciousness relates to itself in the fetish and through the fetish. Fetishism is consequently an act of the self-sublation of the sensuous into spirit, the fetish a finitely speculative object. Whether stock, stone or serpent, it is always the writing in which the desire of the subject negates its own sensuousness and relates to itself as universal significance. It is a

writing in the sand, which slakes itself – its thirst – through the movement of the material and transforms itself into 'independent spirituality' (16: TWA, *Phil. Rel.*, 295). Yet the spirit is still unfree in this
movement of the thing, since its bondage to objects, signs and pictorial
representations is retained.

If the consequence of Jewish fetishism was a transcendent God and
the unknowability of that God, and hence a rigorous delimitation of
the sphere of human mastery, in the African religion of fetishes humanity retains power over the things which it has produced. This convert-
ibility of the fetish – its ability to be now the subject and now an object
of power – cannot be explained simply by differences in social forms or
in their respective statuses in the system of spirit. For even if the maker
of the fetish faces his product as an object which is at the disposal of his
capricious desire, he also remains under the sway of this fetish to the
extent that he receives an intuition of his power and self-consciousness
only through this arbitrary product. Not only, then, is the fetish
always latently at once the subject and object of power, but through it
its dynamic man, its producer, himself becomes a fetish. In Hegel's
exposition of Negro fetishism, for this reason, man appears in the
highest place amongst the range of things to which 'independent spirituality' is attributed: 'The last thing in which independent spirituality
is contemplated, is essentially man himself, a living and independent
thing which is spiritual' (16: TWA, *Phil. Rel.*, 295). And, indeed,
man, not as a natural substance, subject to the natural power of death,
but as one which, like the fetish-object, is freed from its merely object-
like character by the fact that it is exposed to the caprice of desire and
to death as a capricious act. Murder, which sublates the limit of finite
determinacy, thus becomes an indispensable determinant of fetishism.
Hegel attributes the highest importance to the fact that through murder man steps out of nature's sphere of mastery on to the threshold of
spirit. Just as he notes in the account of love in the *Jenaer
Realphilosophie* that

>   'the north American savages kill their parents; we do the
>   same' [24: JR, 202]

so in the *Philosophy of Religion* he points out how the Galla and Gaga
hordes and the Indians kill their old and infirm parents,

*'a practice which unmistakably implies that man should
not be deprived of life by nature, but rather this honour
should be done him by another human being.' (16: TWA,*
Phil. Rel., *284)*

The domain of the purely self-relating spirit is not yet entered with
the murder of parents. For although the validity of Spirit's immediate
physical existence is indeed abolished [*aufgehoben*], the 'remaining contingent modes of its particularity', the remnants of its organic life, the
'immortally sensuous' element of bone, the idea of organic survival, are
not relinquished and continue, as something heterogeneous, to exercise
power over the living.

Bones and remnants of the images of ancestors are indeed spirits,
but they are not spirit. The empirical time of the sequence of generations is indeed sublated by the fact that it is only by murdering their
parents that the children give them the power of parents, that they first
beget them as parents; the restriction which the fetish-forming desire
experiences in this death brings this desire closer to its infinity which
returns into itself – yet to the extent that what remains has only the
contingent existence of images and bones and not the absolute form of
spirit free from sensuousness, which can unite with itself in its other,
both the fetish and its creators remain unsatisfied. The parents are, as
corpses and as an idea, still a sensuous writing and they need – once
again – to be read. The reading which, like the shamans' figures, they
require, is as sensuous as they themselves have remained. They require
to be fed, not on the thought of life, which a conceptual reading might
offer them, but with material food, which preserves the living too.
They require food and drink.

The medium of their demand is the sorcerer, who declares before the
assembled people what the 'departed spirit' demands. He is 'the speaking corpse'. Hegel quotes the Capucin missionary Cavazzi:

*'The influence of a hellish demon is manifested in him,
and he screams horribly, he demands the blood which has
not been brought to him; he seizes a knife, stabs someone
in the chest, hacks off heads, cuts open stomachs and drinks
the blood which flows out; he devours heads and shares the
flesh amongst the others, who gobble it up indiscrimi-*

nately, although it may even be the flesh of their own rela-
tives; they know this in advance, yet go to this assembly
with the greatest delight.' (16: TWA, Phil. Rel., *299)*

In the second example which Hegel cites, 'The Gaga imagine that
the dead are hungry and thirsty. If someone becomes sick or especially if he has dreams or visions' the Singhili interprets these to be
the apparitions of a dead relative, who demand to be appeased and
'reconciled':

> *'. . . if he had only recently been buried, then the corpse is*
> *dug up, the head is cut off and cut open; the various fluids*
> *which stream forth must then partly be consumed by the*
> *sick person as food, and partly applied to him in the form*
> *of plasters . . . spirit has thereby reliquished any right to be*
> *regarded as something worthy in itself.'*

The examples which Hegel has chosen from the travel narratives
with which he was familiar are not arbitrary. They are moments of the
systematic architecture of his philosophy of religion, in which the various forms of cult, including those which, like the African ones, remain
at the untruest stage, are expounded as pre-figurations of the absolute
religion of self-knowing truth. The cult of the Galla and Gaga hordes is
to be read as a prefiguration of the Christian cult. What Hegel explicitly confirms in the exposition of anthropo-fetishism ("the presence of
the spiritual in human beings and human self-consciousness as essentially the presence of spirit') – that divinity has its actuality in human
beings, whether in the shape of a magician, a lama, or a Christ ("the
Christian religion explains this and transfigures it' [*er- und verklärt es*]
(16: TWA, *Phil. Rel.*, 297) – this is true in the same way of the Gaga
totem feast. This appears explained and transfigured in the Christian
communion, stripped of its sensuousness, externality and immediacy
and reduced to its essential form, its spiritual significance. If the
eucharist for Hegel is the interpretation, the spirit of the bodily sign
constituted by the cannibalistic rite of the Africans, then such an interpretation, which as a concept is always already present in the fetish-
feast itself, must at least in its presentation be realized through the
system of religions: in the circle of the system the highest stage of the
self-presencing of spirit must re-unite with the lowest. To the extent

that the communion explains the cannibalistic feast, the latter must contain not merely a genetic but also a structural explanation of the latter. The articulations of self-consciousness read each other.

This reading is the whole and a part of the whole. It formulates the way in which the individual shapes of consciousness are reciprocally determined within their totality and interprets this totality through each of its individual figures. What is worked out between the whole and its parts, between the eucharist and – for example – the totem feast, is worked out according to the law of the system which assures the repetition of the one within the circle of the different, once again in the totem feast and in the eucharist. The meal – whether the meal of the system or of the Gaga – is a meal of reconciliation. A reading of love. The deified fetish of the corpse, the bones of the parents, the written characters in the sand: they make good their power over the living and demand to eat and drink, to read sensuously. Resurrected from the dead, they begin, through their privileged readers, the magician, the priest who makes himself their medium, to speak, to kill and to drink of the substance of the sensuously living, whom they need in order to survive. The priest distributes the flesh and blood of the sacrificial victim to the assembled congregation, he offers – in the other scene cited by Hegel – his own body as food in order to be able to slake his own thirst and hunger through the one who ingests him, who sensuously identifies with him. In the fetish-meal the dead do not merely devour the living, the living also devour the dead, in order to receive their power and immortality in their own life. The allelophagy by which the sons devour the father and the father the sons, as in each case other to one another, is transformed, in the feast's circle, into autophagy. The dead man, as a living man, devours a dead man – and in him, devours himself; the living devour the living as assimilated to the dead – and in this devour themselves. The differentiation between gonephagy and teknophagy is dissolved in the circulation of corpses and life just as much as is that between eating and being eaten.

What I read, reads me, and, in me, reads itself. I read what reads itself in me – my own reading.

The feast of reconciliation which is played out in this scene of an exchange of equivalents is based on the absolution of murder. For just

as the murder of the father turns him into spirit, 'explains and transfigures' [*er- und verklärt*] him, so the father is to be eaten in order to turn
oneself into the father and into a participant in the substance of society, the murder of murder, the negation of negation, which extends its
power over organic life and guarantees its immortality. The reconciliation is not only a reconciliation between organic life and a life which
has become inorganic; rather, through the incorporation and reincar-
nation of the 'departed spirit', it is also a reconciliation between the
father and himself in the shape of his sons, between the sons and themselves in the shape of their father – an intensive infinity, which no
longer has a limit in anything but itself. The fetish is sublimated, generalized, absolute. It is no longer a heteronomous power against the
desire of the individual subject, no longer the other, which stands over
against the one as its negation, as its death and its victim, but the
corpse which has been consumed, negation which has returned into
itself, the socially generalized form of desire itself.

Just as Freud shows in his analysis of the totem-meal in *Totem and
Taboo* that through the incorporation of the murdered father the prohi-
bition upon the exercise of absolute power is internalized and elevated
into a moral law, so Hegel shows that in the meal of the fetish the
desire for the death of the other in fact refers to itself, and, self-
restricted, driven back into itself, that its self-negation crystallizes in
the law of an exchange between the living and the dead, the individual
and the universal. Through the totem-meal the fetish, now sublimated,
becomes the law of socialization.

The fetish is the dead entity which digests itself; a tabula which sublates itself.

In this way all the means which sensuously determined subjectivity
uses in order to validate its universality, objectivity and ideality, point
to the success of subjectivity's self-realization, even though all of them,
reification in the fetish, murder, cannibalism, appear as forms of self-
destruction. Through their implicit self-negation, however, they reveal
themselves to be mediations – in the strict sense that what is merely
material is idealized, in the sense that murder is absolutized, and cannibalism is sublated into a social synthesis. The meal of the Gaga, whose
'example' Hegel incorporated into his system, realizes the sublation of

the fetish so completely, that it has only to be 'explained' [*erklärt*], in order to be 'transfigured' [*verklärt*] into the authentically speculative meal, into communion.

The sublation is realized too completely, yet not completely enough. Wherever the system of incorporation, the system *tout court*, is always already realized, it is for that very reason always not yet present to itself, since although the system's individual moments, once totalized, enclose themselves as their own parts, its process cannot comprehend its whole and its parts at once. Even the Christian Eucharist must collapse from this lack in the face of the substance of absolute spirit. And in the face of the demand made by the Eucharist for a subjectivity which is universal in itself, the Gaga-meal which has been transfigured in this Eucharist disintegrates. The sign of this meal determines how it is interpreted, structures its process, but cannot completely grasp this process within itself. Its part falls out of its whole, the whole falls, unsublated, out of its part and is only reincorporated through a hierarchically regulated repetition of the self-inclusive process of knowledge. This split, at which the system of knowing must slave away, and without which it would not be an internally differentiated totality, is effected in the cannibalistic meal of the Africans through the insistence and the superfluity of contingent sensuousness. For what remains of the murdered parents does not have the form of spiritual, but of material life, which 'indeed can die once again and hence twice' (16: TWA, *Phil. Rel.*, 300) and dies on still another occasion together with the sensuous existence of the one who eats it. Always once too often. And the meal itself, as something bound to sensuousness, is in any case too much. This is not the meal of conscious knowing, in which something spiritual, itself, is devoured, but the meal of unconscious knowing, of sensuous self-identification; a meal of forgetting:

> *'the situation of this mastery (over nature) is a* numbing of the senses, *in which the particular will is forgotten, extinguished and abstract sensuous consciousness is intensified to the highest degree. The means of producing this numbing are dance, music, shouting, eating, even sexual congress, and these elements are what at a higher level become the cult.'*
> (16: TWA, Phil. Rel., 301–2)

Not only are the particular will and the individual consciousness forgotten and obliterated through the activity of the body, through its dance, its devouring and its sexuality, but also the self-identity of the subject, which nevertheless at the same time begets itself in these practices. Bodily excess allows the sublation of the fetish immanent to the subject to be forgotten, and allows the objective power of subjectivity won in this sublation to be exhausted in the transient feast. The subject is not yet what it already is. Its being, the sublatedness of the fetish, is still 'veiled in the black hue of night' (12: TWA, *Phil. History*, 120) which the unconsciousness and incapacity for consciousness of corporeal excess spreads over it. The very mode of sublation has cast the veil of forgetting, another fetish, over the sublation of the fetish itself.

But what is this sublation of the fetish, if there is one sublation which preserves the fetish and one which sublimates it, which recognizes its truth and which grasps this cognition itself as the process of its truth? All rationalistic critiques of fetishism, beginning with that of the Enlightenment, proceed from the assumption that fetishism must be unmasked as an illusion – a necessary illusion, but one determined by the history of the individual or determined socio-historically – behind which the truth, whether about the relations of production or about the fact of anatomy, is kept hidden. Critique wishes to lift up the veil of the fetish at all costs. It wishes to discover the truth, whether this is announced as a presence or as a lack. The detective-like gesture of these theories of fetishism, however, is itself a fetishistic gesture in that they proceed from the presupposition that a manifest truth could be revealed to them behind this veil and that this truth is disclosed in their theoretical analysis: the fetishism of theory, of the gaze, which makes of itself a substitute for the lacking sensuous presence of its object, of divinity, of truth, of real anatomic relations or of relations of production. The gaze of theory, fascinated by the fetish and its equivalents, sets itself up, petrified, in the face of the truth of its object as an *apotrope* against its threat: itself, like the fetish, at once an assertion and a denial of this truth, itself, like the fetish, at least partially still in a state of untruth, of illusion, and of the veil.

In his text on 'Fetishism' Freud insisted on the fetishist's ambivalence towards castration. In his analysis of the fetishism of the thief of the lock of hair – and which critic of fetishism would not wish to distinguish between the truth which is concealed behind the veil, behind the hair, and this veil 'itself', which critic of fetishism fails to perpetrate a rape of the lock? – he emphasizes that in the aggressive operation against the fetish, 'the need to carry out the denied castration has been pushed to the fore. His action unites in itself two mutually incompatible assertions: the woman has kept his penis and the father has castrated the woman' [34: GW, XIV, 317]. The fetishistic position of the gaze of theory is not altered by the fact that an organic fact has been posited in place of the phantasized castration. Even in this positing the wish for truth and self-certainty, the denial of the sexual and epistemological difference which dissolves every certainty is in play.

The critique of fetishism has always also been a critique of writing, of materiality, of the corruption of spiritual presence through the unconscious and through bodies, of the inversion of the hierarchy between sensuousness and idea, between actuality and its mere sign, a critique of perversion. Just as the great idealistic polemics against the fetish and its alliance with political despotism were carried through on the secure ground of an ethics of self-consciousness, so they were obliged, with respect to the ideal of the freely self-willing subject, to conceive of its connection to sensuousness and its fetish-creating power as itself a principle, as an anti-subject, against which the true subject, the subject of truth in its historical process, was obliged to assert itself.

This danger is not entirely escaped even by that analysis of fetishism which furnishes the material for the economic and sociological critique of the fetish which currently prevails – the Marxian analysis, whenever it begins investigating theoretical, religious, political and economic practices from the unity of the ideology-creating subject. – The table, 'an ordinary sensuous thing' becomes a 'sensuously supersensuous thing' full of metaphysical subtleties

*and theological imaginings' once it enters into the circle of
capitalistic production – the table as a moment of the
reproduction of capital is a fetish (60: MEW, XXIII, 85 et
seq.). What brings the table to these imaginings is not its
material character, not its 'natural form', but its value – a
social relation, which is not graspable in an object-like
[gegenständlich] form, yet must be embodied in the objective form of a commodity. The character of the commodity's
producedness has been erased from its material shape.
What it embodies is really displaced by the table: and this
is its fetish-character, that it exhibits as a material relationship what is in fact a social relationship of different
acts of labour to each other. The table, which as a commodity is endowed with a life of its own and is apparently
emancipated from the way in which it has been produced
through work, becomes capital, becomes the automatic
subject, becomes the self-produced divinity from which
bourgeois society reads off what that society itself is and
what it ought to be. The ideological self-understanding of
capitalistic society flows, therefore, according to the way it
is expounded in the fetish-chapter of* Capital, *from the
single source of the objectification of labour, as it is rendered possible through the exchange of equivalents. The
subject of fetishism is the 'fetish of capital' (60: MEW,
XXV, 837). The expropriation of sensuous work in the service of the phantasmagorical self-appropriation of the
worker in the form of capital – this is the negative utopia
of self-relation, which inevitably hovers over bourgeois
society. Yet just as in the fetish of capital the traits of its
being produced are erased, they are equally erased in the
analysis of the fetish which Marx presents in the manifest
formulations of this chapter and which in many respects
facilitated the revisionistic reinterpretation of those texts by
Marx which had a different emphasis. For here the site of
production of ideologies is, economistically, posited in the
unity of the subject of capital [Kapitalsubjekts], a unity*

*which is itself merely ideological, without any exposition of
its conditions of possibility in the 'material work' of bodies,
of language, which does not merely reproduce capital but
also generates the conditions for its destruction; without
taking into account the relatively autonomous production
of ideologies in sectors other than the economic. The condition of the possibility of the class struggle on ideological
grounds, of the class struggle tout court, lies, however, in
the difference which opens up in the 'automatic subject'
(60: MEW, XXIII, 169), in capital itself – in the collision
between different fetish-making practices, which are not
reducible to a single one according to the dialectical logic
either of capital or of absolute knowing. The strategy of
this struggle cannot simply oppose itself to fetishism as such;
rather, it must permanently and without any teleologically
anticipated end oppose all those kinds of fetishism in which
society has the material illusion of being an autonomous
unity, the illusion of a proprium. Against, therefore, the
traditional, restrictive concept of the fetish, which suggests
that there is something free and authentic which is free
from displacements and objectifications, from fetishisms.
Even the ideal of transparency, of the rationality and universal self-determination of society, which has for so long
guided the struggle against capital, is ideological, a fetish,
which could only dissolve the system of unity, of property, of
the subject, by articulating practically its difference from
the fetish of capital and thereby from its own structure centred on self-relation.*

Hegel's 'sublation' of fetishism only in part relies on the arguments
of the rationalistic critique of fetishism. Instead of immediately opposing knowledge and reverence for the true to deceptive knowledge of
and reverence for deception, as the rationalist critique does, he
attempts to expound the genesis of knowledge from false immediacy,
and, in this way, to exhibit false cognition as a step which cannot be
leapt over on the way to truth. But the *sublation* of the fetish preserves
the fetish which is removed elsewhere – a trap set by polysemy and the

many-levelled character of the dialectical process which this polysemy signifies.

He – or she – lifts, and preserves, a veil.

The act of sublation is doubled, as ever, and is especially clearly so in the case of the fetish. If the speculative fetishism of Christianity and philosophy sublates the fetishism of sensuousness, which forgets itself, speculative fetishism itself forgets the corporeal and unconscious moments which distinguish the fetishism of sensuousness and forgets what should be conserved and recollected in speculation. The process of absolute self-consciousness towards itself must always also drop what it sublates, must always also forget what it recollects; and must always retain, without knowing it, what it forgets. Just as, in the absolute, everything in it is conserved in this process; just as in self-consciousness the pre-historical forms of its genesis are forgotten in this process: so absolute self-consciousness relates asymmetrically to itself and, wherever it brings itself together, must always at the same time open up its circle.

By virtue of this structural doubleness of sublation – which, further-more, once again, reveals the determining trait of fetishism, that it 'unites' two 'mutually incompatible assertions' – the split between the self-forgetting fetishism of the Africans and the self-comprehending fetishism of the Christian philosophers, between knowing and what is corporeal and unconscious, appears all the greater the more they resemble each other. Just because 'we do the same' as the 'North American savages' and the negroes, when they kill and devour their parents, this must be 'incredible' and testify to the 'most disgusting brutality' (16: TWA, *Phil. Rel.*, 121),

                        for it is a question of nausea [Ekel] *here* of what they do. Through the sublation of the excessive sensuousness which forgets itself, a part is split off from the truth of the fetish and set aside, a part which must, however, haunt the system like its own unappeased corpse, as this part of the system and as the whole, in that it at the same time contains the whole truth of the fetish. Fetishism is the spectral double, the ghost of speculative dialectic. An uncanny element, which determines its economy.

The determination of the speculative through the forgetting excluded by it cannot, as Hegel himself emphasizes, be seen as a limit of dialectic; it cannot be seen as *its* limit and consequently cannot be dialectically surpassed. The bodily practice of the Negroes stages a negation of the negativity of self-consciousness, a negation which is incapable of consciousness, which precisely because it circumscribes the Absolute, can nevertheless not for its part be comprehended and re-collected by the Absolute. It remains on the threshold of the history of consciousness, on the forestage of its theatre. Yet this remaining cannot be thought according to the model of substantial existence. The remnant of the fetish *is* not in the emphatic sense of being, and it does not remain at the place allotted to it by self-consciousness. Just as it deforms the framework of spirit and its circular history of re-collection, so the threshold which this remnant marks actually invades the inside of history and never ceases to obstruct spirit's path towards itself.

This frame contracts. The veil is drawn over once again.

A figuration of the unconscious, which does not know itself, does not know itself as a Self, the forgotten fetishism, in the form of a witch, 'steals' even into those contemporary representations which are determined by self-consciousness:

> '. . . *but sorcery also insinuates itself, in a secondary way, into higher standpoints and religions; as for example in the idea of witches, even though such sorcery is there recognized as something partly impotent, partly Godforsaken, and unfitting.*' (16: *TWA*, Phil. Rel., *279*)

And in the *Lectures on the Philosophy of History*:

> '[The Negroes] *have* [in worshipping the dead] *the idea that the dead can revenge themselves and can subject people to this or that misfortune, just in the way that this was believed of witches in the Middle Ages.*' (12: *TWA*, Phil. History, *124*)

In the Nuremberg Encyclopaedia *(1808): 'Inner Light; communicating with higher spirits; Hyosycamus or witches' bane; the witches intoxicated themselves and fell into the most terrible ravings which spread like epidemics. They were burnt in their thousands.*' (4: *TWA*, 48)

This ahistorical fetishism, which here insinuates itself 'in a secondary way . . . into higher standpoints', does not remain incomprehensible,

relegated and forgotten beyond western history, but is defined within it
as one of its moments. It becomes the conceptual negation of the
abstract ideal of self-consciousness, becomes evil. As Faust did with the
devil, the witches have made a pact with the 'monstrous powers of
worldliness' (which is how faith perceives evil). Thus does the
Philosophy of History set out the characteristics of medieval witchcraft:

> *'but those poor women who were called witches enjoyed
> merely the satisfaction of a petty revenge on their neighh-
> bours, when they turned their cow's milk sour or made
> their child ill. However, the magnitude of the transgression
> involved in spoiling the milk or making the child sick was
> not taken into account; rather it was the power of evil as
> such which was abstractly persecuted in them.' (12:
> TWA, Phil. History, 506)*

The witches' kitchen of history – the milk was turned sour, but not
by the 'poor women'; the 'monstrous plague' which raged for several
centuries through the western history of self-consciousness, was incorporated into the process of spirit not by the ravings of the women, but
by the 'infinite lie' which governs the Middle Ages (12: TWA, *Phil.
History,* 125). The structuring principle of history, that it is the course
of self-conscious spirit through the forms of sensuousness, itself contains what is authentically witch-like, the contagious material for this
plague. The power of the sensuous, the impotence of the spirit, prove
so strong that the African 'condition' is revived in Europe: just as in
Africa '(human) flesh was sold in the market' (ibid.) so in the European
Middle Ages, an equally black epoch, 'human flesh was sold in public
in the market' (ibid., 450). Manifest cannibalism has indeed come to
an end. But just how little the externality which has not been internalized can successfully be placed under the guardianship of self-conscious
spirit and ruled by it, becomes clear from the fact that only with the
epoch of the French Revolution, once the power of positive religion
over society had collapsed, did the epidemic of witch-hunting die
down. But even after the Revolution, as will be shown, the process of
self-consciousness on a world-historical scale is corrupted through sensuous demands and fetishistic fixations which cannot be brought to
consciousness.

Hegel finds himself confronted by the witch. Witches play a role not only in his later, systematic writings, in which they appear as an historical form, but also as early as the account of Judaism in the 'Spirit of Christianity' – as the allegory of the hiding, poisoning deity which castrates its adherents and is itself castrated, the deity of positive religion.

> *'The great tragedy of the Jewish people is no Greek tragedy; it can rouse neither terror nor pity, for both of these arise only out of the fate which follows from the inevitable failing of a beautiful character; it can arouse horror alone. The fate of the Jewish people is the fate of Macbeth who stepped out of nature itself, clung to alien beings, and so in their service had to trample and slay everything holy in human nature, had at last to be forsaken by his gods (since these were objects and he their slave) and be dashed to pieces on his faith itself.' (21: Nohl, 260; Knox, 204–5)*

The Jewish deity, as it has previously appeared in the Gorgon's image and then in Cybele's, figures here – following the implicit quotation from Shakespeare's *Macbeth* – as a witch. The witches, upon whom the Jewish people and Macbeth come to depend, are also, conformably with the analogy between the Jewish model of a positive religion of law and Kant's religion of reason, an allegory of Kant's threefold divinity, which Hegel denounces elsewhere (16: TWA, *Phil. Rel.*, 43) as an 'infinite ghost'. And just as Christ sets himself against the legal ethics of Judaism and the highest guarantor of that ethics, the fiction of a transcendent deity, so Hegel, as the founder of a new speculative relgion of love, sets himself against Kant's own horrible 'witches-faith'.

It is, then, to begin with, not concepts which are here confonted with each other, but *imagines*. But why the *imago* of the witch in particular? Why these 'poor women' who have nevertheless become overpowering through the imagination of an entire epoch, who are supposed to spoil the cow's milk and make the children sick? Certainly the *imago* of the witch functions in Hegel's text on the one hand as a counter-image to the Greek nurse, whose pure milk provides nourishment to a free, republican constitution, on the other as an equivalent of the gorgon and the threatening mother-goddess Cybele and, beyond that, of the totemistic fetishes of African cults. But it cannot be overlooked that this *imago* – beyond the metaphoric-semantic context which establishes its meaning – appears in a text which performs a rigorous critique upon names, upon the ideological and fetishistic implications of the power of the proper name. The witch figures in Hegel's text, then, not merely as the image of a conceptual content, but, even if without Hegel's conscious intention, as a name and so in the first place as an unconscious *imago* of the threatening mother, against whose representative in historical and philosophical reality war is declared. 'Witch' is another name for Hegel, for another Hegel than the Hegel who is officially recognized.

> *Here, displaced, is an etymological fantasy on the name of the witch, a form to which Hegel (who loved to exploit pseudo-etymological and etymological relationships of words for the articulation of speculative thinking) was no stranger. It is cited from the Swabian Dictionary, with etymological and historical notes, by J. C. v. Schmidt (79: Stuttgart: 1831), which appeared in the year of Hegel's death. Under the words 'eggäs, hekkas, hekgais, hekgaus', for lizard, it is noted that 'The final syllable ehsa, esse, which has become ex in the later form, and which in the western south-west is used in the diminutive Essässele as the name of the lizard, is the same which is contained in Am-ei-se [ant], Ilt-is [polecat], Horn-is [hornet]. It is remarkable that in Ulm an old miserly, dirty woman is called Hekkäs, and a witch [Hexe] is called haegesse in Old Swabian. One might be inclined to infer from these common elements of names a common quality, either that of rapid disappearance or that of the terror which they cause, for the sake of which quality the same element is inserted. But the name of the fiendish woman has a different origin, which, despite the differing*

*derivations given of it, can easily be discovered, when it
is noticed that they may be traced back to a common
root. In* Hagg, Haag, Hag, Schalk *(*hake *in Swedish)*
Hagsch, Haagsch, *a mischievous woman, a witch,*
Hägele, *a fiend of male or of female sex (. . .) and* saga,
a witch, a sorceress (Latin) there is a connection with hag
*(which for Skinner already, without a suffix, means
witch,* strix*)*, hug, *understanding, cleverness,* hagur,
klug (Icelandic), sagus, *prophesying,* sagi, *according to*
Cato = pontifices et sacri expiatores *amongst the
Etruscans,* ἄγιοσ, sacer, *(*saker*) and* sagax, *capable of
tracking something down, clever, artful, unmistakeable.
And since* sagax *derives from* sagire, *whilst this itself
(. . .) is related to* sapere, *and* σοφοι, σοφαι, *sorcerers,
witches:* zaubern *[to practise magic] may also belong to
this family. . . .*

(. . .) Hallenberg, holding particularly to the Spanish
hechizera, *derives it from* hacio, facio *(since it is also
called* fechizera*): for in the Middle Ages the sorceresses
were called* facturae. . . . *In Swedish they were called*
görninger, *from* göra; *amongst the Greeks* μαγγανον
*meant both a machine (*Mang*) and sorcery: s. de nom.
Luc. et Vis. p. 45. Let the expert linguist choose! Kant was
joking when he derived* Hexe *[witch] from* hoc est corpus
meum.

Kant makes this joke in his Anthropology *(51: tr.
M. J. Gregor [The Hague: Martinus Nijhoff, 1974], BA
42), where he also asserts a connection with*
hocus-pocus. *He explains the transformation of the
transubstantiation-formula from a 'pious reluctance to
name the right name and to profane it; just as superstitious
people are in the habit of not naming unnatural objects, so
as not to desecrate them.' For Kant, in the transformation
of the host into the body of Christ this body of Christ itself
is transformed – out of 'pious reluctance' and therefore
inevitably, once again – into the witch.*

In his discussion of the speculative proposition in the Preface to the
Phenomenology, Hegel recommends that an exposition of the dialectical
process should avoid not only the 'sensuously intuited or pictured self'
but also the 'name as name', which indicates the grammatically fixed
subject (3: TWA, *Phen.*, 62), because it does not contain the concept
of the subject and suggests the substantiality of something external. So
too in his earliest writings, on the critique of the positive character of
Christianity, he is already directing his polemic against the fixation of
truth and ethical life to a single name, the name of Christ. As an
external vehicle for the dissemination of Christianity the name has had
a ruinous effect upon authentic religiosity: 'the shibboleth of its friends
– the citizens of the kingdom of God – was not: virtue, uprightness –
but rather "Christ, baptism", etc.' (21: Nohl, 33). Hegel refers in this
context to Lessing's *Nathan* (59: tr. W. A. Steel and A. Dent [London:
Everyman, 1930], Act II, scene 1):

> '(. . .) –*Not his virtue but his name*
> *Shall cover all the world; shall shame*
> *The name of every worthy man,*
> *Engulf them. Only with the name*
> *Shall they have aught to do'*

The name is indispensable to the dissemination of a pure religion of
virtue, since without it the merely abstract attitude, itself anonymous,
would lack any relationship to social reality. As a substitute for the lack of
reality in the pure requirements of reason, however, the name must at the
same time displace or even corrupt these requirements, since the loose
compromise between the moral law and sensuousness, whose place is
indicated by the name, permits the name itself already to be taken for the
presence of what it merely signifies; permits meanings other than the
originally intended one to be foisted upon it. The name, the substitute
for the concept, opens up a series of ideas which suppose themselves to
be the concept, which usurp and pervert the concept. Whilst the name
indicates the border between the moral idea of a pure life and the claims
of a heteronomous, historically, socially and physically determined sensuousness, and, more precisely, whilst it forms the veil with which both
spheres are interwoven, it profanes the former and hypostasizes the latter.
Hegel leaves no doubt on this matter: the name functions as a fetish.

The fetishism of the name is most explicitly indicated by Hegel (apart from the decayed forms of Christianity) in the constitution of Jewish society. Along with nourishment, private property and ceremonial law, the name too is for that society a form of individual and social self-constitution. Yet the self which clings to the name is nothing substantial; instead its substance has always already been wrested from it by an infinite deity. In the name of this deity the Jewish people – each tribe, sect, family and individual person – are cut off from the rest of humanity and from the universality which is inherent in themselves, from reason and from their own being, by the mark of distinction which they bear like the mark of circumcision. In the name, therefore, the tear repeats itself in a displaced form, the tear against which the name was supposed to protect. Every name is false when measured against the claim to personal autonomy, the claim to the ethical unity of the self-willing will or the free self-determination of a society; every name is a pseudonym. What it names is shown through just this naming to be incomplete and, furthermore, dead. The 'pious reluctance', of which Kant writes, the fascination in the face of the name, to which Hegel refers, the subjection beneath its power, against which Lessing polemicizes, all originate from the fact that something dead is at work within the idea of pure life. The name, and not only the name of the one who has died, expresses the death of its bearer, and only in this way keeps the one who is dead in his name alive. The relationship between the bearer and what is borne, between the sign and what is signified, is reversed: it is the name which bears the particularity and property, the life and survival of the one who is named. Hence the power of names, hence the reluctance to 'profane' and 'desecrate' them by speaking them. The names, which are supposed to protect the person, are the most vulnerable spot of their autonomy. In this sense Freud in his *Totem and Taboo*, like Hegel, also characterized as fetishistic the 'primitive', childlike and neurotic cathexis of the proper name (38: GW, IX [1912], 71 ff., 133 ff.).

Hegel, in whose major writings –, the *Phenomenology*, the *Logic* and the main text of the *Encyclopaedia* – scarcely a single name appears, but who in his Jena essays vents the annihilating power of his polemic precisely on names, always strictly avoided speaking of his own person, of his own name, and explains that what he *merely opines* [*meine*] is false. This almost aggressive abstinence from opining, from what is merely mine, which goes so far as a demand that the individual who expresses the thought of the world-spirit is obliged to forget himself (3: TWA, Phen., 67), is a reaction to the danger which emanates from names, not because they are nothing, but because they are something dead which nevertheless survives. The name, like every other fetish, exhibits an amalgam of the living and the dead, of presence and absence, of assertion and rejection, yet is incapable of synthesizing these into a unity, as the self-knowing concept demands. If what is negated lives on in the concept as spirit, mediated through sublation, in the concept as spirit, then what has died lives on in the name only as a ghost. In the name the concept itself finds its false copy, a spectral double of the speculative. And where the opinion of the one through whom the absolute expresses itself is the absolute, the place where opinion would be both opinion and absolute, there the false copy would threaten to become an archetype; the spectral double threatens to become an authentic persona. If the talk were affirmatively of a name, of the proper name of the philosopher of the absolute, this proper name alone, as the determinant of a historically, socially, physically fixed opinion, would already suffice to disqualify the absolute as mere opinion. The circle of the speculative would be marked by the tear of the mother, the plenitude of the present by withdrawal, knowing and self-consciousness by something corporeal and unconscious. The text of that which identifies itself with the resurrected Christ and beyond this with the absolute must belie its own name, since this name, a totem, the living dead, a castrating and castrated mother, would be the name of the witch. Hegel's text: a witch-text. A text, a veil.

This text which always also shows that which it withdraws in the very gesture of withdrawal itself, leaves each of its forms, not excluding the highest, between the absolute unity of the subject and something not appropriable by this unity; leaves itself oscillating between speculative dialectic and its written articulation, between the writing of its authentic name sublated into the concept, and a reading which replaces and denounces this name with a homonym which deforms it.

The absolute would always also remain the absolute fetish, a mere representation, a curtain, a foretaste [*Vorstellung, Vorhang, Vortisch*], a first course or passage beyond which there would be no other. But – and this is also an effect of seduction by the fetish, and its oscillation – Hegel, Christ, would offer, for the moment, to advance nonetheless.

That which is past, without reuniting itself with the present; that which is merely represented, without its distance from what it represents being susceptible of annulment; a Before which cannot be its own After; a first, which cannot be its own second – is dead. But even the present which is not its own past, the representation which is not what it represents, the second whose first is not itself, must also be counted as dead, since it is incapable of overcoming its own division. This is the reason for the ambivalence of Hegel's diagnosis, never so open in the later system, that the fate of Judaism, the fate of Kantianism, carries in itself no possibility of healing the life which it has injured, and even murdered. If, that is, the system of religious and epistemological fetishism is recognized as fetishistic in Hegel's critique, it is nevertheless on the one hand localized into a non-fetishistic context of authentic life, yet on the other this system and its knowledge, which are categorially distinguished from each other, remain dead with respect to each other. 'True unification, true love take place only amongst living people who . . . are dead to each other on no side; it excludes all oppositions' (21: Nohl, 379).

Jesus came amongst the Jews as one who announced this love. His gospel is characterized as revolutionary (21: Nohl, 385), his epoch as one of ferment (ibid., 261). Yet the process of the unification of unity and division, which this revolution is supposed to inaugurate, can be described appropriately only on the basis of a phenomenology and a logic of love. This structure explains first how love relates as infinite life to the dead matter which stands in opposition to it, how it attempts to dissolve this dead matter into itself, and then what resists this dissolution, despite Hegel's attempt.

The simple argument against the hypostasis of the before and of the fetish, that difference can only be known as difference if unity is presupposed, requires complementation through a further argument. For this argument does indeed take account of the abstract structure of difference, but not of the specific content of this different element; it names the logical implication of difference, that there must be unity, but this unity, which is supposed to be capable of dissolving the division between Before and After, itself remains pre-reflexive and therefore caught in this opposition. The unity which merely precedes difference still has the character of a representation. Hegel therefore distinguishes between an 'unconscious, undeveloped' unity (21: Nohl, 379) and a 'unity brought to completion' in which life unifies itself and its divisions 'without any further lack'. If the undeveloped unity stood opposed to the possibility of division and reflection, this possibility is sublated in the process of love.

The organ of this sublation is shame.

Shame must enter the scene of love, because it is shame which reacts to the possibility of division, as it still persists in undeveloped unity. Possibility signifies: the possibility of recidivism into picture-thinking, into oppositions of understanding or of reason, into categories of property, into the possibility that living unity may be mutilated. 'To say that the lovers have an independence and a living principle peculiar to each of themselves means only that they may die. (. . .) Love, however, strives to sublate even this distinction, this possibility as mere possibility and attempts itself to unify the mortal, to make it immortal.' Love turns into shame against the possibility of death which is immanent in love itself. Hegel's concept of shame is distinguished from other current conceptions by a difference which appears minimal and which he himself indicates: 'it is not a fear *for* what is mortal, for what is one's own, but a fear *of* these' (21: Nohl, 380). As fear *for* what is mortal or one's own, shame would keep hold of these and ascribe them a value of their own, like the prostitute or the tyrant; it would be the representative of a deathly order of property (ibid.). As fear *of* what is mortal or one's own, rather, shame promotes the sublation of property which is based on a system of separations; it is not retention but surrender. Shame, then, appears first as an affect, which arises in the domain of a being which is indeed one with itself, yet which has disintegrated into its actuality and its as yet unrealized possibilities. It is directed, as the power of love, against everything which resists its unity, which resists the copula of its being: against the veil of clothing, against the oppositions of pictorial thinking, even, as Hegel explicitly remarks, against the 'rec-ollection of the body', against death. Shame, then, is indeed impossible without the unity of love which precedes it and is, as Hegel formulates it, 'an effect of love' – yet the original being of love can be brought together with its developed form, undiminished by any restriction, only by means of shame. Shame is the organ of the self-sublation of love. It prepares the transition from the deficient to the fulfilled form of love's being. Shame thus turns, as a function of love, as its 'fear', its 'reluctance' and its 'anger', against representation, body, possibility and death, in order to dissolve them in the unity of being. Shame is the negative-synthetic power through which this – ontological – difference contracts.

Hegel insists that 'love is stronger than fear; it is not fearful of its fear, but accompanied by its fear it sublates divisions . . . it is a recipro-cal taking and giving; its gifts may be scorned out of shyness, through shyness an opponent may not yield to its receiving; but it still tries whether hope has not deceived it, whether it still finds itself every-where' (21: Nohl, 380). Love, driven by shame, gives up all property.

> *'The lover who takes is not thereby made richer than the other; he is enriched indeed, but only so much as the other is. So too the giver does not make himself poorer; by giving to the other he has at the same time and to the same extent enhanced his own treasure (compare Juliet in* Romeo and Juliet: "the more I give to thee, The more I have"). *This wealth of life love acquires . . . for it seeks out differences and devises unifications ad infinitum; it turns to the whole manifold of nature in order to drink love out of every life.'* (21: Nohl, 380; Knox, 307)

Whoever gives, has more. Not that what he gives is restored to him increased, since unlike the exchange entered into by the prostitute, the exchange of love is not based on the rule of equivalence. It is asymmet-rical, it gives property for the sake of something shared, it gives some-thing distinct for the sake of unification; it gives up the possibility of death, in order to receive pure life. Shame is the agent of this exchange, an agent for which it is a question of the acquisition and protection of a property which is greater than any private property could be, in that

shame is, as an organ of love, directed towards the negation of ownership. Shame could not indeed be as infinite as the process which it
accompanies and compels, since the infinite difference, which love
seeks, and the infinite surrender, in which love is satisfied (in the
Aesthetics [13: TWA, 310] Hegel cites Juliet's phrase 'The more I give
to thee, the more I have' once again), both envisage another kind of
infinity than the empty infinity of a mere approximation. Hegel
emphasizes that shame 'disappears' together with the 'separable' element to which it refers. But yet when all 'separability has been dis-
carded', when all distinctions, and therefore also the distinction
between possibility and actuality, have been sublated, and being has
been united with itself, one object [*Gegenstand*] of shame remains: the
'lack of consciousness' [*Bewußtlosigkeit*] in the consummate copula of
love.

> 'What in the first instance is most the individual's own is
> united into the whole in the lovers' touch and contact; con-
> sciousness of a separate self disappears, and all distinction
> between the lovers is annulled. The mortal element, the
> body, has lost the character of separability, and a seed of
> immortality . . . has come into existence.' (21: Nohl, 381;
> Knox, 307)

The subject under discussion in this text is the sublation of separation, already in an entirely speculative sense – the term does not simply
mean eradication, but rather, beyond this, a transformation of the
modality, an alteration within the categoriality of the 'as', which is also
expressed in another formulation from the same text: 'In love what has
been separated remains, but no longer as something separate, but as
unified' (21: Nohl, 379). It might be added that it is only in this unity
that what has been split off *is*, in the emphatic sense of the word, since
it is only in this unity that what has been separated is no longer
opposed to being, but taken up into its fullness. And beyond this, separation *as* separation is only thinkable, *is* only separation, once it is elevated to the unity of being. Unity is the truth of separation. The 'lack
of consciousness' in the complete unity of love is accordingly not
straightforwardly identical with the original unity which is equally called
'lacking in consciousness'. The veil which is cast over consciousness

with love is not an object of shame, as a fetishistic line of separation, but rather a veil which flutters in the unity of oneness and separation. This lack of consciousness, then, does not come into force in the absolute copula of love as a pre-speculative distinction, or as a potentially always already sublated opposition, but as a restriction within synthetic unity itself. In the conception of unrestricted being, in the conception – since the theoretical conception is here inseparable from the practical conception – of the 'germ of immortality' in the act of love, which at its peak contracts to 'a single point', and must therefore run through the circular path of development which has led up to this peak once again and over and over again, a restriction of being asserts itself, a restriction which is not contained in the concept of being but which is also not excluded from this concept. On the basis of this restriction, the unity which has already been attained must once more venture out into the field of separations and journey forth to more comprehensive acts of synthesis.

> 'The seed breaks free from its original unity, turns ever
> more and more to opposition, and begins to develop. Each
> stage of its development is a separation, and its aim in
> each is to regain for itself the full richness of life.' (21:
> Nohl, 381; Knox, 307)

The surplus of possibility, in the unity of death and life – of lack of consciousness, in the unity of consciousness and pure feeling – of shame, in the unity of love with what stands over against it – marks like the sublated veil of the fetish a remnant within pure unity, of which it can be said neither that it is nor that it is not; a relic of totality, which by the same token renders this same totality impossible, as it makes possible the conception of this totality, its 'germ of immortality'. If the synonymously used concepts of love, pure life and being, just like the concept of the concept later, represent a quantity which behaves towards the Kantian categories as a transcendental, the transcategorial of the concepts of actuality, possibility and necessity – then shame, which even in complete unity still turns against this surplus of possibility and death and drives its process further, represents a category which stipulates the path for the transcategorial of speculative unity. Shame does not function as mere affect any more than love does. It is effective as a (self-) detranscendentalizing transcendental, which closes the difference of being from itself and once more opens the restriction of its unity, in order to make possible a more comprehensive closure. But since in this way the sublation of the veil of shame is exhibited as a veil, absolute synthesis is bound to shame as its conditions of possibility, as to the condition of its impossibility. The figure of shame remains irrecoverable for the process which it urges forward, and impossible to sublate for shame itself.

The life of dialectic pulses through the closures of shame. But even in this process it is no different; shame will survive it.

> *Hegel's reduction of shame to an organ in the self-fulfilment of love has the paradoxical consequence that shame – according to his own presentation, rather than his intention – is elevated to a form which can no longer simply be grasped under that unity in the service of which it operates. The concept of shame behaves otherwise, and yet comparably, in a text of Rousseau's which Hegel must have known well and from which he excerpted a passage concerning the equivocal relationship between love and virtue (44: Dok., 174 ff.) According to Rousseau, shame increases desire, and makes pleasure ambiguous in that it relates both to lust and to the restraint upon lust. 'The apparent obstacle which appears to make this object distant is, at bottom, that which brings it closer. Desires veiled by shame become only the more seductive; in obstructing them, modesty inflames them . . . the less he obtains, the more the value of what he obtains increases; and it is thus that he enjoys at once his privations and his pleasures.' (74: Letter to D'Alembert in Oeuvres, XI, 125 ff.)*
>
> *In a tradition descending from Rousseau, also one affected by the influence of Heidegger's concept of aletheia, the psychoanalyst Jacques Lacan specifies a central place in his theory for the function of shame as sublation [Aufhebung] – this concept, together with that of shame [Scham], appears in German in his work – as the sublation*

of the phallus into the transcendental signifier: the phallus 'can play its role only when veiled, that is to say, as itself a sign of the latency, with which any signifiable is struck, when it is raised [aufgehoben] to the function of signifier. The phallus is the signifier of this Aufhebung *[sublation] itself, which it inaugurates (initiates) through its disappearance. This is why the demon of* Αἰδώς *[Scham, shame] surfaces precisely at the moment when, in the ancient mysteries, the phallus is unveiled (cf. the famous painting in the Villa de Pompeii)' (57: Jacques Lacan,* Écrits: a Selection, *tr. Alan Sheridan [London: Tavistock, 1977], 288).*

In that the phallus disappears, it erects itself; as the phallus it unveils itself in its concealment: where it is afflicted with the stigma of castration. Shame — both the German word and the Greek Αἰδώς *have the double meaning of 'concealing because of shyness' and 'the genitalia' — is* aletheia: *concealing unconcealment. What emerges in the aletheic interplay of shame, which is also entrusted by Lacan with the functions of the logos and of nous, is not only the structure of the signifier; as the truth of this structure, shame is the signifier of the signifier, a transcendental, which founds every possible empirical relationship, without being able to lose even the smallest element in such a relationship. As that which it is not, shame is always itself. Pure significance is what shame signifies. There is no pleasure which, according to this logic of what Jacques Derrida has called phallogocentrism, would not be an immediate gain; there is no excess and no difference, no residue, which could still fall away from it in the process of sublation.*

Shame, in Hegel's work, is the organ of the self-sublation of love. Where the unity of love is exhibited as an object of shame, shame ceases to be a mere instrument of this unity, ceases at the same time simply to prosecute the affirmation of its own being and becomes more and less than a merely existent movement of the production and dissolution of unity and being. If shame is described from Hegel's perspective as a cyclical-linear movement towards the goal of consummate love, it goes behind Hegel's back, and goes, in his own text, beyond this goal, which would at the same time be its origin; it splits the unity by itself and works towards a further unity. But there is no unity which would not necessarily be dissolved as a restriction by shame. For shame being is given – its own not excepted – only in the plural. If shame in Hegel's perspective is described from the standpoint of a teleologically anticipated unity, this perspective is so transformed in his hands, in his text, that it is unity which is articulated from the perspective of the movement of shame. The text of shame writes being, which is supposed to have cast off all shame. As always more and less than this being, the shameful text is the signifier of a signified, into which the text allows its difference to penetrate to such an extent that the text's being only *is* by virtue of its difference with itself. That being itself is more and less than being. Shameful being.

A shameful reading, which seeks no other correspondence for this text, no other unity, than that which opens upon its difference. It is not shameful, however, in that it holds to difference; but rather in that it seeks to dissolve difference, whose mark is still borne by unity, and to keep in motion the movement *between* being and difference, between the unity of actuality and possibility and the surplus of possibility, between the pure life, in which there is no longer any death, and death, which still makes itself felt within the purity of life, between signifier and signified, between the signifier and the truth of the signified. Between both, in the spasmic rhythm of contraction and expansion, it is also shameful over and over again as a reading of love.

To close the difference between the 'undeveloped unity' (21: Nohl, 379) and the possibility of death in such a way that this closure [*Schluß*] does not remain merely a moral demand and so prolong the sway of diremption, but rather so that, in advance of any social realization, this conclusion is already realized in the programme of this unity – such a bringing together of being and language is the *experimentum crucis* of a philosophical ontology which aims at liberation from ideological and political relations of domination. Hegel first explicitly develops the implications of this experiment in his commentary on the sermons of Jesus, which sketch the programme of a religion from the spirit of speculative unity. Jesus, confronted like Hegel with the problem that a morality of oppositions cannot be answered with a morality opposed to it, emphasizes that he is not come to destroy the law but to 'fulfil' it. He does not therefore demand 'respect' before the law, as Kant assumed in critical fashion, since respect, as a feeling of particularity, still remains different from the law as a universal, and permits only an infinite approximation to the subject of pure practical reason, even though respect is the priviliged path to *a priori* moral cognition. Hegel remarks: 'Respect is the opposite of the principle which is appropriate to action; the principle is universality; respect is not; for respect, commands are always a given' (21: Nohl, 388). As Hegel emphasizes against a passage from the *Religion within the Limits of Reason Alone* (55: *Religion . . .* , A 254), commands are a given, the mere letter of the law, even where its command is internalized, unlike that of the shamans of the Tungus, who subjugate themselves to an external fetish. Respect for the command of reason merely subjugates itself to an internalized fetish (cf. 21: Nohl, 265 ff.). If Christianity is to be a religion of love and therefore of unity, 'fulfilling the law' must mean something other than 'respecting' it. The most far-reaching aporias arise in the explanation of this central concept of fulfilment and fullness, of pleroma.

In an early note Hegel characterizes the Christian strategy of cultural transformation, using this word from scripture, as πληρωσαι: 'Thus Jesus set up the principle of virtue, and at the same time also directly attacked the statutes of the Jews which were destructive of morals, or attempted to πληρωσαι them, to restore their spirit' (21: Nohl, 363). A proposition from the positivity essay, here still entirely in the spirit of a Kantianizing religion of virtue, translates the Greek word into the Latin '*complementum*' and adds the remark that 'Jesus tried to draw his people's attention to the spirit and disposition which had to vitalize their observance of their laws if they were to please God, but under the government of the church this "fulfilment" of the law was turned once again into rules and ordinances which in turn always need a similar "fulfilment". The church's attempt to provide one has failed in its turn,

because the spirit or the disposition is too ethereal a thing to be confined in formulas, in verbal imperatives' (21: Nohl, 207; Knox, 138). If
this interpretation of the complement still emphasizes, in critical fashion, that the 'ethereal essence' cannot be 'presented' in such a way that
presentation and essence could be brought into concordance, but only
in such a way that the universality of spirit always transcends the laws –
the pleroma-concept in the 'Spirit of Christianity' appears to be aimed
at just this concordance and unity. Yet neither the passage from
Matthew, to which Hegel quite explicitly refers in his annotations to
the 'Spirit of Christianity' –

> *'Matt. 5.17:* πληρωσαι, *to complement, to make com-
> plete through conviction [Gesinnung], through the addi-
> tion of the internal to the external.' (21: Nohl, 395)*

– and *The Life of Jesus* translates: 'Do not believe that I am come to
preach the invalidity of the laws, nor to annul [*aufzuheben*] their bind-
ingness; I am rather come to make them complete' (21: Nohl, 82): neither this passage, nor its citation in the letter to the Romans (8.4;
13.10) – 'Thus love is the fulfilment of the law' – contains a reference
to the *unification* of the fulfilling with the fulfilled, to the *unity* of love
and law. Yet such a strict connection is certainly envisaged in the gnostic application of the pleroma-concept, which for its part represents an
allegorizing reinterpretation of both the gospel concept of pleroma and
the cabbalistic concept of ha-Male'.[1] Hegel may have been familiar
with this cabbalistic-gnostic tradition, at least through conversations
with Schelling.

> *In his reminiscences of Hegel Schwegler reports that 'A
> fellow doctoral graduate of Hegel's told me that during his
> years at the* Stift *Hegel principally studied Aristotle in an
> ancient worm-eaten Basel edition, the only one available
> at that time, whilst Schelling read the gnostics, particu-
> larly the ophitic and valentinian system.' (65:
> Nicolin, 13)*

From his letter of 30 August 1795 it can be seen that Hegel knew
Schelling's dissertation 'De Marcione Paullinarum epistolarum

---

[1] Cf. 80: Gerschom Scholem, *Ursprung und Anfänge der Kabbala* (Berlin:
1962), 60 ff.

emendatore', in which a careful attempt at the rehabilitation of the heretic from the courts of orthodoxy is undertaken. The theme of plenitude which is so important for Hegel is only fleetingly touched on there, and the form of the treatise did not allow it to be otherwise (77: *Werke*, ed. M. Schröter [Munich: 1927–8], I, *Ergänzungsband*, 60 ff.).

The most explicit exposition of the gnostic system, Irenaeus's *Adversus Haereses*,[1] defines the pleroma in the Valentinian system as the totality of all aeons, as the fullness of that which *is* in the strict sense of the word. The limit and the law of this being are laid down by Christ in his function as horothete, who excludes the desire for the impossible and unnameable from the sphere of fullness. The fruit of the totality of all aeons, as they are limited by Christ and mutually united by spirit, is, as 'the most consummate beauty and the star of the pleroma', Jesus (48: Irenaeus [Kempten: 1912], I, 2; 6). A concept of Jesus – who, let it be added, is not here the historical Jesus, but the idea of Jesus before the creation of the world – can therefore be extracted from gnostic doctrine, in which he appears as the unity of the fullness of being with what limits this fullness. – But this unity is accomplished only through the exclusion of what once originated in the longing for the impossible – through the exclusion of matter. Although the Valentinian system also regards the sublation of the opposition as figured in Jesus's act of redemption, its ontology – in contrast to that projected by Hegel – remains dualistic in that every sublation is bound to the exclusion of the material, the barely existent and the non-existent. However fruitful a recollection of the process of division and unification which gnostic doctrine regards as allegorized in the gospel texts may have been for Hegel – the concept of pleroma and of fulfilled being in Hegel's early writings takes up with the gnostic tradition and the cabbalistic and Platonic tradition which it reworks, yet without developing out of gnosticism in linear fashion.

Just as Hegel, with the concept of the pleroma, plays upon an entire tradition of interpreting this word and on an entire epoch in the history of philosophy, and thereby allows it to resonate, so too in his complementary commentary on this word in the *Spirit of Christianity.*

[1] Cf. also 49: Hans Jonas, *Gnosis und spätantiker Geist* (Göttingen: 1964), 362–75; and Wolfgang Schulz, *Dokumente der Gnosis* (Jena: 1910), 164–88.

> *'This correspondence with inclination is the* πλήρωμα *of the law; i.e., it is an 'is,' which, as used to be said, is the 'complement of possibility,' since possibility is the object as something thought, as a universal, while 'is' is the synthesis of subject and object, in which subject and object have lost their opposition.'* (21: Nohl, 268; Knox, 214)

'As used to be said' means: as Wolff and his school expressed themselves in their exposition of Aristotelian metaphysics and Leibniz's philosophy of substance.

> *Wolff gives the following definition in his* Philosophia Prima sive Ontologia *(1730):* 'Hinc *Existentiam* definio per complementum possibilitatis: quam definitionem nominalem esse patet . . . . Dicitur existentia etiam *Actualitas.' And Alexander G. Baumgarten follows him in his* Metaphysica *(Halle: 1743):* 'Existentia *(actus . . . actualitas) est . . . complementum essentiae sive possibilitatis, quatenus haec tantum, ut complexus determinationum spectatur.' (See 30: L. W. Beck, Early German Philosophy [Cambridge, MA: 1969], 453, who refers to both definitions. Cf. also 39: Harris, Hegel's Development, 507n., 316n.)*

Hegel now applies the concept of the complement, as he previously applied that of the pleroma, in a different manner from these thinkers, who also 'expressed' themselves with this concept, not in order to list an ascending scale of categories of actuality and possibility, but rather in order to see in it the condition of possibility of possibility itself and its difference from actuality. For the complement is a 'being', which grounds, as though in their unity, those spheres which have come apart in possibility: subject and object, universal and particular, freedom and necessity. That which is added to what is lacking, precedes it as fullness. In its act of connection, the complement supplies once again that which falls apart in the disintegration of the unity of this fullness. Thus pleroma is the fullness of being, which fulfils the deficient forms of life and connects the opposition which holds sway in these forms with its unity. The complement, then, no more corresponds to the Kantian than to the Wolffian type of 'complement', which leaves open the 'abyss' between subject and object. pleroma is what fills up every lack, and, as such, is both a part and the fullness of being at once. Like being and love, pleroma unites what has been distinguished.

> *Schlegel notes in 1798, at roughly the same time as Hegel's sketches, in his* Philosophical Scholia*: 'A very* χα *[chaotic] concept: that exist(ence) = complem.(entum) possibilitatis.' (78: F. Schlegel,* Kritische Ausgabe*, ed. E. Behler [Paderborn: 1962], XVIII, 42)*

Although in the concepts of the pleroma and the complement the whole history of western ontology is concentrated and simultaneously subjected to a new interpretation; although the expression 'to fulfil the law' combines the two functions of the pleroma, to be both Being itself and a mere addition to Being, an addition which *is* not, in the fullest sense – nevertheless the unity which is thought in the pleroma collides with the limits of language. Just as the 'expression' 'complement of possibility' could not be applied in its historical meaning, but only as a distanced quotation, the form of which was to be amplified by new conceptualization, so the central 'expression' of the Hegelian text itself, that is, 'agreement of inclination with the law', must appear 'unsuitable':

> *'for in it law and inclination, as particular, come forward as opposites ... and since the elements which agree are different, the agreement between them is also merely contingent, only the unity of strangers, something thought.' (21: Nohl, 268; Knox, 214)*

This impression is the consequence of the fact 'that what is living is thought, expressed, in the given form of the concept which is alien to it' (21: Nohl, 267). If language were to prove heteronomous to life, then the possibility of misunderstanding, of the confusion of alien form with authentic content, would remain indissoluble. Kant was guilty of such a confusion when he misunderstood the commandment to love, in which Jesus summarizes his doctrine, as a *command* to love. Yet if Hegel were content to let matters rest with such an abstract critique of language, to assert the fundamental inadequacy of thinking to being, and thereby implicitly to expel both the conceptual and language as such from the realm of philosophical articulation, such a critique would not only exclude his own writings and the critique of

language they undertake, but also contradict its own principle, the unification of language with that which is foreign to it. The source of the
confusion, of false appearance, of contingency, of Kantianism and of
Judaism, must therefore itself constitute a moment of the most fulfilled
unification.

If it is a question of truth in language, as an 'affirmation about something actual' or an 'affirmation about something to come', that is to say
a question of the 'fixed connection' between word and actuality (21:
Nohl, 270), this Being of language cannot, in turn, be indicated by
something materially existent, without falling subject to a semantic
restriction. It is in this sense that Hegel comments upon the Sermon
on the Mount and its criticism of the Jewish practice of oath-taking:

> *'When the Jews swore by heaven, by the earth, by*
> *Jerusalem, or by the hair of their head, and committed*
> *their oath to God, put it in the hands of the Lord, they*
> *linked the reality of what they asserted to an object; they*
> *equated both realities and put the connection of this object*
> *with what was asserted, the equivalence of the two, into*
> *the power of an external authority. God is made the*
> *authority over the word.' (21: Nohl, 271; Knox, 218)*

Whilst the truth of a proposition is attached to a heaven which is
conceived of as object-like, or attached to hair, this truth itself, the
unity of the proposition with what it expresses, is restrictively equated
with one side of its relation and petrifies to a fetish-like object. The
onto-logical knot between language and thing is pulled together into
an alien, thing-like power over language. 'Being itself, exhibited in an
entity, made present in an entity' (21: Nohl, 270) itself contracts to a
mere entity. The unity of the sign with its meaning, as soon as it is tied
to the isolated sign, to a representation, to hair, loses its foundational
character, is displaced into the status of a sign, a representation, hair,
and thereby itself becomes groundless, lacking Being, lacking unity,
lacking significance. Once reduced to the function of a sign, language
loses even this function. Yet language does not lose this function by elevation into the order of Being and fulfilled meaning. It is lost in the
non-sense of a necessary fiction. The language of the oath, of affirmation, of institutionalized agreement – this language is the language of

sacrilege perpetrated on Being. It is a heaven which conceals heaven; hair, which usurps the place of the spirit, 'which alone can bind together its words with an action'; a non-homogeneous weaving together of remnants from the onto-logical connection. Every text in which the signifier, even if only partially, resists being synthesized into its truth – and Hegel's text, which is compelled by an 'agreement of inclination with the law' to speak as though those elements which are in agreement were still different, cannot be excepted from this law; every text in which the sign is robbed not only of its synthetic relationship to its meaning but also of the organic vitality of Being; every text, even when shame at its own difference from the presence of meaning is still at work in it: each and every one turns itself into hair.

Which must be cut. Elsewhere Hegel calls the facial hair that the oriental forbade himself to cut 'the most inessential element in his organic totality', the 'most indifferent thing, in which there is no life', for which reason 'cutting one's nails is an equally great, and circumcision a greater, mutilation' (73: Ros., 518). But only this cut, which curtails the independence and the non-living fixity of hairs and nails, the positivity of the concept and the unattractive aspects, especially, of the philosophical usage of language as it has been handed down, dissolves its restriction to the inessential and the finite and allows its identification with an organism of infinite meaning replete in itself. There must be a cut, so that no cut remains. This dialectical figure, which persists identically from Hegel's earliest to his latest texts, is given a significant metaphorical formulation in the text on 'Faith and Knowledge'. The abstraction from sensuous finitude, regardless of whether it is from that of the body, of language, of the cultural or social institution, 'is conceived of as the painful cutting off of an essential part from the completeness of the whole. But the temporal and empirical, and privation, are thus recognized as an essential part and an absolute In-itself. It is as if someone who sees only the feet of a work of art were to complain, when the whole work is revealed to his sight, that he was being deprived of his deprivation and that the incomplete had been in-completed' (2: TWA, 300 *et seq.*; Walter Cerf and H. S. Harris [eds], *Faith and Knowledge* [Albany, NY: 1977], 66. As with the fetishistic predominance of feet or hair, so the predominance of language is a husk covering the complete form, covering the pleroma of Being, covering the other image of Sais. To speak onto-logically, to read Hegel's text would accordingly be to remove [*aufzuheben*] or to cut this husk in such a way that this image appears in all its abundance.

For it must also appear in its husk, in the husk that is cut and completed through this cut. But how can such a cut be planned, a cut that would not itself work according to the model of the dichotomy it is supposed to dissolve? Like a cut that would not operate privatively upon what is itself defined as a privation of totality? Like a cut that would return to this original totality in such a way that not only the decayed forms of this totality, but also the totality itself, are made complete? How can a cut be thought that repeats, that retrieves, what was lost in separation; a cut of return, which does not separate, but rather, even in the act of separation, unites?

And how must the language which performs this cut be fashioned? And how must the language which comments on this cut be fashioned?

The language which cuts and unites cannot be the language of consciousness. Every language which portrays itself as the expression of a consciousness classifies itself as a particular under the principle of universality contained in consciousness, and makes itself, the universal, 'exalted above itself as a particular' (21: Nohl, 272). Self-consciousness is a shamanistic relationship of domination. Since its language does not speak as *one* language, but, precisely as a particular language, only *contra*dicts [*wider*spricht] the idea of its semantic and moral content, it must remain 'hypocritical', as Hegel puts it (ibid., 273). Despite the indissoluble difference which prevails in this language between what is intended and its realization, the language of self-consciousness is so closely bound up with the demand for equality that every intention in the system of consciousness attempts to realize itself according to the model of equivalence. The law of action as of language is the *ius talionis*: 'an eye for an eye, a tooth for a tooth'. Instead of sublating one lack through the other, it matters only that each lack should be equal to the other. The castration of castration. The economy of equivalence, of semantic and social equivalence and equality of values, is in the service of privation and is, therefore, not at one with itself, the economy of the infinitely self-sustaining difference. The economy of the *ius talionis*,

which establishes the structure of consciousness, lays down the law of
death, not that of life, the law of the regulative fiction, not that of
Being. The law of self-consciousness, instead of being the copula, is
radical disjunction. The blinded eye *is* not the blinded eye. Castration
does not castrate.

It is otherwise with the cut of the pleroma. Castration *is* and is therefore the complement of the lack which it marks. It is, not because it
would supposedly have become equal to itself, but rather because it is
more than its mere concept. If the pleroma has a measure, it is this,
that it is more than can be measured. Being is being-more. The economy of its movement, then, is never that of equivalence, but rather the
asymmetrical movement of surplus. Only the radical non-equivalence
of meaning and sign, of commandment and action, of consciousness
and its relation, removes from each the possibility of orientating itself
to that which is always other as to something heteronomous, only this
non-equivalence makes each reciprocally autonomous and capable not
merely of becoming equal to each other, but of becoming one with
each other. For this reason the material process of language and action
must always contain more than any possible consciousness which could
relate to it. This is the content of the *sententia* from the Sermon on the
Mount, as Hegel glosses it: 'Never let the right hand know what the
left hand is doing' (21: Nohl, 272).

If knowing is a subsumption of particular contents under universal
categories of the understanding or of ethical reason, then Being cannot
be said to know. Being is tied to the condition of its unconsciousness.
Its language becomes onto-logical only when it exceeds the limit which
is set for it by the material which it is to articulate, by its objective
referent, and by a subject transcendent to it. Only this excess in the
language of Being beyond the borderline of consciousness and its distinctions can cut through the semantic relation between description
and meaning in such a way that the difference to which this relation is
tied disappears, and the fetishization of the sign in the unity of representation and presence is sublated. The onto-logical cut of the pleroma
cuts the transcendental-semantic cut between universal meaning and
its particular description. The sign posits itself in difference from the
difference which divides it from its significance. The process of the

negation of the negation through which it travels, leads into the presence of meaning in that which expresses meaning, whether linguistically or in practical contexts. This cut too, therefore, does not cut. Since it *is*, it draws the relation of a sign to what it signifies to form a unity. The cut completes. It raises the life of the particular sign, the sign which is valid only in relation to a heteronomous other, to a meaning which is universal in itself.

This conversion of castration into potentiation – the dialectical movement κατ' ἐξοχήν – figures strongly in Hegel's interpretation as the centre of Christianity and its fate. Hegel glosses the exhortation 'if thy limb offend thee, cut it off' thus:

> *'The highest freedom is . . . the possibility of renouncing everything in order to maintain one's self. Yet the man who seeks to save his life will lose it.' (21: Nohl, 286; Knox, 236)*

Conversely it is the case that 'In order to save himself, man kills himself' (21: Nohl, 285). As a result of the contraction of signifier and signified, the sign must erase itself in the negation of the difference which separates it from its meaning. Only its self-negation, its self-castration, can accomplish the higher life of unity within a nature constricted by categories of the understanding. The acumen of the copula would be a loving unification of subject and object, between conflict [*Widerstreit*] and its unity, a Being in which everything existent, everything objective and all conflict would have died away. It would reduce itself to the point-like experience of the collapse of life and death, subjectivity and universality, the sign and the signified; and would therefore be reduced to a form of unity, which is already lost just at the moment when it is attained. Onto-logical language – if it were to be exhausted in this suicide of the sign – would be the meaningless talk of meaning. The fullness of the pleroma would be empty subjectivity.

What the fullness of Being still lacks, therefore, is the possibility of repeating the suicide of an objectivity, which is bound to objective forms.

What the fullness of language still lacks is the possibility of repeating the cut through its objectivity which is bound to objective forms.

Perfected love is reduced to a mere moment, and however much it cuts open a space for objectivity inside itself, to that extent reflection and its categories of the understanding gain power over love, beyond its consummation. The transience of the unity which is fulfilled in love, leads, together with the realization of love, to recidivism into the realm of distinctions. The pleroma of law, that within love which brings about completion, remains itself 'a nature as yet incomplete' (21: Nohl, 302), because it cannot be objectified in something existent. The complement requires a further complement, just as it already had itself to complete another complement of law, virtue. 'The πλήρωμα of love is therefore religious (religion and love unified, both thought as bound together)' (ibid., 302). Hegel's analysis inserts another type of unification between the exposition of love and the exposition of the religious. If love is the unification of law with the inclination to act as law demands, if religion is the unification of love with the philosophical and social forms in which it is objectified, then the intermediate form constitutes a precarious unification of love with the perceptual representation of a cultic act, which in Hegel's later systematic conceptions assumes an extraordinary significance and, after relatively traditional expositions in the earliest texts, receives its first great speculative analysis in the fragment on the 'spirit of Christianity': the Lord's Supper.

> *'Jesus' leave-taking from his friends took the form of celebrating a love-feast. Love is less than religion, and this meal, too, therefore is not strictly a religious action. (. . .) Yet in the love-feast there is also something objective in evidence, to which feeling is linked but with which it is not yet united into an image. Hence this eating hovers between a common table of friendship and a religious act, and this hovering obscures the clear interpretation of its spirit.' (21: Nohl, 297; Knox, 248)*

The meal is a transition. A transition, certainly, from the subjectivity of love to its objectification in religious forms; but, conversely, as a kind of farewell to the love objectified in Christ, it is the path from a unification 'attached to the actual' to a unification which is almost entirely concentrated within the subject.

The tendency to an objective manifestation of unification accomplished in the form of the meal is twisted into an internalization of the external. Hegel discusses this internally doubled movement of the meal, as a transition from the semiotic to the hermeneutic process, from the act of the production of signs to the act of their interpretation. The circumstance that the meal nowhere dissolves the ambivalence between the material image and the subjective experience of what it presents, that it remains intrinsically equivocal, leads to the difficulty, which Hegel admits, of giving 'a clear interpretation of its spirit'. But it leads, beyond this, to aporias in Hegel's critique of equivocation, which cannot be removed by means of a dialectical theory of unification, but only be ignored.

The communal eating which is celebrated in the farewell feast for Jesus, is no 'conventional sign' (21: Nohl, 297). Eating does not merely mean, but *is* – Hegel insists on this, without yet differentiating, as he later does with great emphasis, that this eating is an eating for enjoyment and an eating for faith.

> *Jesus broke bread: "Take, this is my body given for you; do this in remembrance of me. Likewise he took the cup. Drink ye all of it; this is my blood of the new testament, which is shed for you and for many for the remission of sins; do this in remembrance of me."' (21: Nohl, 297; Knox, 248)*

Not only the eating of the body and the drinking of the blood, but every eating and drinking transcends the restricted circle of the 'conventional sign' and presents itself as a field, on which the restrictive character of signs can be inscribed for the first time. For if signs and what is signified are alien to each other, according to Hegel's definition of them, and are connected only in a Third thought according to the categories of the understanding, the semantic reference which is actualized in the meal is conceivable only as a concrete unification. The model of unification in this case is, as previously for the act of love, eating. In the meal shared in common, objective manifestation and the subjective experience of a single participation are brought together in one.

> *Hegel cites an ethnological example: 'When an Arab has drunk a cup of coffee with a stranger, he has eo ipso made*

*a bond of friendship with him. This common action has
linked them, and on the strength of this link the Arab is
bound to render him all loyalty and help' (21: Nohl, 297).
Freud cites the same example for the same problem in
Totem and Taboo: 'The ethical force of the public sacrificial meal rested upon very ancient ideas of the significance
of eating and drinking together. . . . Customs still in force
among the Arabs of the desert show that what is binding
in a common meal is not a religious factor but the act of
eating itself. Anyone who has eaten the smallest morsel of
food with one of these Bedouin or has swallowed a mouthful of his milk need no longer fear him as an enemy but
may feel secure in his protection and help. Not, however,
for an unlimited time; strictly speaking, only so long as the
food remains in the body. . . . .If a man shared a meal
with his god he was expressing a conviction that they were
of one substance.' (38: S. Freud, 'Totem and Tabu' in* The
Origins of Religion *(Harmondsworth: Penguin, 1985),
195–6)
And Hegel continues: 'The common eating and drinking
here is not what is called a symbol. The connection
between symbol and symbolized is not itself spiritual, is
not life, but an objective bond . . . to eat and drink with
someone is an act of union and is itself a felt union, not a
conventional symbol.' (21: Nohl, 297; Knox, 248)*

As little as the meal is a sign which remains distinct from what it signifies, so little is its ontological quality exhausted in the mere feeling of
the participants that they are already unified through their common
deed. The object of their common eating, that is, which as food and
drink is still distinct from their community, is already conceived as this
community itself. The cup of coffee or the gulp of milk is already the
materially intuitable unity of the common meal; the gulp of wine or
the smallest morsel of bread is already the body and blood of the loving
unification configured in Christ. Hegel can call Christ's statement that
'This is my body, this is my blood' a religious statement and, more
precisely, a statement which 'approximates' to the religious, because in

it the principle of subjective unification in love appears as bound to the object-like food. In this food, the principle of love is 'not merely represented as in a picture, an allegorical figure, but attached to something actual, and is given and enjoyed in something actual, the bread' (21: Nohl, 298). It is as a sign, exactly, that the meal would still signify in the same way as an allegorical figure does, and would achieve its meaning only in something else, which is not sensuously present, but merely thought. And as with a parable, in which the terms of comparison are materially separated and only conceptually united, the meal as an anticipation of redemption, as 'gain', 'advantage' or 'favour', would refer only to a concept which transcends the present unity of objectivity and idea, particularity and universality. Hegel's differentiations are all directed against the semiological reductions of the meal to a structure of significance, reductions which defer the synthesis of signifier and signified, which defer the understanding of this synthesis to some place beyond the current context of experience. This restriction was presented in exemplary fashion by Kant's critical restriction of the power of judgement to a mechanism of nature, the restriction of teleology to a fiction. This conspires with the fact that in his philosophy of religion Kant denounced the Lord's Supper, conceived not as a means of moral self-assurance but as pleasing to God *in itself*, as a fetish-meal (55: *Religion . . .* , A 282). Hegel attempts to demonstrate, against this mechanistic and, for him, itself fetishistic semiology of the meal, that the latter is something divine in itself. The fact of the unmistakable communication of a truth, and even the experience of the self-contained unity of the self, could be explained only through such apparently empirically grounded and linguistic transcendentalizations of meaning.

The meal is neither a parable, nor an anticipation, nor a sign, nor an allegory; it is a symbol. Hegel speals of 'symbolic action', and his elucidations explicate the strict concept of the *symbolon*, as developed in antiquity. In order to make clear that bread and wine are not merely bread and wine in the meal of love, but are more than materially useful objects, he compares them with the pieces of a ring which are carried by friends as a sign of recognition and an indication of their belonging together, that is, as symbols. In Hegel's text, food and drink, the body and blood of Christ, on the one hand, and eating and those who eat on the other, but also, thirdly, the united eaters and the eaters in their individual particularity, all figure as symbols, as pieces of a circle which belong together. Just as those who are distinguished within a pair are symbolically related, each of the three pairs relates symbolically to the others. The meal is their synthesis. A synthesis of meals, which can in no case refer to a meaning abstracted from them, but which manifests in these very meals, like the segments of a ring, the More, the fact that they belong to a whole. In the meal the parts are the whole. Every individual morsel of bread *is* [*ist*] the bread, is Christ and is the community of eaters. Every individual gulp of wine *is* the wine, is the life of Christ, is the gathering of those who drink. They themselves objectively are their own unity as relata with their relation. The meal conclusively reunites the symbolic segments and actualizes the unity of difference and unity within itself.

But: every individual bite of bread *eats* [*ißt*] and *is* the bread, *eats* and *is* Christ, and *eats* and *is* the community of eaters. Or, as Hegel writes: 'Yet the love made objective, this subjective element become a *thing*, reverts once more to its nature, becomes subjective again in the eating' (21: Nohl, 299; Knox, 251). Insofar, then, as the meal, love objectified, ceases to be object-like and takes its course, insofar as the food of love is devoured and the wine of unity and difference is drunk, the More of the totality which was attached to this material form also disappears with it. The mouthful truncates the objective unity of the subjective with the subjective experience of this unity and thereby destroys its own partaking of what it eats. The meal breaks the ring that the meal itself forms into its symbolic parts. Its segments are no longer symbols which would in themselves already constitute a closed whole. The spirit and feeling of the symbolic objects, the mystical objects, as Hegel also calls them, bread and wine, do indeed become living, but as objects they disappear, 'the intellect is robbed of its own; matter, that which is soulless, is destroyed' (21: Nohl, 299; Knox, 251).

Heterogeneity, which procures entry into cultic action through the annihilation of the sensuous manifestation of the subjective, also makes itself felt in Hegel's own analysis. If the first part of the commentary on the Lord's Supper, the speculative interpretation of the formula of investiture, had treated the intuition and the spirit of love as a unity, now – as though the text itself had felt this bite, and were multiplying distinctions under its pressure – their irreconcilability is asserted. It is stated that:

> 'There are always two things there, the faith and the thing, the devotion and the seeing or tasting. To faith it is the spirit which is present; to seeing and tasting, the bread and wine. There is no unification for the two. The intellect contradicts feeling, and vice versa.' (21: Nohl, 300; Knox, 252)

Under the bite which, intending to combine the objective unity of love with the subjective experience of it, destroys its own closure; under the bite which reintroduces between itself as objective and itself as subjective that difference which was already sublated in its object through the sacramental magic of symbolization – the spiritual meal in which the logos proffers itself as Christ reveals itself as writing.

> 'Yet the love made objective, this subjective element become a thing, reverts once more to its nature, becomes subjective again in the eating. This return may perhaps in this respect be compared with the thought which in the written word becomes a thing and which recaptures its subjectivity out of an object, out of something lifeless, when we read. The simile would be more striking if the written word were read away, if by being understood it vanished as a thing, just as in the enjoyment of bread and wine . . . the objects vanish as objects.' (21: Nohl, 299; Knox, 251)

The difference between eating and reading, between the *corpus mysticum* and writing, a difference which Hegel attempts to stabilize despite his own comparison, is expounded once again through a further comparison. The writing is a stone, which resists transformation into the subjective totality which is exhibited in it.

> 'When lovers sacrifice before the altar of the goddess of love and the prayerful breath of their emotion fans their emotion to a white-hot flame, the goddess herself has entered

> *their hearts – yet the marble statue remains standing in*
> *front of them. In the love-feast, on the other hand, the cor-*
> *poreal vanishes and only living feeling is present.' (21:*
> *Nohl, 299; Knox, 251)*

If the stone, then, on one side resembles writing, as a material object
which remains external even to the subjective experience of it, it also
resembles in turn, once eroded and turned to dust, the crushed communion wafer, in eating which the sensation of love and its material
form fall apart, and forcibly dirempt the symbol in which they were
formally unified. The feeling produced by either – the Greek gods now
crumbled to dust and the divine food now melted in the mouth – is
not love as objectified in an individual figure, but rather 'melancholy
over the incompatibility between living forces and the corpse' (21:
Nohl, 301; Knox, 252).

The same is true of reading. All reading is melancholy, because it
must work through the experience of the irreconcilability of the corpse
of writing, in which the thought has petrified to an external form, with
its subjective revivification in understanding. Reading is the work of
mourning over the loss of this unity of objectivation and subjectivity, a
loss which the act of reading itself produces. Reading is therefore
potentially infinite, a melancholia, because it repeats the very tear
which it attempts to mend.

> *Twenty or thirty years after writing these fragments Hegel*
> *once again noted, in his lectures on aesthetics, the connec-*
> *tion between reading and mourning in the form of the*
> *sculpted Gods of Greece: 'The blessed gods mourn as it*
> *were over their blessedness or their bodily form. We read in*
> *their faces the fate that awaits them, and its development,*
> *as the actual emergence of that contradiction between*
> *loftiness and particularity, between spirituality and sensu-*
> *ous existence, drags classical art itself to its ruin.' (14:*
> *TWA, 86; 15: TWA, I, 485)*

Reading the text, like eating the communion wafer, opens up difference, precisely insofar as it seeks to supply the lack immanent in its
objects, their persistent externality, precisely insofar as it seeks to close
the difference.

Reading the drama of the Christian eucharist likewise repeats the 'tragedy of the Jewish people' (21: Nohl, 260).

If the divinity which was promised melts away in the mouth, the unification manifested in the meal also then reverts to the harshest opposition, since the promised divinity remains something other than the bread which can be eaten and the wine which can be drunk.

Insofar as eating transforms the perceptible representation of a unity of eater and food, a unity of the eater with the partners in the meal, and a unity of the mere representation of this unity with unity itself, into pure subjectivity, without leaving a remnant, and in this way sets out the content of the sacramental food, it annihilates just this content – the unity of subjectivity and objectivation – through its restriction to merely subjective experience. The subjectification of the objective unity of sign and signified leaves this unity behind as a merely objective representation. The result of the symbolic meal is therefore quite other than symbolic; it divides irreconcilably into two relics of the original unity of the meal, into a perceptible or intellectual representation on the one side, and empty feeling on the other. The eating of the meal – like the reading of the writing – has the paradoxical character that this meal, as symbolic – like this reading, as meaningful – is not eaten, is not read. The symbol of onto-logical unity disintegrates through its performance, through the practical reincorporation in which it can alone be realized; the symbol literally collapses through itself into allegory.

This dialectic of the meal, which shatters the symbolic ring of speculative dialectic in such a way that its pieces can no longer be fitted together, means that the meal, insofar as it annihilates objectivity, is 'not objective enough' for a religious act (21: Nohl, 300); but insofar as it remains distinct, as material, and as a representation of unity, from its onto-logical content, the meal is too objective, that is, it does not have its objectivity as a unity of subjective and objective. Too subjective, too objective; too much and not enough has been eaten. The infinity figured by the food not only remains ungraspable for the bite, but also remains unsuitable for the system of the gradual progressive completion, into which it is supposed to be incorporated as a moment, since – although Hegel would like to believe otherwise when he characterizes the Lord's Supper as a transition between love and religion – there is no path from the system towards religion leading out of this system which would not also constitute a path back into the forms of a dead opposition.

With this tear in the ring of progressive synthesis, which destroys the symbolic character of its pieces, Hegel's text itself, in which the speculative food offers itself as a writing, meets a mouth, which reads it neither in the sense of a transcendental hermeneutic, nor in the sense of a speculative sublation of such a hermeneutic – a mouth for which the writing proves illegible and inedible. For just as Hegel presents the foundation of a religion of love in the allegorical form of Christ's foundation of such a religion, so he proclaims the original eucharistic formula at the Lord's Supper not merely with the voice of the commentator, but, indistinguishably, with Christ's voice as well; citing Christ's voice and imitating it at the same time.

> '[Jesus] *broke the bread and gave its to his friends: "Take, eat, this is my body sacrificed for you". So also when he took the cup: . . . this is my blood. . . . Not only is the wine blood but the blood is spirit. The common goblet, the common drinking, is the spirit of a new covenant . . . and of the fruit of the vine I will not drink again until the day when all shall be fulfilled.'* (21: Nohl, 298 ff.; Knox, 250)

Not only is what Christ offers to his disciples and to his congregation as his own flesh and blood named and interpreted by Hegel, but this gift becomes the gift of the text, a writing mimetically repeated in flesh and blood. But just as bread and wine is not flesh and blood alone, but also 'is' that which begets their unity, spirit, in which they are brought together into a new union; so the meal, which this text once more serves up, is not merely writing and stone and flesh and blood, but Being, which begets the identity of all these as spirit. If, however, Being is in this way writing, if the meal of the spirit is a stone, it falls, as a stone, out of the encircling ring of unity and remains, as a writing, interpreted in its reading, set over against the unity which is completed in it. Being writes itself as an entirely onto-logical relation, and not (Hegel insists upon this) as a paralogical or parabolic relation; Being does not merely externally resemble the writing which attempts to renew its covenant, nor does it remain alien to writing in what Hegel scorns as the 'harsh combination' of allegory (21: Nohl, 298); rather Being is this very writing, and as such transforms itself in the ontological process of its transubstantiation into the characters of an ontography. Hegel – once again – is reading. And insofar as he reads the scene of the Lord's Supper as a writing, and writes it as he reads it, the scene of the meal and that of its writing and its reading are instantly exposed to that cut through which unity separates itself from itself within unity, through which Being separates itself from itself within Being. Hegel, the writer of a new gospel and the favourite disciple of the Lord, whom he himself is, is beheaded, and can neither eat nor read what he proffers in the cup and in the bowl of the text, the gift of his word, his flesh and blood, his writing. As in Hölderlin's 'Patmos':

> *His head falls and, golden, lay like inedible and*
> *imperishable writing*
> *Visible upon a dry dish.*

This writing of the meal, which Hegel provides, would, once read and gathered, disappear in the pure subjectivity of its meaning, and would show itself in the sheer inwardness of its signification as empty, cut off from the unity of the subject with its objective form. The promise [*Versprechen*] of the divine word would be unfulfilled, merely promised [*versprochen*], a *lapsus calami*. If merely read, this writing would still, even after the reading, remain external to the understanding of its content, would remain a dead object, without any connection with the unity sedimented within it. Gathered [*aufgelesen*] or read – the writing of the speculative meal remains unread. And just as the spiritual food of the *corpus mysticum* remains inedible, because it is destined for eating alone, so the writing of the ontological word remains unreadable, because it is destined for reading alone.

Being is what goes away empty. It is left behind as refuse and scraps after the meal, in the form of a fetish-like remnant, either of the representation of possible unity, or of its material sign. The complement, which was to add writing and food to the subjective synthesis of love, ruptures the immanent unity of love and subverts its own function. The addition subtracts. The bond cuts. The complement diminishes.

The title, the head, of the pleroma falls and transforms
itself into something else, into the travesty of another title
and another head:

APEPTOS; OR, HOW TO EAT

Just as the reading which Hegel adds as a complement to the text of
the gospel comes up against the unreadability of what is only readable
and read, so a reading which, following Hegel's example, adds itself as
an interpretation to Hegel's text, posits that text, which is destined for
readability, as different from itself. How can a reading which comes
up against the impossibility of a speculative reading of the writing
still be read; how can a meal, which proffers its matter as inedible, be
eaten?

How can the Hoc est enim corpus meum *presented over*
the corpse of the writing be understood, in the absolute
mass, which Hegel, or another, reads?

The question of readability is that of the speculative-dialectical sublation of the writing in an understanding which unifies its objective
characters with its subjectively intended meaning and restores the circle
of significance without remainder. A question which dashes the reading
of the texts of speculative philosophy against its own impossibility –
against the impossibility of sublating the sublation and continuing the
circulation of its meaning as this reading itself demands. This impossibility is not imposed upon reading and its writing like an external
boundary, one which would, as a merely empirical objectivation of
onto-logical process, always already have overstepped the mark; it
emerges, rather, from the principle of the philosophy of unification
itself, which would have to objectify the unity of subject and object
symbolically, and would have to be able to complete this objective sub-
ject-object as an objective-subjective relation. The difference between
signifier and signified, which no rationalistic, psychologistic, sociological or speculative reading, nor any hermeneutic or pragmatistic
metatheory of readin, can close, is opened up by the very system which
attempts to restore unity. The bite of incorporation into the pure Being
of the word itself cuts into Being and word and splits any possible self
off from itself. In the unity of Being and language, subject and object,

something else is written, something which is not reducible to the relation between them. Symbol and system circumscribe a rupture, which
remains open even in the act of its assimilation. In this rupture speaks
– if indeed it does speak – not something other, but – allegorically –
another kind of speaking, one which cannot be re-collected by ontological speech.

> *On the interpretation – which was, incidentally, current
> amongst the church fathers – of the lamb of Passover in the
> Lord's Supper as holy scripture and of the holy scripture as
> the lamb of Passover, Origen writes (in Joan. lib. 10,
> 18–): 'In eating, one should begin with the head, that is to
> say with the most important and most fundamental doc-
> trines about heavenly matters. One should end with the
> feet, since the last things which one should seek to get to
> know are the slightest of natural things according to their
> worth, the purely material, the subterranean, evil spirits
> and impure demons. For the doctrine about these things,
> which is also contained in the mysteries of scripture, can
> figuratively be called "feet" of the lamb. The "entrails" (of
> the lamb), the inside . . . and hidden parts (of scripture)
> must not be thrown away, but one must rather treat scrip-
> ture as if it were a single body entire. And the extremely
> firm and solid harmonious composition should not be
> reduced or hacked apart in any way. For this is what is
> done by those who wilfully tear apart the spiritual unity of
> the spirit which breathes in all the scriptures.' (Quoted
> from 81: H.-J. Spitz,* Die Metaphorik des geistigen
> Schriftsinns *[Munich: 1972], 20)*

A reading which reads its text from the perspective that its totality
cannot possibly be restored, must not only read things other than those
written in the text, and thereby relate to the text not as a living context
of meaning, but as a written, broken, worm-eaten and battered corpse;
it must also read otherwise than do the other participants in this
totem-meal of the text. In their metalepsis of the corpse, those who
read this writing and eat this meal, are – for the symbolic surplus of
unity is still effective even when it has allegorically disintegrated –

related to each other as dead people, and as in this bread which is flesh and this wine which is blood, they eat and drink of each other, so this unity which has died, the corpse of writing, eats of their flesh and blood. As I read them – the writing and the others – and in this Other read myself as universal, so the writing and the others read me and in me themselves as particular. Reader and writing are the limbs and members of a necrophilological syllogism. We are to be concluded in the concept; but the conclusion cannot be brought to a close in the concept. The writing and its other readers read me, a piece of the corpse like them, even though I would not be readable; they eat this piece, even though it could not be integrated without remainder into the now dead organism of its universality. To break – with me. Since writing and reading remain external to the speculative content of what is given and received in them, the relation between the meal which they offer, which they have in their readers, and that of the readers upon each other, cannot be speculative either. Indigestible, like stones, each of which has petrified the other – medusa'd Medusas – which grind upon one another.

Even in his very last works, Hegel never gave up the wish to erase and to eradicate writing, a wish which he takes so rigorously to its limits in this passage on the Lord's Supper, perhaps the most fully developed amongst the writings of his youth. And like this wish, the analogy between writing and food remains alive in his texts from the earliest to the last. At a very early stage he reproaches Klopstock on the grounds that sensitive hearts 'may reject much' in his *Messias* 'which is digestible and credible for coarser people' (21: Nohl, 358), and criticizes objective religion, which imprints its written signs on the memory of the believer, for the fact that 'the fair and delicate plant of the free and open mind, is borne down by the burden [of dead knowledge], or just as roots work their way through a light soil, and are entwined in it and suck their nourishment from it, but are turned aside by a stone and seek another path, so the burden laid on the memory remains lying there unbroken until the mature intellectual faculties either shake it off completely or leave it aside and draw no nourishing sap from it' (21: Nohl, 7–8; 39: Harris, 485). In the rejection or the displacement of the indigestible stone, however, an alien externality remains and restricts the area of life. That which has been left to lie undissolved, the stone, must be sublated into the order of Being, must be transformed, as nourishment, into a moment of life. The heterogeneous and petrified element appears in language as its written and grammatical form, as a mechanically reproducible abstraction performed by the understanding upon the sensuous-unsensuous organism of language itself. The late systematics of the *Encyclopaedia* can thus demand, in its analysis of the semiological process, 'that learning to read and write an alphabetic writing is to be esteemed as an infinite means of education' since it directs attention to the formal and abstract elements of language, in which the peculiar forms of spirit, the forms of the transformation of the external into spirit's own inwardness, become knowable (10: TWA, Enc., III, §459, Addition; cf. 6: TWA, 521). The path to what is one's own leads through – one's own – alienness.

In his rectoral address in Nürnberg at the end of the school year 1809, Hegel describes the path through this alien land of grammar and writing – and grammar, in Hegel, is always to be understood as the science of the written character of language. There this alien land has the concrete form of foreign, and, especially, ancient, languages, which Kant had also assigned to a privileged role as a 'pattern of taste' (52: *CJ*, 55) on account of their dead and unchanging quality. These languages, as a 'spiritual immersion' and 'secular baptism', must 'initiate' every speaker into taste and science. Hegel evokes the picture of a *scene*: 'we must', he emphasizes, 'take up our lodging with them so that we can breathe their air, absorb their ideas, their manners, one might even say their errors and prejudices, and become at home in this world' (4: TWA, 318; Knox, 325). This food is not permitted to be the 'sensuous *material*' from which the plant 'sucks its nourishment,' the forces for its own reproduction, but must be 'only the intellectual content', the 'substantial inwardness', which as '*mother*' of the spiritual present offers support, nourishment and shelter (4: TWA, 319). Language is a mother, a mother tongue, but a mother who has become alien and distant, divided from us by the 'partition wall' of death. It must be experienced as something alien, in order to provide appetizing nourishment, for its translation into the sphere of our familiar language can only –

another communion wine – 'taste like Rhine wine, which has lost its flavour' (ibid., 320). What is foreign cannot be transformed into what is one's own, nor enjoyed as the spiritual nourishment of this mother tongue, by means of translation, imitation, or copying.

Remoteness must both lead spirit out of its natural proximity to itself and then lead spirit as remoteness into a proximity which it can only consciously and objectively arrive at by means of this circuitous route.

For the sake of closeness spirit seeks distance. 'What is strange, and far away, attracts our interest and lures us to activity and effort: it seems to be the more desirable the more remote it is and the less we have in common with it' (4: TWA, 321; Knox, 328). This is the ruse of reason: that it exhibits its property to itself in the form of something alien; it exhibits what is close at hand as distant. For the distant proximity, which is how spirit determines its own relation to itself, is also the mode in which it feeds off itself as off its own mother tongue.

It is, conversely, from the hardest, most petrified aspect of what is alien, the mechanical side of the grammatical categories, that it sucks the forces for its reproduction and self-appropriation.

> *'For it is the mechanical that is foreign to the mind, and it is this which awakens the mind's desire to digest the indigestible food forced upon it, to make intelligible what is at first without life and meaning, and to assimilate it.' (4: TWA, 322; Knox, 328)*

With complete consistency of metaphor, Hegel characterizes the nourishment drawn from what is distant as 'undigested' – not, it should be noted, as indigestible. But this nourishment, which spirit draws from its mother, is at the same time nothing other than its own substance, is, once again, the secret secretion which spirit itself is. With this nourishment it digests its own proximity – as yet undigested in the circuitous diversion through remoteness. The categories of the understanding, which are sedimented in language as 'elementary philosophy' and, as the Encyclopedia calls them, 'pure spirits' of logic (8: TWA, Enc., I, §23, Addition 2), present themselves in the 'lifeless' and 'mechanical', in the written character of grammar. Grammar is the dead mother, writing, Grammeter, from which spirit can be nourished all the more surely and lastingly, since in its shrine life is conserved, removed from all alteration and decay. And, conversely, this approximation, the digestion of the undigested and the appropriation of the alienated self, is completed in a formal and mechanical process: that of the reading of a writing:

> '[The abstractions of the intellect performed in learning grammar] *are as it were the individual letters, or rather the vowels, of the intellectual realm; we have to begin with them in order first to spell and later to read the language of mind.' (4: TWA, 322; Knox, 329)*

Spirit reads and eats itself as the nourishment, which has become writing, of the departed mother tongue. And conversely it is as this mother that spirit reads itself as its own writing, technography, and devours itself as its own product. The reciprocal relationship between spirit's nourishment through the writing of the mother and the nourishment of the mother grammar through the revivifying reading of the son is the process in which the relationship between language and thinking, the self-relation of spirit to itself as its own language, is realized.

> *Marx amused himself on the topic of this self-relation as the law of speculative dialectic, according to which ultimately the son is the father or even mother of the mother, that is, his own grandmother: 'Herr Szeliga' (so he writes in* The Holy Family *about the 'speculative flower of Mary') 'Herr Szeliga faithfully follows Hegelian speculation, if, for him, the daughter can be taken as the mother of her father according to "logical consistency". In Hegel's philosophy of history, as in his philosophy of nature, the son gives birth to the mother, spirit to nature, the Christian religion to the heathen world, the result to the beginning' (60: MEW, II, 178). But even today this conversion is taken by its critics, as though they were writing only after Marx and not also after Freud, as a practical joke. Nobody would dispute that it is comical – and only the philosopher forces himself to keep a straight face. But we should also ask where the joke lies, and what relation the knowing which it expresses bears to the unconscious.*

This is a perpetual Lord's Supper, which spirit and language share together. In this Lord's Supper, since even in the lifeless-mechanical forms of the grammatical categories of the understanding spirit has to do only with its own alienated form, no remnant of dead literalness appears to be left over, no corpse, which is not resurrected, and no stone, which is not removed. The oral copula of the son, who becomes his father, spirit, with the mother tongue: one which eats.

> *And yet another meal, once again, that of Novalis:*
> *'Communal eating is a symbolical act of unification. . . .*
> *To enjoy, dedicate, and assimilate everything, is to eat, or*
> *rather eating is nothing more than a dedication. All spiri-*
> *tual enjoyment can therefore be expressed through eating.*
> *– In friendship one in effect eats of one's friend, or lives off*
> *him. It is a genuine trope to substitute the body for the*
> *spirit – and at a memorial feast to a friend to enjoy his*
> *flesh, with bold, supersensuous imagination, in every*
> *mouthful, and in every drink to relish his blood. . . .*
> *Who knows what a sublime symbol blood may be?*
> *Precisely what is repellent about the constituents of the*
> *organism leads us to conclude that there is something very*
> *sublime in them. We shudder before them, as before ghosts,*
> *and sense in this curious mixture, with childish horror, a*
> *mysterious world which perhaps resembles a woman we*
> *once knew. . . . We enjoy the Nameless (genius of nature)*
> *in our sleep. – We awake, like the child at the mother's*
> *breast, and recognize how all that refreshes and strengthens*
> *us came to us as a result of favour and love, and how air,*
> *drink and food are the constituent parts of an inexpressibly*
> *dear person.' (72: Novalis,* Schriften, *ed. R. Samuel*
> *[Darmstadt: 1965], II, 620 ff.)*

That there is no unity between the letter and its substantial content; that the meal of love and of friendship, even when it has been consumed, remains object-like and opposed to the principle of subjectivity – this argument against the speculative dignity of reading and eating is not ignored in Hegel's later system, but it is indeed moderated. In that system, the mechanical aspect of eating stands only on the threshold of the authentic sphere of spirit, in which the mechanics of reading and writing have their place, on the threshold of thinking. However different they are in other respects, neither can ever enter the field of the unity of subject and object, since both are mechanical; yet they indeed participate in this field as its material presupposition and its formal self-mediation. The formal form of mediation means, on the one hand, that it obeys an abstract legality of the understanding, but, on the other, that it obeys a principle of contingency, which cannot entirely be governed by the autonomy of consciousness, still less by that of self-consciousness. Recollection, then – the first stage of the second main stage of intelligence before thinking – is characterized throughout the *Encyclopaedia* as the 'unconscious pit' of intelligence where 'at first, I do not yet exercise full command over the images slumbering in the shaft or pit of my inwardness, am as yet unable to recall them *at will*'.

> '*No one knows what an infinite host of images of the past slumbers in him; now and then they do indeed accidentally awake, but one cannot, as it is said, call them to mind*' (10: Philosophy of Mind, 205). In the Jenaer Realphilosophie Hegel considers such '*accidental*' recollections: '*In phantasmagoric representations we are surrounded by night; here a bloody head suddenly shoots out, there a white shape, and they disappear again as suddenly. One perceives this night when one looks another human being in the eye – one peers into a night which inspires terror; the night of the world which here lowers towards us*' (24: JR, 180 ff.).

The intelligence is not master of its own recollected images. They have a time and a causality which is independent of the intelligence. Nor is this night-time – 'at first not yet' overcome – completely illumined even in the forms of writing, which enter at the summit of the next stage, the imagination, and where the time of thought, which disappears into itself, is paralysed and spellbound in the 'sculptural' externality of a spatial figure. For the 'hieroglyphical reading', which is what the reading of alphabetical writing, a writing which is 'in and for itself more intelligent' than hieroglyphs, eventually becomes through habit, when it no longer requires a representation of the sounds which are heard in time – such reading is 'for itself a deaf reading and a dumb writing' permanently bound to an externality heterogeneous to consciousness. Against this, the 'proper relation' between space and time in language is 'that the visible language relates to the sounding language only as a sign; the intelligence is expressed immediately and in an unconditioned way through speaking' (10: TWA, Enc., III, §459, Addition). Writing exhibits itself, then, like a residue of the nocturnal pit of recollection. The sensuous aspect of its spatiality cannot be completely dissolved by the time of consciousness, which is more unsensuous and which de-sensualizes. Reading, even if in the written signs of imagination it relates to objects posited by the intelligence, rather than merely offered to it, remains a repetition of the 'phantasmagoric representations' from the unconscious pit of imagination and a reproduction of their 'contingent' temporality.

Hegel's subsequent construction, once again, passes through and beyond the night which, in this way, hangs over thinking, not merely from the viewpoint of the other, but from thinking's own form of articulation. For what has been surpassed, and what has been surpassed in the form of the memory which preserves and reproduces names, returns transformed in this construction. The object, to whose mere image the intelligence was still restricted in recollection and in the sign-forming imagination, is in the memory the image- and intuition-less *name* of this object. What is presented to intelligence, in the name, as intelligence's own product, cannot 'as it were be read off from the tableau of the imagination'; it is not a pictorial or alphabetic writing, to which meaning could be opposed like something perceptible. The name no more refers to a meaning [*Sinn*] than it still possesses a sensuous character [*Sinnlichkeit*] itself. It is drawn from a pit other than the pit of recollection, that is, from the 'deep pit of the ego', and appears rather as the being of the matter itself which is retained 'from memory' in the intelligence itself (10: TWA, Enc., III, §462). The shaft of the I has become, in its 'difference from the thing, something quite empty, a spiritless container of the word, that is, it has become mechanical memory' (ibid., Addition). In memory the '*excess of recollection*' is converted into the most extreme evacuation of meaning, and the complete abandonment of subjectivity by spirit (ibid.). In this way the subject relates both to the being of the names produced by it, and to itself, as to the meaningless objectivity of a mechanism. By virtue of the identity of the intelligence and its content, word and meaning, language and subject-matter, subject and object, appear equally hollowed out. For this reason Hegel calls this hollow subjectivity 'the universal space of names as such, that is, of meaningless words' (10: TWA, Enc., III, §463).

In order to justify giving abstract subjectivity the title 'mechanical memory', Hegel refers to the exposition of the 'object' in the 'doctrine of the concept' (8: TWA, Enc., I, §195), where the immediacy of the concept in natural relationships, such as pressure and impact, and, beyond this, in the treatment of piety, regulated by 'ceremonial laws', and in intellectual activities, 'like for example reading, writing, making music, etc.', is characterized as a 'formal mechanism'. The mechanics of such relations and operations shows itself to be a subordinate form of the concept insofar as it only arises within the general organism of nature and spirit in the case of some 'disturbance or restriction'.

> *'Thus a sufferer from indigestion feels* pressure *on the stomach after partaking of certain food in slight quantity; whereas those whose digestive organs are sound remain free from the sensation, though they have eaten the same things.'* (8: TWA, Enc., I, §195, Addition, 263)

The 'examples' have systematic rigour, as always in Hegel. Reading, poor digestion and the ceremonial activity of piety are all, like memory, forms of an assimilation of the external by the organism of the concept, an assimilation which itself remains external. It is in memory that this externality and objectivity are most clearly turned inwards to become an empty form of subjectivity itself. The difference from the space of writing, whose 'intelligent', but not inward, objectivity still resists the self-relation of thought, becomes absolute in the 'space of names', because memory is here confronted with its own complete spiritlessness – memory itself is writing, an 'empty bond', to which meanings are no longer alien and opposed, but into which these meanings, themselves empty, have transformed themselves. In this meaninglessness of language the distinction between meaning and name is erased in a way which was not possible in sensuous writing; the objectivity of the subjective is therefore no longer merely empty, but, as a *reflectedly* empty objectivity, is also a true and fulfilled one. The transition to thinking and the unity of subject and object which is produced in the course of this transition are stamped with this reversal, which is completed through the radical internalization of the external in memory. Language has passed over into thinking and thinking is one with being, which thereby offers itself to thinking in language.

The problem which concerns Hegel in the systematic discussion of the relation between language and thinking in the *Encyclopaedia* is the same as that treated in the *Spirit of Christianity*: how can a unity of subject and object be thought which is not merely a subjective unity, but both a subjective and an objective unity? If the unity of the subjective and the objective remains something subjective in the domains of recollection, imagination and memory, the borderline between this unity and a subjective-objective unity is crossed in thinking. If memory's content is still, for memory, a representation, thinking knows itself to be the subject matter which it thinks (cf. 10: TWA, Enc., III, §465, Addition). Thinking is the recollection of the unconscious pit of recollection and of the deep pit of the I – but it is at the same time the recollection in this pit of images and names and this pit's own recollection of itself. It is the re-collection into the pit, from which a 'bloody head' and meaningless names emerge and hover over thinking, and the re-collection of the names which are now known by heart, in which the names have been relieved of their threatening externality and meaninglessness. This dialectical inversion of the wellspring, an inversion of recollection, from a recollection of contingent images, to a re-collection or re-inwardization of thinking into its objects as into itself, can, however, succeed only on the condition that thinking relates to its own anticipatory forms, the realm of representations, as to *its own* other, therefore as to itself. In its Before its After is already there and in its After its Before still remains; and it is nothing else than the transition from Before to After, the re-collection of recollection, the transformation of the 'bloody head' and of the machine into a self-determined and complete thinking, of the meaningless into its meaning.

Not merely the abstract structure of this self-relation, but also the images in which it is articulated – for the realm of images persists, although subordinated, in thinking – remain invariant for the self-determination of this thinking. Thinking likewise relates to its grammatically fixed categories in the mode of re-collection, and, according to the account given in the rectoral address, in the mode of reading. Just as in the *Encyclopaedia* thinking delves into the hollow of empty names and contingent images, in order to unite with it, so, in reading the ancient languages, thinking is the house of mother language in which the son 'takes up his lodging' in order himself to become a dwelling for what he has himself devoured. Thinking recollects its recollection into language and is itself fulfilled thinking, a third term: the unity of the son – who, as his father, lives with the mother – with the mother, a son who only is the son through this unity of mother and son. The son, the unity of thinking with its linguistic and phantasmagoric anticipatory forms, begets himself as begotten and thus is for the first time what he is, the son. The image which the speculative self-relation of thinking recognizes as its own is a family portrait – the triad of father, mother and child, according to whose paradigm the early phenomenology of love as a self-relation of being is developed ('The child is itself the parents' [21: Nohl, 381]). But it is not the static relation between different positions within this family which provides the image for the speculative triad, but the reciprocal identification of these positions, the act, in which every relatum and every particular relation is united with all the others and becomes the whole relation. The paradigm of the speculative process is the image of incest.

Thinking, which reads its writing as that of the mother; and reading, the onto-logical family meal, are also a speculative incest.

A speculative sublation of incest. For just as the son *is* only the son as the son when he unifies himself as his own father with his own mother, and thereby makes himself his own mother; just as thinking is only thinking so long as it issues into the pit of recollection and mechanical memory: so, nevertheless, the unity and the self-relation which they both realize are at the same time more than merely this specific unity and this specific concept and are on the way to stepping beyond themselves into a further unity. In every such self-reunification a progress to something other is already at work; in every triad already a fourth, in every unity already a difference. But every possible difference – and in this the double sense of *Aufhebung* is retained – is determined in Hegel's work in such a way that it once more dissolves into a speculative unity; every fourth is so determined that it is reduced to an element of a new triad. The incestuous self-relation in the speculative circle of the family affects each difference with the principles of its trinitarian economy. But what cannot be protected by the law of its house, but only erased, the mechanical externality of the repetition of images, itself nonetheless prevails in the paradigmatic status held by the continually repeated image of the family triad in the articulation of systematic unity. As something external, a *determinativum*, it is itself inscribed into the law of its re-collection and marks in recollection the trait which gives the lie to its immanent infinity. The mechanical repetiton of this image of the speculative unity of being and thinking in language binds this unity itself to the site which it is supposed to have transcended by virtue of its structure of inversion and reflection: the site of a 'formal mechanism', of a 'disturbance and restriction', the site of a language which presents itself as meaningless writing and which is accessible only to a deaf reading and a dumb writing. The son, the unity of father and other, remains separated from them, from his own being, precisely insofar as he is that being. The trinitarian structure of self-relation is, in relation to itself, an irreducible fourth.

The ontological reconstruction of Christianity in the early writings also encounters a similar limit.

The defectiveness of the meal, since it can be measured against the paradigm of unity in love, is thereby known as defectiveness and can for this reason be superseded in the direction of a more developed form of unity. This higher unity, both subjective and objective, is envisaged in the 'religious domain' as the 'πλήρωμα of love' (21: Nohl, 302). The religious sphere is not principally expounded by Hegel as a social cult, but as the unity of reflection and love. If he formulates the corresponding programme – 'the task is to think pure life' – in terms of *thinking*, not merely *being*, this constitutes a demand which only a theory of pure being which understands itself as a religion can fulfil. If Hegel could object to the concept of self-consciousness yielded by the Kantian *Critiques*, especially that of practical reason, for condemning self-consciousness to remain an imperative power and an abstract universality beyond the concrete context within which the subject might act, and hence to remain, as it were, a shamanistic tribunal, which obstructs any possibility of unification, then it is equally the case that fulfilled unification is fulfilled only when it does not allow consciousness to stand as a power beyond it, but rather still contains the reflected universality of consciousness, its linguistic objectivation. For the sake of a distinction between a dualistic concept and a concept conceived speculatively, Hegel replaced the term 'pure self-consciousness' in his manuscript with the formulation 'the consciousness of pure life', clearly revealing that the ontology of the young Hegel is developed at a conscious distance from the aporetic reflection-theory of self-consciousness, which turns on the hinge of a hierarchically pre-ordered abstract subject – that is to say, the ontology of the young Hegel is developed out of the critique of the structure of moral self-consciousness, and Hegel's own early theory of self-consciousness is then built on the foundation of this ontology. Pure life's consciousness of itself as pure life – and Hegel defines pure life as Being – has an apparently aporetic character to the extent that Being is something in itself infinite, whereas consciousness is something particular and therefore finite – 'therefore his consciousness and the infinite cannot be completely in one' (21: Nohl, 303; Knox, 254). Yet this aporia appears as the signature [*Signum*] of a Kantianism which continues to work latently in philosophical language, which still retains the hierarchical relationship between the moral idea and its empirical realization. In a theory of pure Being we cannot speak of opposing finite thought to an infinity which it would relate to as itself (21: Nohl, 303 ff.).

The difficulties of providing a diction for philosophy appropriate to its speculative content, and, to put it differently, the difficulty of thinking pure being in such a way that the thought of pure being is one with pure being, so that its language is this being itself in its unity, which is both subjective and objective – this dilemma of Hegel's onto-logic on the terrain of a language ruled by Kantian dualism is the dilemma with which the form of Christ and the language of his gospel are confronted in the domain of 'Jewish culture'. This 'Jewish culture, which was so poor in spiritual relationships, compelled him to avail himself of objective ties . . . for expressing the highest spiritual realities' (21: Nohl, 305; Knox, 255), and to 'force' the most spiritual of things into such 'matter of fact and everyday ties' as 'I am the door; I am the true bread, who eats my flesh', etc. (21: Nohl, 306; Knox, 256). Even in this most philosophical of the gospels, whose text, written in Greek, not Hebrew, Hegel is preparing to interpret with these words, the speculative thought of Christianity 'labours' beneath the compulsion of the Jewish language of actuality and reflection. The proposition 'God *was* the word' is not an ontological proposition, because it implicitly insinuates that Being and its word is a past actuality, which no longer enjoys validity in the presence of the contemporary word which refers to it.

As little as spiritual being and its relatum, the logos, can be expressed in the medium of the language of reflection, just as little may the language of reflection, on the other hand, passively be taken for what it presents itself to be. It must be read. That ontological relationship which inheres in the language of reflection despite the pressure exerted by inauthentic ways of speaking must live again, without compulsion, in the relationship between its content and the reader:

> *'this language, which is always objective, thus obtains meaning and import only in the spirit of the reader'* –

and Hegel insists on the diversity of possible meanings and on the polysemy of what has been read – 'a meaning which differs according to the different ways in which the relationships of life and the opposition of life and death have come into his consciousness' (21: Nohl, 306; Knox, 256–7). With this argument, that the tension between the language of reflection and a speculative meaning can be brought into a unity of being and language only in the reader's spirit, not only is Hegel's reading of the gospel ontologically legitimated, but the praxis of the reading itself attains an ontological status. Religion, according to an etymological derivation of Cicero's which was certainly not unknown to Hegel, meant reading the sacred texts once again and over and over again. Hegel's reading and his writing are religion, the philosophical cultus, in which the unity of being and logos, God and world, thinking and life, is to be fulfilled.

'[A]ll reflection's expressions about the relations of the objective being . . . must be avoided. . . . Only spirit grasps and comprehends spirit' (21: Nohl, 305; Knox, 255). But how can the divine be spoken of with enthusiasm, as Hegel demands? How can the existence of God be expressed (21: Nohl, 397)? How can God speak, without what is expressed relating to this speaking as though to something heterogeneous? In the relation between speaking and what is expressed, between reading and what is read, the 'rending of life, a lifeless connection between God and the world' (21: Nohl, 308; Knox, 259) as presented in Jewish and Kantian doctrine, cannot be repeated, if the substance of ontology itself is not to be torn apart. The relata must be 'mystically' connected in the same way as the mystical pieces of the speculative-symbolic ring.

In order to clarify their relationship, Hegel cites the first sentences of the prologue to John's gospel. What is expressed must relate to speaking in the same way as the logos relates to God. But what is expressed is not, as the word 'ex-pressed' suggests, a merely externalized being. If the actual is to be regarded as divine throughout, then the gnostic model of emanation cannot suffice to explain the connection of being and language. Yet the logos must be emanation at the same time, that is, 'a part of infinite partition' and the life in this part. The logos relates as the son towardss the father; as the branch to the whole tree.

> '*The single entity, the restricted entity, as something opposed [to life], something dead, is yet a branch of the infinite tree of life. Each part, to which the whole is external, is yet a whole, a life. And this life, once again as something reflected upon, as divided by reflection into the relation of subject and predicate, is life (ζωη) and life grasped as such (φως, truth).*' (21: Nohl, 307; Knox, 258)

Hegel can refer in this exegesis to a syntactical ambiguity in the prologue to John's gospel and to the metaphor of the relationship between generations, one which belongs amongst the 'few natural expressions accidentally preserved in the Jewish speech of that time, and therefore to be counted among their more felicitous expressions' (21: Nohl, 308; Knox, 260).

*One of the few expressions in which the speculative iden-
tity of being and language, thinking and pure life is prefigured – 'accidentally preserved'. Yet this 'fortunate' and
'natural expression' of the father–son relationship appears
within the Jewish context, as Hegel elsewhere indicates, as
a denaturing fetishism of the genealogical table and of the
name (21: Nohl, 75), as the formula for an external self-
relation which is restricted to the sensuous sphere. The
absolute world-historical contingency of this 'expression' is
absolutely necessary, because of its substantive determinacy,
for the necessity of the history of the absolute; the decayed
metaphor of the relationship between generations is
absolutely necessary as a generative moment for the ontological theory of a pure self-relation. The transition
between the two systems – the fetishistic system and the
Christian system – is provided by the fortunate accident
which closes the gap which hovers in the uncertain middle
space between historical contingency and the teleology of
history, by an interpretation which follows this fortunate
accident and which places it in the service of necessity, in
its own service. The generation of the system of autogeneration remains bound to the heterogeneous alien body
of this expression; the appropriative interpretation of this
expression remains bound to its contingency, to the irreducible alterity of its ideological context. The system of historical self-production has its origin elsewhere than in
itself.*

'The relation of a son to his father is not a conceptual unity (as, for
instance, unity or harmony of disposition, similarity of principles, etc. .
. . On the contrary, it is a living relation of living beings, a likeness of
life' 21: Nohl, 308; Knox, 260). This relationship, equally removed
from the relationship of natural reproduction and from a unity under
concepts of the understanding, is not only the relationship of the person of Christ to God, but in general the relation of humanity to God,
of language to being, of truth to life. It is, then, not a relation between
different substances, but a 'transubstantiation' (21: Nohl, 391), which

takes place between speaking and what is spoken. The copula in the proposition 'Humanity (Jesus, as the Son) is God (pure life, as the father)' is accordingly, as has already been explicated in the logic of love, to be read dynamically and to be understood as an act of generation, which first of all begets its relata as relatives, as father and son, and, at the same time, identifies each with the other. In this way each relatum is the whole relation; each part, to which the whole is external, is at the same time the whole, pure transition. The son is son only insofar as he is at the same time his own father; the father is father only so long as he is his own son. And, since the ontological copula 'is' proves to be a genealogical copula here, it can be said more precisely that the son begets himself as the father who in turn begets himself as his son.

> *'. . . at home, where he is perhaps more important than his father.' (Chr. F. v. Schnurrer on Hegel, 10 September 1793; see 65: Nicolin, 24)*

In the speculative circle of generation every moment relates to the position of its own father, of its own son, and, since the son is the father of his own father, to the position of its own grandson. Hegel's text itself, which, as a spiritually inspired speech about spirit, shows itself here to be the logos, the language and the truth of Being, Being which is both the father and the son whom this father begets; yet is, as this son, at the same time this father, Being itself, which is purely at home with itself even in what has been separated from it, which reproduces only itself in its product, and which sustains itself in its own gift. Hegel's language – an economy of autogeneration – would be the pure, surplusless and remnantless transition from the son to the father, from being to consciousness, a sacramental transubstantiation in the speculative mass which he reads.

Hegel's language glosses the pure transition [*Übergang*] (and, indeed, since there are no differing substances, the pure *passage* [*Gang*]) which it displays, and which Hegel's language itself is, by a figure of transition, a metaphor. After the citation of a second Arabic example – 'Even in the expression "A son of Koresh", for example, which the Arabs use to denote the individual, a single member of the stock, there is the implication that . . . he himself is just the whole which the entire stock is' (21: Nohl, 308; Knox, 260) – Hegel develops

the metaphor of the 'infinite tree of life', which the interpretation of
the prologue to John's gospel already introduces, the metaphor of
another stock and its sons.

> 'A tree which has three branches makes up with them one
> tree; but every 'son' of the tree, every branch (and also its
> other 'children', leaves and blossoms) is itself a tree. The
> fibres bringing sap to the branch from the stem are of the
> same nature as the roots. If a tree is set in the ground
> upside down it will put forth leaves out of the roots in the
> air, and the boughs will root themselves in the ground.
> And it is just as true to say that there is only one tree here
> as to say that there are three.' (21: Nohl, 309; Knox,
> 261)

This 'example' of the tree and of the inversion of the trunk or stock,
of the whole and its parts, is introduced once again in the *Jenaer
Realphilosophie*, with all the restrictions which pertain to the merely
organic as such and which must necessarily be omitted in the explication of the speculative cycle:

> 'Root – a tree placed upside-down with its boughs in the
> earth, bursts into bud; the roots become complete branches
> . . . and branches are converted into roots; but Foliage, the
> free process, no longer has such solidity in itself that it can
> survive independently. This self does not arrive at its own
> proper full circle.' (24: JR, 130 ff.)

Kant, before Hegel and in no less radical fashion, indeed penetrating
literally to the root of the matter, had already described such an *ordo
inversus* of the tree and its branches, of the whole and its parts, as an
'example' of a natural teleology which would be more than mechanical.
For Kant a tree, provided that 'it [reproduce itself] according to its
species' and continue to sustain itself, is its own cause and effect.
'Secondly', Kant continues, 'a tree produces itself as an *individual*'
through the process of assimilating its nourishment, a process to which
Kant does not hesitate to 'accord equal respect' with reproduction
itself. 'Third, part of the tree also produces itself inasmuch as there is a
mutual dependence between the preservation of one part and that of
the others.'

'Hence even in one and the same tree we may regard each branch or leaf as merely set into or grafted onto it, and hence as an independent tree that only attaches itself to another one and nourishes itself parasitically. The leaves, too, though produced by the tree, also sustain it in turn; for repeated defoliation would kill it, and its growth depends on their effect on the trunk.' (52: CJ, B 287 ff.; Critique of Judgement . . . , *tr. W. S. Pluhar [Indianapolis, IN: Hackett, 1987], 250)*

That Hegel proceeds from the natural totality of the tree and the autonomous self-generation of its parts and its whole, whereas Kant in his exposition presents a digression upon grafting, and thereby upon the intervention of something heteronomous, which allows the totality of natural teleology to be thought of as something heterogeneous in itself, has its ground in the fact that for Kant the idea of the whole cannot be the cause of the connection between the parts, but only, heterogeneously, the 'ground of the cognition' of their unity. The idea of the whole does not originate in the objective context of nature itself, but is a merely subjective maxim for judging that context according to a 'distant analogy' on the part of self-determining reason. Since according to Kant's exposition it is the idea of unity which determines the manifold of nature as a whole, just as 'conversely (reciprocally)' (52: B 291) the latter itself combines into a unity; since the causality of reason and the causality of freedom, which come together in this reciprocal determination, nevertheless remain heterogeneous kinds of faculty [*Vermögenszweige*] – then their context, the context of teleology and mechanism, cognition and object, must be read according to the analogy of the grafting of a scion on to another tree. If Hegel's Christological tree explicitly includes the knowledge of totality as one of totality's own moments, and makes the self-conceived life into the universe of life itself, in Kant this knowledge behaves like a branch which is grafted on to another tree and feeds as 'parasitically' off the tree as the tree feeds off the branch. The knowledge of immanent teleology is thus indeed indebted to the totality of nature, but to a nature which is no longer merely natural, but at the same time rational. From the perspective of the idealist systems, which appealed from the start to the concept of teleological judgement, because the unifying link between the causality of freedom and the causality of nature could be seen in teleological judgement just as in aesthetic judgement, Kant's thought appeared inconsistent in presenting the idea of the whole, although analogous to the objective process of nature, as something heterogeneous to this objective process. But the 'gulf' between the causality of nature and the causality of freedom, over which the tree of teleological judgement is laid in order to build a bridge, cannot be closed by such a bridge, since the connection between reason and nature which is realized in teleological judgement remains bound to the grafting-on of something heterogeneous and accordingly must remain limited by its heteronomous *moment*.

Hegel cites the Kantian 'example', the prelude on the threshold of absolute idealism, in order to free the analogy put forward there from its *aná*, and to transform it into a relation of the pure logos. Here we can no longer speak of a 'holy mystery' in the 'connection of the infinite with the finite', nor of an 'unbridgeable gulf' by which the father is supposedly separated from the son, as the idea of ethical reason is separated from the categories of the understanding (52: 304). In the ontology of the Logos, which is one with being, there is no longer any room for the parasitism of an analogy which always leaves open a small remnant of the teleologically bridged gulf between father and son, between being and its word. In the speculative tree, whose roots are its branches, whose branches are its roots, whose movement is an unrestricted circulation of origin and result, space and time, its material determinants are sublated. But together with space and time, the linguistic articulations of the speculative tree's status had also to be sublated, since these articulations, as vocal utterance and as writing, are intrinsically bound to these two forms of intuition. For – once again – if it is the case that not only is the trunk the father of the leaves, but the leaves – and no leaf is missing – are also the father of the trunk; if being is not merely the father of consciousness, but this consciousness and its language are also at the same time the father of being, then this language, this pure consciousness just as much *is* this entire process of generation as it is its product. It can no longer be said of these terms that they relate to each other, that they mean each other, or describe each other, or testify to each other. Onto-logy is meaningless. The copula between father and son, species and individual, is so complete that they can now no longer even be said to beget one another, but only to be their own generation. Being and consciousness, pure life and language, are the act of their own generation. Yet if the argumentative reading of Hegel's text is to remain *strictu sensu* immanent, and to convey its meaning, then one can also no longer speak as though Hegel's text is *about* the being of the generation of these terms – for they *are* their generation *as* this text, and also as *this* text. My discourse is its own generation as discourse and being: a speculative semontology.

> *This reading is the generation of its text. Just as this text itself, a trunk, has produced this reading as one of its branches, so this text itself must be begotten ever anew as a living trunk whose meaning feeds off it. Without this inversion of the genealogical tree and without this self-eating there is no language and no speculative reading which could satisfy the demands of speculative ontology.*
>
> *In this way I would be the father of the text which I read. The relation between us, however, is trinitarian – I am only the father to the extent that the text copulates with me as the mother – since I am also the mother of the text, which I have to feed with its logos – the text is a teknovore – and produces me as the son who reads it. The father is the mother. This, grasped as a particular form, is the son. In the son both father and mother have, as their unity, their developed being ('The child itself is the parents' [21: Nohl, 381]). But these three no longer have this being as individual contingent figures, any more than they have it in an external institution -, but, rather, only in the fulfilled life of its whole relation, which dissolves all externality and erases particularity. It is not, then, I who read and am read, but instead through me the process of reading between its different relata reads and is read. The I and its name are devoured in this process.*
>
> *Reading and text – they beget and bear witness to each other – eat and feed each other.*

> *The process of speculative reading moves in the circle of the Holy Family.*

Hegel's reading unites with what it reads; the reading of Hegel with Hegel's reading. Referential discourse shows itself to be implicative. Only in this way does it become *religion*.

> *Thirty years after the interpretation of the prologue to John's gospel Hegel says in the* Lectures on the History of Philosophy: *'The spirit's testimony to the content of religion is religiosity itself; it is a witness that testifies* [bezeugt]; *this is at the same time to beget* [zeugen]. *Spirit begets itself, and does so only in bearing witness; it only is, insofar as it begets itself, testifies to itself, and shows itself, reveals itself.'* (18: TWA, Hist. Philosophy, I, 94)

Hegel reacts to Kant's critique of the anthropomorphism of the ideas of God and the ban on images which this critique produces with a theomorphizing of humanity. A human being – and not only Christ, who as the son of God and son of Man is only a paradigm of humanity in general – a human being *exists* only as a 'modification of divinity' (21: Nohl, 315) and thus is the concrete totality of the divine itself. Only in God does humanity have its essence; only in humanity does God have his essence. The consciousness of pure being, this self-consciousness of humanity as God, begets its self as something which begets it, and is itself nothing other than the pure copula of thought and being. Even Hegel's later religio-philosophic conception of self-consciousness is to be read in this sense: 'The Son's self-consciousness of himself is at the same time his knowledge of the Father; in the Father the Son has his knowledge of himself' (16: TWA, *Phil. Rel.*, I, 439). The synthesis of self and consciousness, of being and language is accomplished in all relata in such a way that consciousness, before all time and throughout all time, has always already generated itself as self-consciousness; that language, beyond all spatial and temporal articulation, has always already generated itself as ontological; both constitute the process of the be-getting of these moments and their sublation. Language, therefore, is this language only as the language of being and of its unity. This language itself is the concrete presence, the co-presence, and the transition, of language and being, of God and humanity into each other: not a metaphor in the sense that it is the image of a pre-existing meaning, but a metaphor in the sense that it exhibits a relation between image and meaning, which is still prior to its relata and without which these relata do not exist. The sign shows only where it – as what is shown – also itself *is*; Being is only where it also shows itself – as a sign.

> *Nietzsche – and how could Hegel's interpretation of Christianity be read without Nietzsche's interpretation of it – wrote of Christ in his* Antichrist *that:*
> '*The condition making it possible for these anti-realists even to speak is precisely that nothing they say is to be taken literally . . . Blessedness is not promised . . . : it is the only reality: everything else is a sign allowing blessedness to be spoken of.*
> *. . . only practising the gospel leads to God, indeed it is 'God'! – What the gospel did away with was the Judaism of concepts . . .*
> *The concept of 'the Son of Man' is not a concrete person who belongs in history, something individual or singular, but an 'eternal' reality, a psychological symbol freed from the concept of time. . . . by the word 'son' an entrance into the feeling-of-total-transfiguration of all things (blessedness) is meant, by the word 'father' this feeling itself, the feeling of eternity, of perfection is meant.' (66: F. Nietzsche,* Werke in drei Bänden, *ed. K. Schlecta [Munich: 1966], II, 1194–6)*
> '*The remnant is a sign': Nietzsche's interpretation of the gospel differs from Hegelian speculation in the fact that in Hegel's ontological dissolution of the sign, in the system of semontology, there is no remnant. Yet even in Hegelian speculation – this remains to be shown – the remnant, the sign which is not dissolved in being, the remnant and the rest which is silence, is not erased.*

The pure path of language to itself as being, the path of consciousness to itself as subject and substance, is a path back. In the language of the gospel, it is the 'return to oneness, to becoming like children', in which what has been lost through objectification and diremption is won back (21: Nohl, 316). Just as in the phenomenology of love, the diremption of the parents was sublated in the child, so in the ontology of religion it is the angel-children in whom the difference between a merely subjective unification in love and its objective determinateness is to be sublated – 'As an angel, the childlike spirit is represented not simply as in God without all reality, without existence of its own, but at the same time as a son of God, a particular' (21: Nohl, 316; Knox, 270). Hegel's angelology specifies the relationship in which subjectivity and objectivity are sublated in the figure of the angel as intellectual intuition – although this concept, which Kant reserves for the divinity, is not explicitly named: 'a man wholly immersed in seeing the sun would be only a feeling of light, would be light-feeling become an entity. A man who lived entirely in beholding another would be this other entirely, would be merely possessed of the possibility of becoming different from him' (ibid.). This relation is neither an abstract relation nor a purely philosophical one; rather, it is that social relation which is formed as a religious relation in the *name* of Christ (following his own theory of language, Hegel translates ὀνομα in Matthew 10.41 as 'spirit' [*Geist*]). Hegel's angels are this name, in which the unity of sensuousness and spirit, subjectivity and objectivity, unity and difference is completed socially. Every difference, even that between names, is erased in the name of the angel, the name of Hegel, of the absolute pleroma and the absolute ὀnoma; the son is the sun of the father and every sound of language is a 'unison in the harmony of the whole' (21: Nohl, 316). In this name the 'infinite tree of life' is erected.

But where is the earth in which this tree is planted, whether upright or upside-down? If its movement exhibits the reciprocal generation of father and son – where is the mother? Where, so far as the names of the angels are concerned, does this leave the witch? And where does it leave that reflection which, as external, castrative, 'repels' unification and 'reunification' (21: Nohl, 316; Knox, 270), which threatens the self-begetting of the father, of the son, of the grandchild, and which insinuates another language into this ontological language?

If the question as to the earth can be answered by saying that the
tree is rooted in itself and is without limit; if the question as to the
mother can be answered by saying that she is nothing but the very relation in which father and son are one; – there is still no answer to the
question as to the other, which for ever divides this same mother, the
witch, the father and the son from each other, and no answer to the
question as to the external reflection, in which speculative language
degenerates into an objective language – no answer which would satisfy
the philosophy of unification. In the life of the historical Jesus this
brute non-sublatable externality is represented by the state and by the
language of the Jews. In the religious life, as it is worked out in the
unity of father and son and in the further unity of father, son and congregation, the law is indeed sublated in such a way that it remains pure
life, even though it is realized in the form of law (21: Nohl, 268). But
it is precisely to pure life that the restriction which has already limited
subjective unity applies: that it must result in a destruction of all objectivity in itself and must, for this reason, provoke all the more massive a
resistance from a transcendentalistic language and culture. The Jewish
language of difference reawakens within the extended unity of being
and reflection in Christian onto-logic, and rebels against this unity,
since it is still unity and is therefore defective.

'Union and Being are synonymous; in every proposition the copula
'is' expresses the union of subject and predicate – a being' (21: Nohl,
383; 39: Harris, 513). In order to *be* a word of love, to *be* a word of
being, rather than merely to 'express' such words, the connecting word
'is' must be separated from its character as a sign, and the cut which
divides the signifier from the signified must itself be cut in such a way
that being is present in it in abundance. But the copula, in order not to
disappear itself as a word of being with this cut, which separates everything objective from it, in order to subsist as being, requires a complement. If the copula were a pure cut, suicide, self-castration, both
language and the being present in it would be erased once the unity of
language and being were fulfilled, and the *dea abscondita* of transcendental materialism would be restored. The *objective* unity of reflection
and love can repair this lack within a unity that is merely momentary
and ideal, by *exhibiting* this self-castration and the unity accomplished

by it. In the ontological philosophy – in just this unity of love and reflection – the pure, suicidal self-relation is therefore not erased, but extended by means of a relatum which allows it to be permanent. The copula, a self-castration set against itself in difference, is suspended in its complement. Being is not fulfilled in itself, it is fulfilled only in a presentation which delays its plenitude in the act of preserving it. The philosophical exposition of being therefore has the double function of sublation – it is the negation and the affirmation of pure life, the synthesis constituting the abstract idea is delegated to this exposition as to something external, an externality which is its own and into which *eo actu* it returns.

The exposition of pure life in the philosophical logos stands to pure life itself as the son does to the father. Hegel's ontology, the complement of the copula, is Christ. Suicide and self-castration, whose imago is figured in the Father, is exhibited in the, as it were, homosexual relation between father and son, being and language, pure life and philosophical reflection, in such a way that its merely negative identity is preserved and prolonged precisely through being inhibited. Dialectical ontology would be a self-castration objectified by means of a heterogeneous moment into a homosexual act, a self-castration postponed and sublated in its postponement.

But in this homogeneous relation between language and being the dilemma of the copula finds itself repeated – even if the objectifying court of reflection introduces a heterogeneous element into this relation, and even if the material difference involved in a language of presentation delays the realization of the pure self-relation of a language immediately replete with meaning. For the relation between copula and complement is, for its part, to be thought as a copula. Being and language beget and testify to each other; language does not express being, but is being; being is its own language. In the immanent circle described by the ontological tree, merely subjective unity is shown to be the model of its own objectification. This means, however, that what is achieved in the complement of religio-philosophical reflection – the suspension of subjectivity, the concrete articulation of a merely ideal ontological discourse – degenerates in the mode of its articulation. The model of merely subjective being still persists and with it the aporia of a language which, because it is, does not remain. The repeatable character of being, which is inaugurated by its philosophical exposition, is, then, at once combined with and closed to this being by means of the ontological determinacy of this exposition – which is impossible. Dialectical ontology returns, in a necessary short-circuit, to ideal ontology and, beyond this, to the meontological language of transcendentalism, to which the mother shows herself only in her concealment, to which being shows itself as its own nothing.

Ontological language is the language of revelation, in which nothing remains concealed. As that open language which excludes nothing, however, it must precisely exclude exclusion; as that language which conceals nothing, it must conceal concealment; as that language which unifies everything, it must precisely separate from itself whatever resists unification. Ontological language, which is intended to complement meontological language, must banish the latter from its own totality as a language bound to the difference between being and language. Its immanent lack of oppositions arises only through an opposition to what is external; the unity of Father and Son in the logos of Christ and in philosophical ontology arises only in opposition to the allegorical language of those who subject themselves to a transcendental mother-divinity. With this opposition unity turns itself – once again – into the object of something heterogeneous, turns itself into something which is in itself heterogeneous.

Hegel characterizes this lack in Christian ontology with a reference to the 'harsh expressions (σκληροι λογοι)' which it uses – Christ is one with the Father, he is bread, he has come down from heaven, etc. – expressions which can be misunderstood as parables: 'then every image must be set aside as only play, as a by-product of the imagination and without truth; and, instead of the life of the image, nothing remains but objects' (21: Nohl, 309; Knox, 261). Not only the images which Christ and the writers of the gospels use to express themselves, but also the images which his speculative reader, Hegel, takes over from them and adds to them, such as the images of father and son, of the trunk and its branches, of the angels and the sun, are in their context endowed with the life of unity of which they speak, but are degraded by the reading which is not integrated with them into a 'by-product', an exemplification of concepts in whose truth they do not participate. It accordingly remains possible, not only that the Christian gospel will be misunderstood by its Jewish audience, but also that Hegel's speculative gospel will be misunderstood by its readers, and that its logos will be reduced to a corpse. Like the writing of the Lord's Supper, dialectical ontology, even as the both subjective and objective unity of subject and object, remains a totality that is distinct from its realization, and, hence, is merely objective. A withered leaf, scraps fallen from the table of the rich: the totality falls out of its own framework.

> *The speculative-ontological relation between the branches and the trunk, between father and son, between logos and being, between the reader and his text, is gone. The reader – whether Hegel as the reader of the Christian gospel, or the reader of the ontological gospel which Hegel preaches – is no longer merely the son who begets his father, the subjective unity of subject-object, and thereby himself as the subjective-objective unity of language and being. With the remnant of the objective language of reality, which he can no longer redeem ontologically, the reader asserts the rights of semiotic, epistemological and sexual difference, the reader asserts the rights of the mother in the relation to the text as father, the mother who eludes any completed unification. Whilst the father expresses himself in the son, both are none the less separated through the disjunction of these linguistic-sexual differences; whilst the reader, in his ontological reading, produces his text and, with his text, produces himself as a reader, the text which is supposed to have been completely devoured in this reading nonetheless remains opposed to him as an alien fact, a fact which remains exposed to a reading which is not speculative, to a reading which does not read its meaning, being, but reads the irreducible difference against the meaning; a reading which is not and which therefore does not read.*
> *Ontological and non-ontological readings are not opposed to each other like two different possibilities. The former, the unifying reading, proves defective when measured*

> *against its own principle and as distinguished from unity*
> *by its unity; the latter, the reading of difference, invades*
> *the synthesizing reading and, as an unsublated possibility*
> *of the objective, pushes the developed unity of subject and*
> *object to an immanent difference. But although neither*
> *reading is external to the other, they do not enter into a*
> *speculative synthesis. They intersect each other in such a*
> *way that they are neither distinct from each other nor one*
> *with each other. Their entanglement at once sings of self-*
> *conscious being with the voice of angels and yet remains as*
> *silent as the grave.*

Self and consciousness, father and son are supposed to eat together at a common meal, which they themselves are. But just as something is missing from their meal, because those who are not one with their father are excluded from it, so there is also something in their meal which is too much. For the lack there is a corresponding excess, for the less a corresponding more. The Jews – and the 'Jewish' reader of onto-logical philosophy – feed

> *'off what is given to them, off the scraps which fall from*
> *the table of the rich.' (21: Nohl, 312)*

That is, something which belongs to the ontological unity of self-consciousness and, as a part of it, is already the whole unity, falls out of this unified circle and can no longer be brought back into it by ontological means. The dialectical structure of self-consciousness begets an excess, through which self-consciousness turns itself into the object of a merely parasitic participation in self-consciousness. It is not only the Jews and the Jewish language of difference which are excommunicated from this communion supper: self-consciousness itself, the pure communication of language and being, culminates *a limine* in its own self-excommunication. A difference inscribes itself into the structure of absolute consciousness, an unconscious difference and one incapable of consciousness; a difference which opens within the closure of this structure; the tear which was merely hidden by dialectic opens up, an otherness which is not the other of the one, which is not *its own* other, which shatters the economy of being, of logic, of truth.

For if truth is 'comprehended life' (21: Nohl, 307), but through its
unity with life is different from life, how could one still unreservedly
speak of the truth of being, of the self-verifying character of the concept of being, of a true reading? Nor can this truth, penetrated by the
falsehood it excludes, be restored by asserting that the false *as* false is
not a moment of the truth. Hegel uses this argument in the early writings when he complements the formulation 'agreement of law with
inclination' with the additional remark that the relata in this relation
no longer appear *as* inclination or *as* law (ibid., 268); and the Preface to
the *Phenomenology* uses the same argument, in order to assert, against
the semantic concepts of truth and falsehood, the transemantic concept
of these concepts:

> *Just as the expression* 'the unity' *of subject and object,*
> *finite and infinite, being and thought, etc. has the awk-*
> *wardness that object and subject, etc. mean that which*
> *they are outside their unity, that is, they are not meant as*
> *that which their expression says, just so the false is no*
> *longer, as false, a moment of the true.' (3: TWA, Phen.,*
> *41)*

If the requirement that the dialectical movement must be immanent
is to be followed, however, the concept of the unity of true and false, in
which the false is no longer to appear *as* false, cannot lie beyond the
boundary of semantic content. The transemantic concept of true and
false, its unity, which includes true and false as no longer different, can
be no other than the movement of the immanently self-negating
semantic difference between the 'unity of true and false' and the 'unity
of true and false, in which they are no longer present *as* true and false'.
It is not synthetic unity itself, however, which is expressed in this complement to the meaning of the concept of unity, but rather this unity
under the form of a determination of difference, through which even
the semantic fixations of 'as false' and 'as true' are inscribed in the concept, in which the categoriality of the 'as' is no longer supposed to have
any validity. In order to erase even this remnant of difference and arrive
at a sublation of the false in its unity with the true which would be
more than merely negative, speculative dialectic would be compelled
into an infinite progress, in which each further determination of unity

would necessarily reproduce difference, which would no longer have any effect *as* difference in this dialectic. Hegel's negation of grammatical-semantic identities would therefore culminate – against the intention of his theory – in a process of difference, in which difference does indeed separate itself from itself *as* difference, but does not contract into a substantial unity – even that of a negativity which is intended to be *a priori* and synthetic – in which its movement could come to rest as in its own ideal telos. The infinity of the differential process is that of finitude and it is only this finite infinity, tirelessly denounced by Hegel, which produces the concept of an immanent infinity of the self-relation of being and language, self and consciousness as its never final and never consistent result. The closed system of a speculative ontology is possible only on the basis of the open system of a dialectically proceeding difference, which withdraws the condition of their possibility from each of the ontological fixations which is produced by it.

> *Thus – for example – the concept of self-conscious being is affected by the image of the common meal, in which it presents itself; thus the word 'is' [ist], this ontological nucleus, is contaminated by the other word 'eats' [ißt], in which it is supposed to find its sensuous equivalent, in such a way that its own integrity is called into question. In the attempt to separate 'ist' from 'ißt', in order to secure the unity and significance of the 'ist', which guarantees every possible unity and significance, the deficient, subordinate 'ißt' burrows all the deeper into the ontological 'ist' and splits the core. The one 'is' in the other and 'eats' into the other [Das eine 'ißt' und 'ist' im andern] – and there is an end to meaning and to identical being.*

The pleroma – and pleroma means not merely completion and plenitude, but also satiety – cannot still the hunger of the ontological relation for completeness. A remnant, a defect, an excess remains, which is not incorporated into the corpus of ontology; and which therefore, in persisting, does not subsist.

The religion practised by philosophical thinking is just as incapable as the other complements of the law – virtue, love, love-feast – of realizing the self-relation of being in language, the subjective-objective unity of subject and object, except at the price of forfeiting it. The only possibility of keeping the promise of unity, would lie – if one were to disregard the heterogeneity immanent in every language – in the dissolution of the heterogeneous language of the Jews into the ontological language of the Christians, in the sublation of the social difference between the realm of domination and the realm of freedom. The final possibility of combining self and consciousness, subject and object, love and reflection in the ontological conclusion [*Schluß*], would lie in revolution.

The conclusion of the revolution remains open. But remains so only as long as the revolution – in itself – has already been accomplished, as long as it is still possible to close what been opened.

It is Kant who supplies the precedent for Hegel's characterization of Christianity as a social and ideological 'revolution' (21: Nohl, 385; 220). In the first part of *Religion within the Bounds of Reason Alone*, in its first 'Parergon' (55: B 64) which concerns 'The Re-establishment of our Original Capacity for the Good . . .', Kant presents the transition from a religion merely oriented towardss ceremonial laws and observances, like that of the Jews, to a religion of morality governed by the law of reason itself, like that articulated in Christianity according to Kant, as a transition which radically reverses the hierarchy of the empirical and the intelligible character. This reversal, since it concerns the ground of our subjective maxims themselves rather than their empirical realization, must be described not as reform – but as revolution. But since a 'proclivity to evil, as a perverted form of thinking' (55: *Religion* . . . , A 52) necessarily belongs, albeit in an incomprehensible manner, to the human race, then man's moral perversity can after all be transformed only through a 'gradual reform' and a process of reversal towardss moral 'holiness', a process which remains an infinite task. The infinitude of this perpetual reform of our moral maxims is concluded, forms a closed unity, only from the perspective of its perfect onlooker, God. The revolution is finally concluded only *sub specie dei*.

For Kant the mechanical religion of law represents the dominant ideological state apparatus that is characteristic of a tyrannical social system. Consequently Kant must deny the very title of religion to the Jewish faith, which he regards as the 'utter epitome of purely statuary laws' (55: *Religion* . . . , A 176), a faith which represents the most radical fetishistic corruption of the ideal of autonomous reason. It is a purely political faith in a God who is defined in purely political and legalistic terms, not in ethical ones (ibid., A 177). But the 'Kingdom of

God' which the Christian revolution attempts to erect on earth, on the other hand, no longer represents merely a purely political society but rather an 'ethico-civil (as opposed to juridico-civil) society' or an 'ethical political state' (ibid., A 122). The constitution of this state excludes the heteronomy, and thus the immorality, of monarchical, aristocratic and democratic systems, and is organized on analogy with a 'Domestic Community (Family)' whose 'invisible, moral Father' , the ideal of reason, is represented on earth by his Son, the 'paradigm of humanity' personified (ibid., A 206). This family group – in which, once again, the mother seems to play no role – is the only appropriate image for the constitution of the Kingdom of God by virtue of its 'consanguinity' (ibid., A 136), a community of blood so complete that heteronomy and fetishistic perversion of the ideal are excluded, that it is possible to speak of a 'voluntary, universal and permanent union'. The family provides the model for an apparently natural and spontaneous form of socialization under an ethical principle that is supposed to guarantee both the sociality and the autonomy of individuals, both their particularity and universality. But since this particularity has always already been defined in terms of the universal, and since in this Kantian family, unlike Hegel's, the positions of father and son cannot be reversed, then Hegel's objection even to Kant's ethico-political economy of an autonomous society remains a valid one: this economy too represents a concealed form of monarchical domination.

We can already see just how insubstantial a part particularity plays in Kant's outline of this Christian revolution when we consider that, although Kant explicitly defines the Kingdom of God as an 'ethico-*civil* society', and thus as a politically constituted one, he regards the political domain merely as a sphere of potential fetishization for social sovereignty. 'The various kinds of political state only represent the *letter* (littera) of original legislation within the civil condition', he writes in the *Metaphysic of Morals*, and therefore belong to the 'mechanical character of the political constitution' (50: A 211 ff.). The autocracy of the law, which itself 'does not depend upon any one particular person' (ibid., A 212) and equally upon no other particular individuals, would then hardly represent a political constitution any more, would rather almost simply represent an ethical constitution for the state, a constitution which would correspond to the *spirit*, rather than the letter, of the original social contract. Kant must therefore deny any essential political intention to the Christian revolution which reverses the attempt to ground political ethics upon the laws of state in favour of grounding the laws of state upon the single law of reason. In the fragments later edited by Lessing, Reimarus had expressed the opinion that Christ did entertain the eminently political intention of overturning the priestly government of the Jews, that he really wanted, in Kant's words, 'to set himself . . . in their place in enjoyment of supreme worldly power'. In a footnote to his essay on religion Kant objects that this political religion must be regarded as a failure, that the injunction to adopt the Last Supper as a commemoration of the person and the work of Jesus would only provoke ill-will against the Founder and to that extent merely contradict itself. Any political intention is thereby excluded. The Last Supper is concerned rather with the commemoration of a *moral* revolution that will replace the social order of the letter with that of the spirit.

> *'At the same time such commemoration could also contribute its part to the failure of the Master's excellent and purely moral intention, namely to provoke a* public *revolution (of religion) in his own lifetime by overthrowing that ceremonial faith which corrupts all moral inclinations . . . and indeed we can regret even now that this revolution proved unsuccessful; yet it was not entirely in vain, issuing as it did, after the Master's death, in a transformation of religion which spread silently abroad, for all the tribulations it encountered.' (55:* Religion . . . , *B 112)*

But the taking of communion is not merely a commemorative meal, but a perpetual act which translates this pacified revolution into the order of 'ethico-civil society', is a 'repeated public ceremony which perpetuates the union of its members into an ethical body' (55: *Religion* . . . , A 282). But since the public revolution – in religion as in politics – has miscarried, then the organic totality of the ethical body, which the act of communion continually seeks to produce afresh, remains incomplete and unconcluded, as a purely formal ceremony still remains exposed to the danger of fetishistic misinterpretation. The commemoration of the Last Supper reproduces at once the ethical revolution inaugurated by Christ and the failure of that revolution. The ethical body, which the Last Supper was to bring to total completion, remains a rent body; the meal, which was to introduce the unity and the spirit of the law into society and transform the latter into a republican family, encounters only the unconsumable remnant of the dead letter. The meal of moral revolution remains a meal which feeds upon infinite difference, upon the failure and the an economy which are sustained by political ideology and the fetishism of the letter. For all the plenitude of the ideal, it is at once the lack which constitutes the meal.

The contradiction within the politically defined meal of commemoration, a contradiction which Kant thought could be overcome in the ethical domain, still remains at work within the latter. And with it, that contradiction between universal and particular, between the intelligible and the empirical, which grounds the entire edifice of Kant's system. This difference, one which would not even be eliminated with the perfect conclusion of the revolution as envisaged by Kant, designates rather the very condition of that unity to which Kant aspires in the moral law of reason. That is also why the law – except from the hypothetical perspective of God himself – cannot actually be reconciled, cannot successfully be introduced into the concrete unity of father and son, into the economy of the republican family. Hegel comments on this as follows:

> '. . . the condition under which this should come to pass can never become impossible; it reposes, as long as this condition does not arise, but is not sublated; but this repose is no reconciliation because the law is not some existing thing which would always be effective, would always separate, but because it conditions, because it is only possible under the condition of a separation.' (21: Nohl, 392)

Wherever the revolutionizing of society and its ideological and political constitution is concerned, then the theoretical grounding of this revolutionary possibility and the presentation of its course is also inevitably concerned at the same time with the structure of the law which is to re-establish that society, with rupture and the reparation of rupture, with guilty debt and the economy involved in meeting it. Social systems that are governed not by the moral law of practical reason, which – according to Kant – presides over their origin, but rather by the dictates of tyranny, inevitably reveal themselves as transgressors with respect to that law. Hegel's analysis of transgression, of guilty debt and punishment, must therefore be read not so much as a critique of some immanent social phenomenon that would already be legitimated by society itself, but rather as a critique of the very ideological structure of society and therefore of society itself. At the same time Hegel's analysis of the entire social complex of guilty debt is directed against the Kantian programme for its dissolution, one which *de facto* represents an attempt at transcendentalized apologetics. If the revolution – according to its own most universal idealistic concept which is binding on Kant and Hegel alike – reasserts the ancient rights of original socio-ethical relations, once the corruption of the latter has been eliminated, then talk of such restitution can only be highly conditional for Kant. The hypostasis of the law sustains the difference between reality and fulfilment in such a way that the concrete re-establishment of the same must remain unattainable.

Any theory which simply rests with this difference between law and the social ideal implicitly postulated by it on the one hand and its purely empirical and therefore perpetually imperfect realization on the other – for this is Hegel's argument – cannot properly serve as a theory of revolution, can serve only the theoretical affirmation of what it pretends to oppose. As long as the condition of the possibility of the law, namely its separation from the particular, persists, then even the punishment endured for transgression cannot restitute an original state. In the punishment the violation of the law, which punishment avenges, remains in force. But more than that: if the law has been broken by the criminal – whether this be an individual or society as a whole – then universality, as the form of law, must continue to pursue the transgressor, and 'even unites itself with his crime; his deed becomes a universal one' (21: Nohl, 278). As punitive agency the law is turned against itself. For the law must – an eye for an eye, a tooth for a tooth – turn what first broke it into its own object: 'this perverse character of the law, that it becomes the opposite of what it was before, is punishment' (ibid., 280). As punitive instance the law itself is a crime. That is to say: the law is conceived *a priori* only as something already violated, as something which violates itself.

This negative form of self-relation, where law as universal transgression turns against itself as particular transgression, is not a possible mode of self-sublation. For the self, which is negated in the transformation of law into transgression, is not an original unity that could restitute itself in the sanctioning of punishment. This self-distorting transformation, which can never therefore come to anything other than a purely hypothetical final judgement or conclusion within the social process of law-making, rigorously derives from the condition of the possibility of the law which cannot itself be contained in that law: the separation between its universality and the particularity of its realization. But with this condition of possibility the law possesses a 'higher sphere beyond itself' (21: Nohl, 279) – for the separation which has been determined as contradiction must itself be grounded in a unity which is merely derivative in relation to the unity of the ideal. What stands in question here, therefore, is the genesis of the law and its perversion from out of the ontological unity of life and the possibility of its restitution. How does the unity break down into law, and how does life reabsorb what is broken, the law, into itself?

Hegel describes the structure of the degeneration and the restitution of pure life in terms of 'fate'. In contradistinction to the Kantian ethic, which can write the law of freedom only on analogy with the law of nature, and consequently *de facto* never enters the realm of freedom, the doctrine of fate can present itself as a theory of self-determinacy that is free of domination. For in place of a relation of domination between the universal and the particular, we are confronted instead with a relation of hostility between them: 'Fate is merely an enemy, and the man equally stands over against this enemy as a struggling power; the law as something universal, on the other hand, rules and dominates the particular, and holds this human being in obedience to it' (21: Nohl, 280). Thus the theory of fate no more simply dissolves the concept of punishment than it does the opposition between universal and particular; but it no longer regards its conceptual objects from the perspective of the law, but rather from the perspective of life. And since the concept of the law can indeed be grasped within the systematic order of life, whereas the concept of life cannot be grasped within the order of the law, then the law occupies an ontologically lower position than fate, which describes a movement in which life is re-established. Fate is first created by the inflicting of an injury on, 'by the killing of' life. But since this injured or murdered life is not itself separated from the life through which it was injured or killed, then fate must also be of like substance with the one who first provoked that fate and is now pursued by it. Since this fate has been caused by the individual himself, it must also be possible for him to sublate it.

Fate is the law of life itself – a law erected by life through the injury which has been done to it, a law capable of being annulled once more by life through the experience of its injury. Something which marks a 'break' or gap in the totality of its being, not indeed a case of non-being, but rather being in the mode of its self-negation, not *ouk* but *me on*, something which can be transformed back into the being from out of which it has first arisen. A wound which, insofar as it reveals itself to be substantially identical with the originally undamaged life, heals itself; a difference which, as a difference within life itself, closes in upon itself of its own accord. This describes, in a cursory fashion, the structure of fate as it arises from the self-violation of life and finds itself reconciled once again in the process of self-healing.

The genesis and the dissolution of fate are outlined here, but not the necessity of this genesis. Although Hegel himself, with reference to the words of Christ, merely speaks of the 'incomprehensible enigma' that 'nature must be destroyed and the holy must be defiled' (21: Nohl, 315), this merely abstractly identified necessity of violation and injury can indeed be grounded ontologically in the structure of life itself. For as a purely original form of being, life still possesses the unrealized possibility of a separation, of a wound, of a break, within itself, life is just as much an object of these possibilities as they are objects of life. In order to sublate the separation which belongs, originally, to original life, to reveal these still external possibilities as an immanent moment of life itself, being must realize them explicitly in terms of itself. A gap or break must open up in original being, precisely that it may fulfil itself as being. The undamaged corpus of its life must mutilate and wound itself, precisely in order to bestow this undamaged integrity upon the wound; the totality must lacerate itself, in order to preserve this totality in and through the laceration. Thus, in the shape of fate, the original unity of being completes itself as a unity of being and violation in which being has lost its limitations and violation has lost its negative character. Fate is a figure of self-mediation – of the self-expansion and the self-appropriation of life.

The violation of life is a way of appropriating the violation in and through life. But what is violated in life is 'the undivided divinity' (21: Nohl, 280), the unity of the Father. Just as Hegel exemplifies the subjection under the Jewish law with Macbeth's seduction by the witches, so he illustrates the consequences of the parricide they inspire with Macbeth's banquet, at which his murdered friend appears as an evil spirit. If the allusion to Macbeth serves to present the unsublatable fate of the Jews in the first case, it serves the possibility of sublating fate in the second case. For even murdered life

> *'proves immortal, and once killed, it appears as the terrifying spectre of life, a life which activates all its branches, which releases its Eumenides. The delusion of the act of crime, which believes it has destroyed an alien life and thereby extended its own power, is dissolved insofar as the dispatched spirit of violated life rises up against the act, like Banquo who came to Macbeth as a friend, who was not eliminated through his murder, but rather immediately afterwards took up his seat at the feast; not now as a partaker of the meal, but as an evil spirit.'* (21: Nohl, 280)

Like the regicide perpetrated on Duncan, so the philicide perpetrated on Banquo represents a murder committed upon the divinity of undivided life, a parricide. Yet the Father remains. He partakes of the meal which is to seal his death, and – not as a spirit and a partaker of the meal but as an evil spirit and a spoiler of the meal – lets us feel the 'power of the dead'. This 'terrifying spectre' of life 'stands before me as fate; it is satisfied . . . if I have felt its power, just as I myself merely acted as power in the act of transgression' (21: Nohl, 392). The power of the dead excludes all eating. The one who is dead resists the eater because he stands over against the latter in the meal as an independent power. Yet as soon as the repugnance felt towardss the dead one and his spirit is experienced in the meal, then the delusion of the criminal transgressor, of the eater, namely that the dead one really is quite separate from himself, is dissolved, and the power of the dead one, the dead father and his power, becomes an object for him in the meal. The meal of love and reconciliation – in which the unity of criminal and victim, of son and father, in which the peace concluded between the warring powers of life, in which the totality of consciousness, lacerated by its own deed, all take on shape. 'The unified life is powerless, for no hostile life stands over against it' (ibid., 304) – yet this completed unity also includes, along with the hostile moment of life, the moment of power as well, albeit as reconciled power, within itself. The father no longer remains external to the meal, over against it, but rather, since the son has identified himself with him, is absorbed within the meal as the eater and the eaten alike. Banquo – read by Hegel against the grain of the Shakespearean original – within Macbeth.

One remnant apart. Violated life stands over against itself as an objective actuality and has forfeited that absolute freedom which was vouchsafed to it only through its unbroken self-identity. The return to the unity of life, therefore, cannot rest upon an act of free self-determination, but must contain a moment of natural compulsion:

> *'But love then constitutes a need . . . this is the wound which still remains behind, the intuition of itself as something actual.' (21: Nohl, 393)*

This wound, left behind by the mechanism of nature within the corpus of freedom, can be healed only by the plenitude of love; but since the process of fulfilment itself stands under the sign of need, then even this pleroma must continue to bear the traces of violation. Thus a remnant of the law of nature still necessarily remains lodged within the law of freedom which takes shape as fate; a remnant of the power of the dead, of that repugnance felt for its spectre, within the feast of love; a remnant of hostility within the interconnected body of society. Although such a persistence of the negative would not appear to harmonize with Hegel's fundamental theoretical idea of unification, Hegel emphatically refers to it as a 'law of humanity' which governs not merely Christianity but even the Greece idealized by Hegel himself: 'Just as some separation always still transpires amongst people who are united with one another in the most living possible fashion, so too in this unification – this is the law of humanity – in the ideal which utterly unifies what is still separate, the Greeks in their national gods, the Christians in Christ' (21: Nohl, 389). The law of separation, there-fore, is inscribed within fate as the figure of reunification. This rem-nant of separation does not indeed prevent the progressive completion of unity, but does prevent the accomplishment of its positive totality. Even after reconciliation with him, there remains a ghostly remnant of the father, of the murdered Godhead, which does not partake in the feast of reconciliation. A bloody segment which resists the revolution of unity, the return of being to itself. In this economy an aneconomy.

Nevertheless, the origin of fate is supposed to remain bound to being itself, to derive from an alien deed only as mediated in turn through being. With the mere reaction of life, 'whether it be a case of patient suffering or active struggle, the guilt of life, its fate, commences' (21: Nohl, 284). Life incurs guilt both in passive endurance of and in active struggle against external violation of life, for when it endures injury, it relinquishes its own totality, and when it battles against the threat of injury and asserts its rights, it acts counter to the tendency towardss unification. 'The truth' about both forms of reaction can be grasped only in terms of what Hegel dubs 'beauty of soul' and charac-terizes as a 'free elevation beyond the loss of rights and beyond the field of struggle'. This beauty and the reconciliation of fate which it attempts would have to be glimpsed in the integrity of a life beyond rights, a life which, on encountering any actuality that might disturb its purity, would shrink back into itself like 'a sensitive plant' and, in order to preserve its own life, would flee before life in general (21: Nohl, 286). This beauty of soul would be a mimosa that wishes, in shame, to protect its blossoms, and thereby only forfeits it as a result. The retraction before fate is also a fate. The apotrope against castration is a self-castration:

> '. . . *if a member doth offend thee, cut it off. The highest*
> *freedom is the negative attribute of beauty of soul, that is,*
> *the possibility of renouncing everything in order to preserve*

> *itself. But he who would save his life, will lose it. Thus it is that the highest guilt can be combined with the highest guiltlessness, the highest, unhappiest fate with a sublime elevation beyond all fate.' (21: Nohl, 286)*

The apotrope which would prevent castration itself submits to the logic of castration. For the repulsion preserves what has been repulsed; the absolute repulsion preserves absolutely, by absolving what has been preserved from any possibility of guilt, by cutting it off from reality, from nature and society, by annulling the idealized self which has escaped all positivity, and with it annulling the repulsion and the repulsed alike. Reduced to the pure circle of nothingness, in which the beautiful soul of life finds its end and destination, the circling course of its revolution would be completed.

The plenitude of the soul finds this truth, freedom and beauty of life only in an emptiness; the pleroma only in a kenoma. That unity which results from the absolution from all actuality, from all the guilt which oppresses it, cannot prove other than deficient; that guiltlessness which preserves itself by abandoning its property cannot avoid a guilty debt. Of course, the ideal property if being is no longer subject to the laws of material property, has cast off all heteronomous violation through an alien life – but the law here observed by the absolved party is still not its own. It is the law of a fate which stands higher than that which is reconciled in beauty and its freedom, is consequently more than a figure for the mere self-mediation of love. In this it is comparable with the process of shame which is also an agency of unification, but one which still preserves both within and beyond this unification in order to eliminate any last remnant of deficiency through repetition. The fact that love's beauty appears under the image of the mimosa as something 'shameful' is the trace of a fate which is mightier than the fate reconciled in love and therefore visits every such realized unity with a mark of imperfection. Fatelessness is also a fate, the elevation beyond the sphere of property falls victim to its laws, what I keep I thereby precisely lose.

No positive ontological status can be ascribed to this loss – if we may take Hegel's formulation 'to lose in order to keep; he who wishes to keep shall lose' in the strict sense – since it would indeed preserve itself *as* loss and thus, in losing itself, would only gain. But what remains, disappears, and what is sublated, elevated, is precisely that which falls. The logic of fate cannot therefore be a logic which would preserve identical positions, or a logic which would restitute identity with linear consequence: it is a logic of contra-sequence.

I keep, ergo I lose, ergo I keep, ergo I lose, ergo I always keep and I lose at once.

A consequence – a contra-sequence. It is the fate of Christian love and the fate of the beautiful figure of Christ, in which that love is objectified, that they disintegrate in and through the return to the unity of being accomplished in fate, disintegrate in the very revolution they inaugurate. The ontological restitution operated by fate requires the difference over against those deficient forms of life which have violated its original integrity or threaten to do so. But the infinitude that is determined through difference is itself finite, and therefore deficient. The movement of retraction, the withdrawal ('the shameful plant retracts at every touch . . . into itself'), is an apotrope directed against the violation of life, against the threat of scission; but at the same time it is itself castration, hacking off the single offending member. Insofar as the movement of flight is infinite and never actively opposes this castration at any point, it would actually constitute the uncastratable as such; insofar as this movement is itself an infinite act of withdrawal, which even internally separates itself from any vulnerable objectivity, it is at once an infinite castration and one which is absolutely finite and objective. Castration and apotrope, uncontaminated surplus and deficit, living body and dead corpse, the infinite and the finite, these can no longer be thought according to the schema of their mutual opposition – they are the selfsame. Their selfsameness is the absolute difference, difference as the movement of constant and ineluctable withdrawal. This selfsameness is no positive or synthetic unity of different moments, but is rather their unity in difference. It is indeed therefore a modus of unity, and that alone is why Hegel can legitimately insist that guilt and guiltlessness are capable of being 'united' (21: Nohl, 286), that the restitution of autonomous life is successful: 'the divine [is] reconciled with itself and the fate which was first armed against us through our own deed has now dissolved into the breezes of night' (ibid., 287). But dissolved – a consequence and a conclusion this which Hegel cannot afford to draw – in such a way that these nocturnal breezes continue to breathe amidst the radiant light of the reconciled Godhead, that fate is reconciled only in its irreconcilability. Unity in difference – the subjectively determined being of love, as objectified in the form of a beautiful Christian life, is not merely the result of an infinite withdrawal, but this result, this way of being, remains caught up, conceptually entangled, in this process of withdrawal and reduces itself therein almost to nothingness. The mimosa retracts and finds its intended destination in the idea of a mimosa which can no longer be touched by any concept, not even by its 'own'.

If the Christian reconciliation of fate as accomplished in a beautiful life and a beautiful soul is a presentation of the infinite, and thus of freedom, then it is one in which freedom must strive to eliminate its own presentation as a fixation upon the vulnerabilities of finitude. But with the elimination of such a beautiful presentation of freedom the latter has relinquished its very self, the freedom of its own presentation. The Christian unification of subjective being with its objectivation, the unification of unviolated life with the violation of the same, also destroys, along with that damaging objectivation, that being which was thereby to find itself completed – this unification is the movement of a negative aesthetic and a negative ontology. As the very dialectic of unification unfolds, it provokes the emergence of another, a non-synthetic, dialectic of difference.

The Christian revolution culminates in what Hegel dubs its 'failure' (21: Nohl, 261). For with Christianity the speculative-dialectical movement towardss the restitution of the unity of being has failed, the project of supplementing guilt-entangled legal relations through the teleological process of fate has failed, and consequently the projected close of history which was envisaged in the concept of Christian fate and its reconciliation has also failed. But this failure is the very mode under which the ontological principle of loving union establishes connection with the ontologically deficient realm of Jewish legal relations, and comes to unite with the latter through its self-destruction. The principle of unity with the separated moment is realized insofar as the principle separates itself from itself. The ontological dialectic finds its fulfilment by ceding itself to a different dialectic in which both being and its logos are relinquished. However, as if Hegel were reluctant to recognize the movement which he tirelessly describes, he also insists in his exposition of Christian self-consciousness upon the pleromaic power of fate. A subject alien to that of Kantian-Judaic reflection which acts in accordance with ethical maxims and firmly established social rules, namely the subject involved in the Christian revolution, is nonetheless supposed to be capable of the self-reunification which escapes the former, and the representational deficit already identified in the former is supposed to find recompense in a 'beautiful deed' or a 'beautiful consciousness'.

The consciousness of right as a system is defined by the ethical economy of equivalence between guilt and punishment. This is the system of vengeance whose highest executor – its mere 'administrator', as Hegel complains (21: Nohl, 281) – is God. As executioner God confronts the murderer, just as the murderer confronted the tyrant. And the law that has been transgressed confronts the crime in the form of punishment. Hegel describes the infinite interconnection of guilt, taking the etymology of the word '*Schuld*' seriously, as one of multiple debt and repayment (ibid., 290 ff.). Since the consciousness of right hypostatizes the moral ideal in relation to empirical possibility, though categorically insisting upon their equivalence, it necessarily becomes its debtor; while on the other hand the moral ideal, personified as God, cannot help remaining its faithful creditor. The system of ethical equivalence is therefore simultaneously the system of ethical exploitation. Hegel thus attacks the bourgeois economy as a whole, together with its Kantian apologia, insofar as he recognizes the circulating economy of this complex of guilty debt as an internalization of the ideal in which the self-consciousness diremptcd into the moments of debtor and creditor loses this dichotomous structure. For with the absolute internalization of the creditor the debtor now recognizes himself as the creditor, the murder recognizes himself as the victim, the hangman recognizes himself as the hanged man; they all therefore invariably know themselves simultaneously as both more and less than they are. Surplus and

deficit are one and the same. But they are not equal and are not measured by the yardstick of an ideal which requires their equivalence. If,
as Hegel emphasizes, Jewish legal thought is unfamiliar with the consciousness of guilty debt because what underlies the relationship
between debt and punishment here is a normative criterion external to
both, then Christian self-consciousness on the other hand is specifically
characterized by the fact that it is essentially a consciousness of guilt,
that the punishment is itself as infinite as the life which has been violated and therefore transcends the dominion of moral reflection, the
limitations of mere consciousness. It is only this self-consciousness that
exposes itself as consciousness of guilt from the perspective of the violation of its own infinite unity, which is already intrinsically reconciled
and concludes the conflict of guilt and guiltlessness.

> *The contemptuous response of Nietzsche who likewise com-
> poses the* Genealogy of Morals *as an economic history of
> guilty debt and its cancellation: 'A brilliant stroke on the
> part of* Christianity: *God himself sacrificing himself in
> satisfaction of man's guilty debt, God paying off himself,
> God as the only one who can redeem the debt which has
> become irredeemable for man himself – the faithful credi-
> tor sacrificing himself for his debtor, and out of love (can
> one credit it?) – all out of love for his debtor!' (66:
> Nietzsche, II, 832 ff.)*

Hegel exemplifies the process of guilt consciousness, one more time,
with a meal-scene. A Christian meal at which the bite of conscience
strikes itself –

> *and according to Nietzsche only he is really 'healthy' who is
> 'ashamed of his repentance', he whose 'biting conscience
> feels something the way a dog feels something when it bites
> upon a stone.' (ibid., III, 726)*

– a meal at which subject and object are one and the same. It is that
singular scene in the history of Jesus marked out as the only deed
which is ever characterized as beautiful: 'Verse 10 – *kalon ergon*, a beautiful deed – the only deed in the history of the Jews which merits the
epithet of *kalon*, in fact the only beautiful deed which ever transpires
there' (21: Nohl, 397). It is the deed of Mary Magdalene.

> *'Another beautiful example of a repenting sinner appears in the story of Jesus: the famous and beautiful sinner, Mary Magdalene.' (21: Nohl, 292)*

Hegel's attempted reconstitution of the gospel narratives also contains an encounter with another sinning woman, as narrated by the Johannine text. Asked whether an adulteress should be put to death by stoning, as demanded by the law of Moses, Jesus acted as if he had not heard the question, but rather

> *'bent down and inscribed figures in the sand with his finger' (21: Nohl, 97) – like the African sorcerer in the 'Philosophy of Religion' who also inscribes 'circles, figures in the sand'. (16:* Phil. Rel., *283)*

Questioned further by the Pharisees Jesus answers, saying that he who is without sin should cast the first stone

> *– 'and then once again he made figures in the sand as before.'*

And just as the 'scribes' well instructed in the writings of the law must absolve the adulteress, so Jesus, after he has inscribed figures in the sand, after he has written, cannot condemn her either. That he writes – the only occasion, this, on which he writes – is his sin and his act of adulteration, so that he too, conscious of his own guilt, cannot cast the first stone at the woman who has sinned. The consciousness of trespass made manifest in another also proves to be its own forgiveness.

So also in the case of the 'celebrated and beautiful sinner, Mary Magdalene'.

> *Maria Magdalena Fromme was the name of Hegel's mother, Marie the name of his wife, and Maria that of his daughter.*

'Mary, conscious of her guilt, hears that Jesus is eating in a Pharisee's house, amongst a great company of righteous and respectable people . . . her heart draws her through the company towards Jesus, she kneels at his feet and weeps, washing his feet in her tears and drying them with the hair of her head, she kisses his feet and anoints them with unguents, with pure and costly spikenard' (21: Nohl, 292). In response to the indignation of the 'respectable people' and his disciples alike, who regard Magdalene as a sinner and her act as an extravagance, Jesus retorts that her sins have been forgiven her because she has shown much love. Her sin is cancelled by that through which she sinned – by love. Her tears and the spikenard with which she anointed his feet are the 'holy outpourings of a loving heart' (ibid., 293), and it is from such outpouring that she 'drinks' her reconciliation. Her gift is her forgiveness. Insofar as she spends herself she is taken up into the *pleroma*, into the abundant surplus of love. 'Deeply wounded', she transcends her 'shyness', her shame before the proper domestic economy of consciousness, lowers her face in tears over her unguents, immerses herself unselfconsciously in the joy of bestowing them. The guarantee for the economy of equivalence, of measuring up to the ideal, of discharging the guilty debt, also sinks away along with consciousness into a sea of giving. The beauty of this 'beautiful scene' lies in the act which exceeds the spirit of calculating measure shown by the participants in the meal. What is beautiful about this act, which remains one 'without purpose in any practical sense with respect to conduct or instruction' (ibid., 293), is not that 'purposiveness without purpose' which remains entangled in its orientation towardss the ideal and therefore also in the categories of consciousness. That alone is beautiful which transcends the restrictions of conscious life. In unimpeded bestowing, in self-othering, in the 'discharge' of tears as another early Hegel text describes it (73: Ros., 519), in its own mysterious secretion the finitude of the self-conscious subject sinks away, and related no longer to any heterogeneous element, dissolves into the infinitude of a self-relation which no longer knows of opposition and equality, of economy and morality. The guilty debt relates to itself in its secretion, and, bathed in its own tears, finds it is one with itself, finds itself absolved. In the guilty consciousness the self-relation of sin is its exculpation.

Mary Magdalene weeps throughout the meal. Whereas the proper 'respectable people' ingest and incorporate substance that is other to themselves, she pours forth tears and is drenched by the same. It is not their act of incorporation which is beautiful, it is her othering act of externalization; and nothing is more beautiful than to weep while others eat. Insofar as she sinks into tears and bathes Christ's feet with them, supersedes, cancels and transcends the difference between her exteriority and her interiority, between guilt and love, and with this the sexual difference between Christ and herself – for the beautiful act is a copula – Mary Magdalene returns, conscious of her sin, 'once again' into the 'most beautiful consciousness' (21: Nohl, 293).

The representation of the guilty consciousness is beautiful and, in reverse, the beautiful representation is a representation of guilty consciousness, because the latter is able therein to relate to its necessary failure, to its diremption as if to an external given, and to relate to itself in it – a unity which is actualized in this relation to self, appearing not as a finite measuring up to ends or values, but rather in a regulated excess of diremption and inwardizing memory which alone is appropriate to the infinitude of damaged life. The aesthetic is the form in which ontological self-relation is realized in the consciousness of guilt. In the aesthetic the violence inflicted upon life has been made objective, the externalization has been externalized and transformed into a representation with which consciousness is united, but one from which consciousness can also turn away as from its cathartic secretion. The guilty consciousness absolves itself in this representation and reunites *culpa* and exculpation in this 'most beautiful consciousness'. Mary Magdalene's act initiates the aesthetic revolution within Christianity.

The scene of Mary Magdalene – one where the prostitute becomes as devout [*fromm*] as Hegel's mother Maria Magdalena Fromme – is a primal scene of speculative ontology.

> *A scene of reading. Just as Jesus, writing 'figures in the sand with his finger', reads in this writing the image and picture of his sin and forgives the sinning woman, so Mary Magdalene sinks into tears and reaches for unguents as the expression of grief for her sins – an external act that is itself a sin – and finds herself forgiven in the unification of guilty subjectivity and its objectification. She reads and delights in her lesion. Reading is the absolution from the sin of writing.*
>
> *Reading is an apotropaic act. Against the violation inaugurated by the finger or implement that writes she defends herself by following in his tracks, by sinking into tears, and by repeating and following his writing she eliminates the difference between the writing and the reading. Thus*

as organ of ontological synthesis reading strives to abolish not merely the violence of writing but also itself. The apotrope is to fall away, the repetition of externalization shall restitute a pure meaning without externality.

'A great man condemns men to explicate him' (11: TWA, 574). He puts others in debt and their expiation lies in being forced to read him.

Reading protects us against writing insofar as it assimilates itself to the latter. Reading drinks from the effusions of dirempted consciousness, which it recognizes as its own, is a reconciliation with the crime committed against the unity of being, a crime in which it participates, and thus a reconciliation with itself. Beneath the suckling gaze of reading the configuration of murdered father, murderer son and prostituted mother transforms itself into the unity of Father, Son and Holy Mother – reading closes and concludes the the ontological circle of the family.

Reading, which drinks the writing and sinks into it, is both contained and container, part of the whole and the whole which embraces the part. Reading closes the circle between subjectivity and its objectification. But this conclusive closure lacks objectively determined form and therefore cannot be communicated to the Jewish scribes of the law or to his disciples, and even Christ presents it only as a pretext for the legitimation of a beautiful deed. The reading of Mary Magdalene does not only drink the traces of her sin, she attempts to drink them away entirely. The figures which Jesus makes he inscribes in sand where they will soon easily vanish once more – a psammography. Nothing is allowed to remain that still belonged positively to the world of diremption and could offer itself within that world as an agent of unification. The unity of absolving reading remains merely subjective, and therefore rent; an irreligious reading that does not read once again.

This reading has never once read completely, for it has failed to read the distinction between its own reconciliation

and the unreconciledness of others. It has indeed attained
an abundant fullness of its own, but in this fullness it goes
away empty-handed because it has not gathered into itself
the world and language of actuality that objectively stand
over against it. This fulfilled reading – falling now from
its manic into its depressive phase – relates to itself now as
lack, as thirst. It still harbours a fragment of the crime of
writing which it wished to eliminate, a fragment of mur-
der and prostitution.

The reading of Mary Magdalene cannot restitute the orig-
inal unity of being. The revolution in the name of beauty
must fail. Its scene is not the consummate primal scene of
ontology. A rent remains.

The fate which clings to the violation of life is reconciled by the
beautiful act of Mary Magdalene in such a way that this reconciliation
itself tears a wound to which a different fate will also cling. The judicial
categories of legal consciousness, the economy of equivalence, the
hypostatization of the ideal and the fate which perpetuates itself within
its system are superseded in the 'beautiful consciousness' of guilt and
transformed through love. Repentance is the revolution. But in order
to introduce the principles of Christianity into the world of positivity,
this revolution repeats the character of Judaism. Just as the latter had
constituted itself in opposition to the 'outpourings' of Mother Nature
and is characterized precisely by the 'rent' between actuality and its
transcendental law, so too Christianity likewise announces itself in an
'outpouring' which results in a 'rent' between unity and objectivity.
Christ, who preaches the 'Kingdom of God' as a kingdom of beauty
and harmony, must, in order not to fall under the domination of that
Jewish legality which cripples all natural forms of beauty, repudiate all
connection with the institutions of legal consciousness and even separate himself from any natural relations which they still contain. In
order not to be suffocated by the tightly woven net of the law in which
the naturally given familial relations have been swallowed up, he must
himself tear asunder the bond which still connects him to such relations. As the Jewish people separates itself off from Mother Nature, so
also Jesus, in order to dissolve all connection with the 'web of Jewish

legality', separates himself off from his natural bodily mother. Christ must extricate himself from her bonds if he is to establish the kingdom of reconciliation with the father:

> '*in order not to tear apart a relationship already entered into, he would have had to allow himself to be surrounded by all these threads [of the web]; thus he could find freedom only in the void, because every modification of life was caught up in bondage; that is why Jesus isolated himself from his mother, from his brothers, from his family relations; he was not permitted to love a woman, nor to have children, could not become the father of a family or a fellow citizen who might enjoy a common life with others. The fate of Jesus was to suffer the fate of his people. . . .'*
> (21: Nohl, 328)

Thus love and nature must find themselves 'torn all the more terribly' (21: Nohl, 329) because Jesus dissolves all connection with the socialized natural forms of love, precisely in order to keep love pure. Since beauty, which lends form and shape to love, would be contaminated by amalgamation with sensuousness and all the positive legal relations it harbours, this hagalma of Christianity, this objectification of subjectively realized freedom, must withdraw itself from all positivity and vanish into nothing but a 'brilliant shadow' (ibid.). And like beauty, freedom too must then shrink into a mere ideal whose fulfilment can be expected only from isolated acts and awaited in a pure beyond, in heaven.

> '*The existence of Jesus was therefore a separation from the world, a flight from the latter into heaven; the reestablishment of an empty and evacuated life in the realm of ideality; in all conflict a memory and a looking upwards towardss God; but in part an activation of the divine and, to that extent, a struggle with fate . . . apart from that part of fate which appeared in immediate form as the state . . . towards which he relates quite passively.*' (21: Nohl, 329)

The retranscendentalization of ontological unity into an ideal erected beyond the autonomous self-realization of the individual as promise and command is a direct consequence of the de-transcendentalization of the ideal into the concrete unity of subject and object. This counter-sequence is not merely the fate of Jesus, it is the fate of his earliest 'community' as well. This 'community' is baptized in the name of the angel; and that means 'immersed into the relationship of the Father, the Son and the Holy Spirit' and fulfilled through relation to 'the one, the modification (separation) and the developed reunification'. Immersed like Mary Magdalene into the infinite liquid fullness of its relation to self, the ecclesia is the social embodiment of the onto-logical synthesis; it constitutes the socio-ontological circle of self-appropriation, the configuration of beauty in social form. For, according to Hegel's formulation, reflected social unity appears as an object in terms of the beautiful (21: Nohl, 316). But this beauty – and this is its lack and the lack of every ontological circle – cannot succeed in becoming an object solely for itself without relinquishing the character of objectivity. For if ethically and aesthetically determined being is not to remain merely a representation on the part of a plurality of subjects, who do not themselves belong to this being, if it is to be the realized form of these subjects themselves, then it must exclude its representational character as an object; but as a contracted unity it must itself become the object of what is excluded, namely Judaic reflection, and become representation.

Hegel introduces a quantitative argument for this dialectical reversal of dialectical unity – and thus of a specific form of dialectic itself – this reversal from unity into diremption, from beauty into ugliness, from fatelessness into an ineluctable fate: more is less.

> 'Is there any more beautiful idea than a community of human beings who are related to one another through love?', a more sublime idea than that of belonging to a whole which as a whole, as a unity, is God's spirit – and whose sons the individuals are? Could there still remain anything incomplete in this, so that fate might have power over it? or would this fate be the nemesis which raged against too *beautiful* a striving, against an overleaping of nature?' (21: Nohl, 322)

The extension of the principle of subjective unity over the whole community must restrict its possibilities of life to a single one, the shared community of love. Thus its objectification is negatively determined *a priori*. The supercession of the right to property which circumscribes the essential constitution of civil society; the communal eating and drinking in which the forms of objectivity are dissolved; 'the community of wives' which, as Hegel remarks, the early Christians had neither the courage nor the purity to establish or which they were ashamed to admit to; all of these forms in which the early Christian community strove to realize itself after the death of Christ seek to banish the objective character of the political and moral conditions under which they live and to oppose themselves to them in an abstract manner. 'In love's task the community despises any unification which is not the most intimate, every spirit which is not the highest' (21: Nohl, 323). To the extent to which love, the principle of concentration and contraction, establishes itself socially, so must the realm of objectivity which love excludes also expand. Where the interconnected relations of life contract, there also expands the realm of the dead which is unreconciled with it. Expands to such a degree that the morally, economically and politically isolated forms which the socio-ontological synthesis of the Christian community assumes must themselves remain undeveloped and lifeless.

The self-contraction of life issues in its own nullification. The repressed social deadness is still at work in the mechanism of repression itself, and returns – like the spirit of murdered Banquo – to haunt the heart of life. This time unreconciled and irreconcilable. For the social form into which fate returns in this way is itself nothing but an attempt to reconcile fate and to transform it into fatelessness. What appeared to succeed in the domain of philosophical construction, and in the private and thus undeveloped act of Mary Magdalene – namely the unification of fatelessness and fate – is not, however, possible in the realm of social action. As an 'unnatural extension of the range of love' (21: Nohl, 324) the principle of subjective unity entangles itself in a contradiction through which it will be destroyed.

Christianity proves as little capable of becoming objective to itself as it was of establishing itself as an objective form of life. Although the language of the gospels cannot extricate itself from the concepts of reflection and the positivity which clings to it, an objectively realized unity of subject and object nevertheless did seem possible within the context of philosophical ontology. For Hegel saw no substantial defect in the philosophical construction of the religious cultus, only a temporary one in the process of application and execution. But things stand otherwise in the case of the socially realized cultus. Even when its principle is extended to cover the entire community, love is indeed 'a divine spirit, but still not yet religion' (21: Nohl, 332). Love requires a further complement which not merely unifies love and reflection, as in the philosophical cult, but also unites love, reflection and imagination. It is only from such a pleroma, one which also no longer excludes the sphere of sensuous and material experience, that the realization of an objectively determinate beauty in the social sense, of religion, can be expected. It is only by virtue of this complement that the revolution can be realized.

Since the community in its pre-religious condition remains essentially concentrated upon itself and flees from all forms of objectivity which arise within it or oppose it, the subjectivity of its own relations must contradict the factical objectivity in which others are involved. The lack, to which this conflict bears witness, can only be made whole within a unity embracing the relation and its relata. In words which recall Hölderlin, Hegel demands that in this complete synthesis 'harmony and the harmonized should be one'. The 'urge' which is directed towards the 'All in One', the *hen kai pan*, cannot be satisfied or 'sated' (21: Nohl, 333) except through a unification of the invisible spirit of love and the sphere of the visible and imaginatively representable. This appetitus remains, so Hegel stresses, 'ineradicably unsatisfied', just as it cannot capture the self-representation of the spirit of the community in a beautiful image. It will only be fully sated in a Godhead which is reflected, represented and enjoyed in the life of the community.

> *Hölderlin: his fragment 'On Religion' reads as if it were a written continuation of the unconcluded conversations pursued with Hegel, conversations which may well also*

have taken place during Hölderlin's visits to Frankfurt between September 1798 and May 1800, after his enforced separation from Susette Gontard. The fragment commences: 'You ask me . . . why human beings actually represent *the interrelation between themselves and their world, why they must make for themselves an idea or image of their destiny, something which closely considered neither properly allows itself to be thought, nor simply lies there before our senses?' (45: F. Hölderlin,* Sämtliche Werke *[Grosse Stuttgarter Ausgabe (henceforth GSA)] ed. F. Beissner and A. Beck [Stuttgart: Kohlhammer, 1946–85; IV (1), 275). Hölderlin attempts an explanation of the genesis of this image of a communal Godhead from out of the shared experience of 'more than mechanical relationships' (ibid., 276), claiming that human beings alone strive to 'repeat' the satisfaction experienced within their relationships to one another and to the world, to repeat all this in 'spiritual life' and in terms of both* thought *and* memory. *It is only this 'higher law' formulated through repetition, not life itself in its immediacy, that properly represents and expresses the 'infinite interconnection of life' (ibid.). Represents it in the image of the religious cult and realizes it within the practical life of society. The concrete repetition – one that is simultaneously abstract and determinate – of the mechanical satisfaction of 'pressing need' stills that other hunger of a social life which transcends the sphere of nature. It is only this repetition – a spiritual manducation – which generates the infinite interconnection of life, the image of the Godhead.*

This 'higher Enlightenment' transcends that undertaken by Kant, which supposedly subjected ethics to little more than 'vain etiquette' and aesthetic experience to the 'shallow precepts of taste', insofar as the interconnection of life demanded by it still remains, for all its universality, indissolubly related to the particularity of specific conditions (ibid., 277). Consequently Hölderlin must also envisage the possibility that the representation of this interconnection as it is formed within a 'hubristic or slavish life', that this communal Godhead can always bear 'the shape of the tyrant or of the slave' (ibid., 270). Yet even this fate, which befalls the defective repetition of defective conditions, can be reconciled within the universal interconnection of limited modes of life and imaginative representation. While Hölderlin here resolves the aporias of particularity within the cosmopolitan utopia of a 'union of many within one religion' (ibid., 281), Hegel will later strive to show that they are always already sublated, thereby following the same schema now transformed into a philosophy of history.

How then should the community be satisfied? How can it externalize the Godhead which is present within the communal life, in order to relate to its own relation as to a relatum? How can it nourish and sustain itself from its own substance externalized as an image? Not from a Godhead which assumes a personal form in Christ, for he was forced to flee the world of objects and perish for the sake of the principle of subjectivity. Not from the dead Christ, for he lacks the life which continues to endure within the community. Nor from the commemorated image which preserves the idea of the living Christ, for it still remains associated with the 'decaying body' of the dead man. The hunger of the community and the hunger of the concept for self-relation cannot be stilled by a rotting body or the image of a rotting body.

> *'Yet the image found new life in the resurrected one raised up to heaven, and love found here the representation of its unity.' (21: Nohl, 334)*

The resurrection and the 'reunion of spirit and body' which it accomplishes is therefore the pleroma for the lack that clings both to Christ, the ideal which flees life, and to the community, the social union, which for itself is void of actuality. Only with the apotheosis of the dead God does the subjective unity of subjectivity and objectivity find its objective shape and become religion. Not the rotting body but the transfigured body, irradiated by the ontological life of the community, satisfies the hunger for the 'All in One'. What the community receives from such a body is not something bestowed by another, it is itself, giving itself to itself through this body. The image of the dead man resurrected is the image of a society which relates freely to itself.

The relation of the Christian community to the resurrected Christ concludes the circle of socio-ontological self-relation. Baptized into the social body, liberated from its restriction to the spirit and the ideal, the Godhead becomes an actual God, a relatum which is itself the entire relation in which society relates to it. The hierarchy of complements is completed and enclosed within the God of the community.

But even to this complement, the final one, there still clings an insubstantial supplement, to this addition which completes the totality there still clings something 'auxiliary' which depletes it.

For whereas in the Greek religion of beauty the hero alone is the object of veneration, in the Christian religion, which equally has beauty for its substrate, it is not merely the resurrected one, but also at the same time the teacher and the crucified one who is worshipped. Just as the commemorated image of the living Christ would remain associated with the idea of the 'rotting body', so too even the transfigured Christ remains associated with the abused and broken man. Hegel calls this moment associated with the image of socio-ontological unification a further addition, an 'auxiliary' to the complement:

> '*Thus another auxiliary element [Beiwesen], something utterly objective and individual that is paired with love, is joined with the image of the resurrected one, of the unification which has become essential being, but ... one that is to remain fixed for the understanding, that thereby becomes an actuality that continues to hang upon the feet of the transfigured and deified man like lead and draws him down back to earth.*' (21: Nohl, 305)

This complement of the complement, with which no further stage of fulfilment is attained but through which the pyramid begins to be dismantled, this inessential auxiliary, should belong 'in and to the essential being of God' as something 'sure and lasting', and yet must thereby empty and de-substantialize that essence. The reality which Christ had cast off in death, instead of remaining a mere husk within the grave, has only risen again from the grave and 'hung itself upon the resurrected God'. The actual life which was driven from the centre of love thrusts itself back, as addition, into the centre, because the relationship between both is not that free relationship required by beauty, but a compulsive need. It is the 'melancholic need for the actual' which hypostatizes the husk, the outer covering itself, into something substantial and deforms the sublime image of social beauty into the 'monstrous union' of body and spirit (21: Nohl, 335).

The husk of the actual, this curtain hung around the figure of the resurrected God, is a material bound to the imago of the mother from whom Jesus has separated himself; bound up with the texture of objective forms of socialization from which the Christian community isolates itself; bound up with a text composed in the language of actuality from which the speculative language of ontology strives to distance itself. It is always something material which shapes and determines the stuff which inhibits the dialectical movement of the subject and its objectifications, the stuff in which the socio-ontological *ichtos* ensnares the *Christos* as in a net.

> The textile is woven to make a hammock, a net [Hamen] for angling, for Hegeling. A snare for Hegel – the absolute fish. ('If the absolute slips away from us, and from the earth where it struts around finally falls into the water, then it becomes a fish, an organic living being' [73: Ros., 540]). But Hegel must evade something other than himself. He can remain hanging only in a net woven by his own movement, in a web spun by himself. He ensnares himself only in himself. In myself. In the web which is woven like a hymen between his element and his shape, between his substance and his subject, between his outside and his inside . . . between me and him, a web in which both are always already ensnared although they also remain separated. In such a way that the fish cannot recognize the net as its own, a net which fails to hold him and allows him to slip through its meshes. Allows him to be absolute. – Hegel in the text, Hegel in the hammock.

Even the erect shape of the one who has been raised up from the dead still remains caught up in the maternal coils which Christian ontology seeks to sever; bound to the navel which sustains its glittering ideality by feeding upon the sphere of historical actuality; hanging upon this *omphalos* which contracts itself into a knot.

> *The text contracts – if it is the alimentary canal through which the protean logos, the concrete shape of social life, nourishes itself. Thus the materiality upon which it depends knots the navel, closes its throat. The restriction to objectification, the contraction of the omphalos, the oesophagus; the knot in the copulative bond of union deprives it of nourishment and breath, strangulates the logos, chokes the ontological word. The logos, erect at the stauros, the gallows of this motherly text.*

The self-relation of being through which the hunger for absolute synthesis was to be stilled, the self-alimentation of life passes through a 'real bond' (21: Nohl, 336) which does not destroy this unity but does make it depend upon its material conditions, and thus turns the substantial and its subject alike into derivative moments, dissolves the real and ideal bond of the ontological copula. This binding word 'is' – is a rope.

The dialectical-ontological figure hangs. Hangs upon the cross of materiality which it sought to supersede, upon the gallows of what it sought to excise from itself. Like the Mosaic eagle weighed down, drawn earthwards, by the heavy stones of Jewish legalism (21: Nohl, 256), so too the Christ who ascends to heaven is drawn down by the objectivity of his own shape which 'hangs upon his feet like lead' (ibid., 335). The covering which clothes him does not merely hang about him, literally depend from his body, but rather the way around, it is he who depends upon the covering. And likewise the community hangs and depends upon its own objectification in the resurrected one, as upon an alien dominating object. The insubstantial property, the supplement, has become the substance, the covering has become its *subjectum*. Substance and subject depend upon the derived moment which depends upon them. Essence and exemplification, at once mutually opposed and bound together, hang upon one another in a web, a text which is no longer sensible or intelligible, no longer merely subjective or objective, no longer merely shape or Idea; a text rather which is always both at once, although it cannot articulate itself into a unity. Essence and exemplification depend upon 'themselves', upon a self which represents no origin, no primary or conclusive identity. They both remain, between their own extremes, between themselves, wavering in limbo.

The Last Supper 'wavers' (21: Nohl, 297) between the feeling of love and the religious act; the one who has been immersed and baptized into the 'relationship of Father, Son and Holy Spirit' also 'wavers', wavers 'indecisively between actuality and dreaming' (ibid., 319); the apotheosis of social synthesis wavers in the middle between heaven and earth (ibid., 335) – Christian ontology as a whole and at its peak is 'an indeterminate wavering between actuality and spirit' (ibid., 341). But this wavering is not merely undetermined and indecisive, it is also indeterminable and undecidable. The unification from which ontology proceeds and towards which it remains teleologically oriented is, as Hegel emphatically puts it, 'everlastingly impossible' (ibid., 341). Engaged in the history of Christianity, ensnared in the text, speculative-dialectical ontology encounters a limit, one which certainly results from the movement of the former but no longer belongs to it. The logic of opposition and synthesis, the categorial trinity of actuality, possibility and necessity, appears to hang in a logically indeterminable intermediate domain of the historically determined text – suspended in the monstrous copula of life and death. The circle has closed; but precisely because it closes, its conclusive articulation is impossible. The objective social context in which the unification begins to take shape inhibits its own realization, causing it to vanish in the forlorn utopia of its impossibility, as promise and hindrance of the totality that was announced.

It is not merely the metaphorics of textual fabrication – the covering, the threading and tying, the web and the texture – which Hegel insistently brings into play at the end of his analysis, but also the systematic function which he ascribes to the *corpus mysticum* of the resurrected one that ties the appearance of this latter with the presentation of the Jewish Godhead, which in turn is compared with the veiled and hidden image of Cybele. Both are 'castrated' divinities, both of them only offer the promise of being all and everything. Death threatens from behind the veil of Cybele, and, according to Hegel's interpretation, the empty transcendence of a purely imaginative conception; equally there is nothing concealed behind the outer covering of the resurrected one which is not also and already woven into the covering and forfeit to it. For all the distance their history erects between them, both divinities are objects of the understanding, whose form and whose command still remain opposed to subjective life and its unity. The ideal which that veil and this covering intimate is in each case itself incapable of anything but a purely parabolic realization. Transfigured and raised from the dead, the Christ is another Cybele, another witch [*Hexe*]. The reconciliation of his fate becomes the fate of being.

The Kingdom of God, which is always already the kingdom of men, has still not become what it is. As something which men merely represent imaginatively to themselves, the Kingdom turns once again into that of the Jewish God which excludes human participation in it, and even more human unity with it, for ever. This Kingdom becomes an unsatisfiable and therefore empty social ideal, a moral obligation, an imperative. The domination of positive law which was superseded by Christ commences once again in the resurrected Christ. The pure consciousness of life returns once more to the consciousness of right and law.

Love becomes a fetish.

Being – a fetish.

The unity of subject and object, freedom and necessity, the law of nature and the law of reason – the ontological arche and its telos – a fetish.

The beautiful figure of the God raised from the dead – a fetish.

The Christian religion, like the Jewish religion of obligations and observances – a fetish religion.

The revolution, though in quite another sense than that intended, is complete. Christianity has transformed itself back into the Judaism that it wished to dissolve, to repress, to flee, to reconcile. It has become what it had to expel from itself if it was to be itself. The separation which it accomplished, which was to have been a function of unification, has been unable to eliminate the system of diremption; the separation has proved itself rather as the agent of assimilation, the assimilation of unity and diremption. Unity, Being, Beauty and Freedom have turned to stone, have petrified into categories which possess an independent life. But since they are not actual and effective in social life, but merely abstractly actual as conceptual objects, they signify the opposite of what they are. The truth of the logos has become a lie which cannot be denied by any party. The ideological and social revolution which Christ inaugurated and his community wished to perfect has re-established not the eschatological unity prefigured in original unity, but the very condition of corrupted life from which the revolution began. The path of the revolution, which liberates the moments of extreme abundance, describes an empty circle.

Christianity is, once again, Judaism.

> *'[Christianity] is* not *a movement in opposition to the Judaic instinct, it is the very consequence of the same, a further conclusion in the development of its fear-instilling logic' (67: Nietzsche,* The Antichrist, *II, 1183). 'The Christ, this* ultimate ratio *of the lie, is the Jew once more – indeed threefold.' (ibid., 1206). And Marx, for whom religion represents the 'splendid completion' and the 'moral aroma' of a perverted world (60: MEW, I, 378): 'Christianity arose out of Judaism. It has now dissolved back into Judaism' ('On the Jewish Question', in ibid., 376).*

In this *once again*, in this non-revolutionary repetition, more has obviously transpired than a mere re-presentation of what has already been. If before in Judaism being and its social reality had degenerated *a priori* as it were into mere illusion, rendering any alternative to the domination of delusive appearance utterly inconceivable, now in Christianity , once it has dissolved the a-priority of fiction, being and its truth shatter against their own principle. The repetition of the diremption into the world of the ideal, and into a world other than that of sheer actuality, now unfolds as nothing less than the self-supersession of the truth of being. And indeed a self-supersession in which the positions of abundance already attained seem to be preserved only in order to abandon them all the more ruthlessly to their degeneration. The figure of self-relation which Christianity introduced, as fate, demonstrates its complicity with the system of moral diremption and the economy of guilty debt; the fate of Christianity is irreconcilable; the unity of the corpse and life, Father and Son – the condition for closing the family circle – is rendered impossible by the intervention of a logically indeterminable material moment. Being hangs sublated and superseded between its ontological abundance and its fetishistic depravity and simply 'is', without unity, at once both and neither. The contraction to the same is the very movement of disintegration 'itself'.

> In 'The Spirit of Christianity', and already in part in the essay on the 'Positivity of the Christian Religion', Hegel had exposed those elements in the historical and theoretical foundations of Christianity which were prone to pervert it into a sanction for a normative ethics and an ideological instrument of an authoritarian state. Hegel intended a primal history, composed in critical vein, of the prevailing occidental ideology. But over and beyond that, in the form of a theoretical and historical reconstruction, Hegel also ended up describing the construction of an ontologically founded system, along with the mechanisms of its actualization and disintegration. The self-destruction of the fetishistic ethics of Judaism and transcendental idealism, a destruction which reveals itself merely as the reverse of its self-affirmation, has opened up the space for the complement of Christian life, a life which for its own part collapses and degenerates in its attempt to unfold subjective unity into social objectivity and thus for the first time to enclose itself within the ontological context of life. Christianity repeats at its culmination the Judaism it relinquishes; its dialectical ontology of unity and the reunification of separated moments repeats the transcendentalist hypostasis of diremption; Hegel repeats Kant. The lack, which Kant sought to supply for Christianity as a

> *statuary religion of law by substituting the law of practical*
> *reason, reveals itself once again, as Hegel shows, within the*
> *very law of practical reason. But the lack, which Hegel*
> *thought to supply for the pure moral law by recourse to the*
> *principle of love and its various realizations, repeats itself*
> *once again within the religion of love and its own ontolog-*
> *ical premises. The same spectacle repeatedly presents itself*
> *at every particular station of the historical process of phi-*
> *losophy, according to a law which remains unknown to the*
> *contending participants of this procession, even though it*
> *acquires shape and definition in their arguments: the law*
> *according to which the complement is the subtrahend, the*
> *bestowal the withdrawal, according to which excess*
> *becomes difference and closure orifice. Logic of result –*
> *logic of reversal.*

The transition to something other, once 'accomplished', proves to be a return to the same. But the identity of the One is no more fulfilled than was the identity of the other – we can no more speak of a *progressive* path than we can speak of a *regressive* path of return. The process is exposed, the judgement suspended; decidability itself, the presupposition of every judgement, is brought before the bar of judgement.

> *Ceremonial caesura; it is truth which stands in question.*

And not merely a specific, empirical, historically emergent truth but truth 'itself', the truth of history. The social order whose life were nothing but the idea which it possesses of its own life, whose idea of life were nothing but this life itself, would be the truth of being, the objectified form of original unity (21: Nohl, 307). But where the disintegration of this unity is irreparable, where the revolution which should return us to it has failed, and the fate which provoked the diremption is irreconcilable, there the objectification of being in its truth, the truth of being, also becomes problematic. It is the fate of the truth of being to become once more the regulative fiction of the truth of being.

The fate which was to be resolved in fully unfolded and developed being represents Hegel's first speculative concept of history. Since this cannot be accomplished in the developing trial of Christian society, the truth which was the destination remains in a state of fiction. Just as the ontologically founded concept of truth failed and came to grief historically, so too the priority of ontology over transcendentalism must appear questionable and the alliance between Hegel's philosophical programme and the Christian gospel must shatter. Hegel must distance himself from what he has written in order to justify the rightness of the claim to truth he has formulated, in order to posit the questionable process and trial of history as actual and effective in his own philosophy itself.

In order to protect the truth of history from its perversion into lie, ontology from its self-destruction, Hegel needs only to transpose the positions of his theoretical calculus ever so slightly. He does not dissolve the court of judgement but reorganizes the hierarchy of its executants.

> *There is another 'resolution' of this aporia different from that found by Hegel. – Nietzsche's method, which allows truth to testify as witness against itself, allows the lawgiver be condemned through his own law: 'All great things are destroyed by themselves, through an act of self-supersession; this is what the law of life demands, the law of* necessary *self-overcoming within the essence of life – the law-giver himself always ultimately confronts the call:* 'patere legem, quam ipse tulisti'. *In the same way Christianity destroyed itself as* Dogma *in and through its own morality; in the same way Christianity as* Morality *must now destroy itself – we stand at the threshold of* this *event. After Christian truthfulness and sincerity has drawn one conclusion after another, now in the end it must draw its* strongest *conclusion* yet, *one directed against itself . . . a mighty spectacle in a hundred acts which is reserved for the next two centuries in Europe, the most terrible, the most questionable, and perhaps also the most hopeful of all spectacles'* (The Genealogy of Morals, *899). The pronouncement which the actors utter concerning themselves – their masks, their history, and their court of judgement – is spoken in a different spectacle, in*

> *the satyr-play that follows the tragedy. But the words of*
> *this pronouncement are drowned in contemptuous*
> *laughter.*

Hegel continues to pronounce judgement with serious mien. A judgement not upon the court of judgement, but upon the historical forms in which its demands are to be fulfilled.

Initially at least – in the surviving opening pages of the 'Systemfragment' of 1800 (1) – society seems in the forms of a religious cult, no longer necessarily that of Christianity, capable of a complete fulfilment of life that corresponds unreservedly with the absolute synthesis, the synthesis of thesis and antithesis. It is only in the religious cult that the pleroma can be seen, the totality of social being in which all multiplicity, all reflective understanding, all opposition and death find themselves unified and related, as life. The potentially infinite chain of complements in philosophical reflection, which abandons itself to 'this perennial progression without rest', is 'navigated' here by by means of absolute synthesis (21: Nohl, 348) – the sails are set towardss the untroubled sea of concrete infinity where no fatal disturbance, no struggle, no tempests threaten, but where catastrophe is all the more certain. There is a sea change between the first surviving sheet of the Frankfurt system and the final sheet. The criterion for necessary *social* fulfilment of the absolute synthesis anchored at the ontological heart of the system becomes dispensable with regard to final judgement concerning the unfolding process. Since the unification accomplished in the cult leads into insoluble aporias, the historical objectification of *pleroma* in the construction of ontological self-relation can fall away as accidental and contingent.

In the same moment that the social 'completion' (21: Nohl, 348) of pure being sinks down into a merely social and historical fact, the philosophical discourse which grasps and systematically articulates history in its entirety erects itself as the new realized form of speculative unity. In the first part of the surviving system ontological priority had still been unreservedly ascribed to religious praxis, to which philosophical thought must defer inasmuch as it is still bound to reflective oppositions

– 'Philosophy must therefore cease where religion begins, because the former is a form of thought, which thus possesses an opposition, partly over against what is not thought, and partly between the thinker and the thought' (ibid.); whereas in the final concluding part of the system philosophy has exchanged position, if only as yet implicitly, with the religion which here appears bound to the contingencies of history. It is now theory, though not of course a theory merely limited to the forms of reflection, which establishes and co-ordinates the system of history and being, temporality and infinity in such a way that the very actuality which failed the demand for unity imposed by ontological premisses remains related and connected to this demand as to its own vertex. Here already we see the beginnings of what Hegel first explicitly formulates in the *Phenomenology of Spirit*: that time is the power of the concept, which is supposed itself to remain insusceptible to the damage of time. The law which proclaims the rightful judgement on history from within history henceforth possesses its seat within the speculative concept of the system.

Once the highest instances of dialectical ontology, that of the philosophical cultus over against that of the religious cultus, have exchanged positions, then the economy of the circulation and self-reproduction of being is restored, an economy threatened by catastrophe through the insubstantiality of the necessary social objectification of being, through the aneconomical as such.

For the appropriative and self-appropriating structure of pure being it is the law of property which proves eminently aneconomical in the context of the essay on 'The Spirit of Christianity'. Property, defined by the right of ownership with regard to things as external possessions, is a category of alienation – not merely in respect of the owner's right to alienate his property, but in respect of the owner's own alienation from the society to which he belongs and which has rendered the possession of his own goods possible in the first place. Property is *ex definitione* a privation, is determined as private property and relates to the proper economy of the totality of being as its destruction. The possession of wealth cannot permit a 'complete life',

> *'because something is then still given over to life as its own, which yet can never become its property.' (21: Nohl, 434)*

Christian doctrine, from whose potentially unifying perspective Hegel here argues, represents a critique of the ethical and also political economy of domination through property, one which hinders socio-ontological self-appropriation. Against this critique of property, which Hegel in a later note modifies as a defence of the Jacobin politics of expropriation (73: Ros., 525), Hegel himself makes an objection:

> 'Property is a fate which has become too mighty for us even to entertain reflections about it, for us to imagine that separation from this fate were conceivable.' (21: Nohl, 273)

The ultimate issue of the Christian revolution, in which even amidst the community of goods a 'sad need for something actual', for a something objective proper to themselves' still persisted, testifies to the irreconcilable character of this fate and to the unrealizable nature of the ontological principle. In the Frankfurt 'Systemfragment' Hegel now discovers a method which can connect the recognition of the necessity of private property with the continued affirmation of the ontological theory of unification.

In the final page of the Frankfurt system Hegel once again takes up the analysis of the Last Supper which he had presented in 'The Spirit of Christianity', where it represented a recidivism into pure subjectivity, and pursues it in the more abstract terminology of sacrifice and destruction to the point where it becomes, as 'purposeless destruction', the conceptual heart of a cultic praxis, a practice at once absolutely religious and absolutely speculative.

> '[And man gives] over but a part of his property, the necessity of which is his fate, as a sacrificial offering, for his fate is a necessary one which cannot be overcome ... and through this purposelessness of destruction alone, through this destruction for the sake of destruction, he makes good his otherwise purely particular relationship of purposive destruction; and at the same time he has completely fulfilled the objectivity of objects, their utter unrelatedness, their death, through a destruction unrelated to himself; and if indeed the necessity of a related destruction of objects remains, we see the appearance of such purposeless destruction for the sake of destruction, which reveals itself

> *as the only religious one with respect to absolute objects.'*
> *(21: Nohl, 349–50)*

This sacrificial offering – and the Lutheran verse which Hegel cites:

> *'He whom Heaven's Heaven could not enclose,*
> *He lies now in Mary's womb.'*

– leaves us in no doubt that this is the sacrifice of the God objectified
in maternal materiality – this offering also retains as a partial and historically transient one an infinite ambivalence inasmuch as the 'utter
destruction of objectivity' it accomplishes and thus its utter subjectification still represents 'a permanent relationship with objects' (21:
Nohl, 349). And this permanent relationship exists only in the 'utter
lack of relation', in death; the absolute relation is attained only in the
annulled relationship and with it the copula of relation and relatum.
This expropriation of private property, which extends to squandering
the means of subsistence and excluding every process of private and
social reproduction; this destruction of this particular manifestation of
the Godhead, which must destroy not merely its objectivity but the
Godhead itself insofar as it appears in a particular way; the annulling of
all finitude and of every economy based upon exchange and opposition
is the only thing which fulfils the absolute economy of the conclusive
unification of the finite and the infinite. 'This purposeless destruction
for the sake of destruction' is the *pleroma*, the final conclusion.

But if the offering were universal, were not subject to the necessary
fate of material property, then absolute being would be a spark which
vanished as soon as ignited. The pleroma would be the mystical Now
of divine presence. Death 'completed' would be the completion of
objectivity and of the subjective tendency towards unification; would
be the fusion and identification of subject and object and therein pure
being, the negation of its negation: the death of death; as unproductive
consumption, destroying the conditions of possibility and validity for
its own relation, would disappear as a merely abstract empty life.
Completed and perfected being would be the end of being and of its
speculative-dialectical self-relation, the end of social synthesis, of history, of ontology. The sacrificial offering and the sacrificial meal – a
food which does not nourish, is not digested, and does not serve
organic reproduction; a food which purely is and consumes itself as

such; this sacrificial meal, the culmination of the social cultus where
God is put to death and rises up again, may no *longer* therefore constitute merely a *part* of the cultus. There must remain a residue that is not
utterly consumed by the offering, which resists the suctional draw and
pull of the negative totality of being. This resistant, unconsumed
residue – it is what Hegel calls the necessary fate of property – no
longer bears the character of empirical contingency, as it still did in
'The Spirit of Christianity', but rather arises out of the structure of
being itself as the necessary and inevitable delay of its absolutization.

It is only the residue left behind by the empty totality of the offering
which discloses the possibility of the progressive concretization of pure
life in the remaining institutions of religious cult and social praxis. To
consume this residue is the work of history, to reconstruct the cadential
sequence of its path the work of systematic philosophy. The system of
speculative ontology, where the path of history presents itself as the
court of judgement over its own forfeiture to objectivity, continues the
sacrificial meal in the shapes of finite life, where the intensive totality of
the absolute sacrifice should once again repeat itself extensively in its
residue. But this second meal, unlike the first, does not consist in the
unreserved destruction of objectivity but rather in the controlled and
regulated expression of this destruction; as with the 'divine worship'
described in the 'Systemfragment', this meal remains a 'kind of subjective expression which, like sounding speech', can be rendered 'beautiful
and objective through rules' (21: Nohl, 350).

The offering up of the residue, controlled, prolonged and fixated, is
Hegel's philosophy. This philosophy prepares the meal of the absolute
and, sitting down with itself for company at its own table, consumes
even its own objectivity.

Yet by enthroning philosophical discourse as the highest guarantor for
the security and certainty of ontological synthesis, Hegel has
renounced – who receives, relinquishes – the social realization of this
synthesis. It is merely 'some kind of elevation of the finite to the infinite' (21: Nohl, 350) that is necessarily required, not one that is perfect
and complete. This restriction upon cultic self-relation, one which
leaves its traces in the entire path of history and in the system that

comprehensively grasps this history, arises from the oppressive burden of property, a fate that is ontologically necessary and, as Hegel stresses, ineliminable. The material residue does not merely force entry into the historical process; it also regulates the forward stride of history and in consequence that of philosophy. The movements of history and system follow the rule of the material, never eliminable without residue but perpetually postponable. – The rule of the maternal. There is a passage in Hegel's Jena waste-book which can be read as an explication of his Frankfurt formulations concerning the complementary dynamic of divine worship. Here Hegel himself attempted to connect the self-relation of divinity in the community – what he later calls the 'eternal history, the eternal movement that God himself is' (17: TWA, *Phil. Rel.*, II, 298) – with the rhythms of the 'Great Mother Cybele':

> '*The dread shudder before the divinity, the destruction of the individual, permeate the gathering. But soon they breathe again. . . . They recognize themselves as life . . . feel and become aware of themselves and start into movement, into dance. . . . The individuals become articulated members of the objective unity. Like Cybele, the mighty Mother of the Gods herself strikes the drums, who otherwise works her way with a silent and unconscious power. Thus the Godhead enjoys its own being, and man has identified himself with the same.*' (2: TWA, 563)

The philosophical system remains distinct from such objective and corybantic unity. Yet insofar as the system closes the circle and procession of these maenads, philosophy describes the scenography of a festival as the commemorative re-membering of its own objectivity.

Hegel too dances. Hegel's philosophy dances according to the rule and measure of the mother and constitutes the unity of the dance, its rules, its conception. This philosophy is Cybele, immanent and objectified, beating out upon its own belly-drum the rhythm of 'eternal history'. With its own staff – for 'her priests were castrated, emasculated in body and soul' (21: Nohl, 250). Thus the omnipotence of this metaphysics of dialectical ontology articulates itself – thanks to 'the destruction of the individual', the castration of all particularity – in a music which not only resounds with the power of that objectivity to which the subjective has externalized and sacrificed itself, but also works its way within its subjects – who loses, receives – 'with a silent unconscious power'. A tumult unheard of and unhearable, consciously regulating and drowning out consciousness and self-consciousness, a tumult before which 'all seeing and hearing passes away', the musical offering of the absolute philosophy.

If the philosopher is to keep in step with the throbbing rhythm of the true – and the truth issues in the 'bacchanalian revel where no member remains sober' (3: TWA, *Phen.*, 46) – he must, according to another formulation from the *Phenomenology*, 'avoid falling himself into the immanent rhythm of the concepts' (ibid. 56). The retention of subjectivity, the relinquishment of caprice, is a sacrificial offering to the rule, without which the harmony of the whole would remain unattainable. Hegel performs the offering of the residue, of what still resists the harmony of the whole which is to resound in this philosophy. Just as it is an offering of his own subjectivity, Hegel's own offering to the rule, so too it is also an offering of all the historical shapes in which the unity of subject and object has objectified itself. Just as the castrating mother received a sacrificial offering, so too she must now be sacrificially offered up to her own matrix, to the philosophical idea. She must be eaten. It is Christ who – once again – takes the place of the mother in the historical succession of divine shapes.

> *In the notes of his waste-book Hegel continues: 'In* the eating of the Godhead *this enjoyment is overleapt, but it profoundly expresses the infinite pain, the utter shattering of what is most interior. God offers himself up, gives himself over to destruction. God himself is dead; the uttermost despair of total abandonment by God.' (2: TWA, 563)*

Contemporary with these remarks, at the close of the essay on 'Faith and Knowledge', which like the *Phenomenology* once again emphatically repeats the formula 'God is dead', the sacrificial meal in memory of the dead God is explicitly identified as the concern of philosophy. In 'all the truth and harshness of its Godforsakenness' the historical Good Friday repeats itself as the 'speculative Good Friday' of philosophy (2: TWA, 432). But from out of the Godforsaken harshness of this meal, in which philosophy accomplishes the sacrifice of the objective totality and all the forms of reflection, there rises up again 'the highest totality' as the *corpus mysticum* of Hegelian philosophy itself, in which the body of the mother, the body of Christ, is transfigured and illuminated on the Easter Sunday of speculation.

> *If the purposeless destruction for the sake of destruction, the absolute sacrifice, must be sacrificed because it has been annulled as the empty point of the parousia – that which remains, philosophical reflection and every historical form of cult, must also be sacrificed. In every case of sacrificial offering therefore, different though they are, the offering itself becomes the object of sacrifice. And the relationship between finite and infinite, absolute knowledge and appearing consciousness, history and system, is summed up in the proposition: the sacrifice sacrifices itself. The objectification of the absolute is its sacrifice, the negation of objectivity is the sacrifice of this sacrifice, its return to the absolute which, since it alone first preserves the sacrifice as sacrifice, is nothing other than the absolute process of the sacrifice: the operation, the labour and the work of the concept.*
>
> *What still remains then of the material, maternal, supposedly ineliminable residue within speculative philosophy? That which resists, inedible and indigestible, the sacrificial meal to which philosophy exposed it? What fails to dance to the conceptual rhythm of its music, which remains unconscious and yet absolute knowledge? Is it that speculative philosophy itself as idea, system and concept must be materialized in language, writing, text? That the form of the speculative meal itself submits to empirical-historical forms of transformation? That the harmony of the concept merely performs* da capo *the barbaric harmonies of Cybele? That a difference, a residue, perpetually remains between the possibility of socially realized synthesis and the law of the latter as formulated in the system? That consequently the speculative law of the historical process must remain something objective over against that very*

> *process, thereby caught up in difference from its own con-*
> *cept? That dialectical ontology cannot completely perceive*
> *its own structure, cannot digest itself without remainder or*
> *residue?*

In the immediately succeeding and practically conceived political writings concerning 'The Constitution of Germany' and in the subsequent 'System of Ethical Life' and the essay 'On the Scientific Treatment of Natural Law', Hegel attempted conclusively to close this difference between system and history still left open by his first system in a constructive and in an analytical-speculative manner respectively. It is not merely philosophy alone, but also societies, spurred on by the critical impulses of the former and in accordance with the objective tendencies of history, which are supposed to be capable of assuming that ontological structure which was still denied to the Christian community in Hegel's earlier conception. In the 'System of Ethical Life' and in the 'Natural Law' essay alike, it is sacrifice, once again, which supplies the paradigm for the supercession of the fate dictated by the necessity of [private] property. And indeed the ethical life of society cedes that part that is 'bound up' with the 'inorganic element', the 'positive element' that is not entirely integrated into the self-relation of society, the 'subterranean powers' of violence, of suffering, of death.

> *'This is nothing but the enactment of the tragedy of ethical*
> *life which the absolute eternally plays with itself, – so that*
> *it bears itself eternally into objectivity, and in this shape*
> *gives itself over to suffering and death and raises itself from*
> *out its ashes into glory.' (2: TWA, 495)*

Ethical nature must expose itself as objective to inorganic nature and, having become unethical, guilty and evil, can only reconquer its integrity insofar as it 'severs' its involvement with the powers of *thanatos* and opposes itself to them as 'fate' (ibid., 496). Severing the bond that connects ethical and inorganic nature simultaneously produces a new, and double, connection: inasmuch as life has offered its dead element over to death it is once more entirely at home with itself, and the dead element, recognized by the living, becomes indeed its transient but nonetheless organic body. In distinction from the process of tragedy in which the ethical power of the polis is constituted, the comic after-play which presents the subsequent history of the polis is performed in a realm of fatelessness. Yet the comedy, culminating in farce, is mirrored in a world of 'shadow-images' and insubstantial delusions which can no longer return to any genuine unity and ultimately find themselves standing over against actuality as their tragic fate once again. It is not comedy, as in Nietzsche, which represents the conceptual essence of the historical and social process; 'the absolute relationship is presented ... in tragedy' (ibid., 499). In the 'absolute relationship' of 'tragedy in the ethical' the fate of the finite social form is resolved in this way: it is recognized by the idea as something which belongs to the other, inorganic realm, and transfigured in the light shed by the idea. Yet the sacrificial offering still cannot directly present the 'absolute infinity of life' in the finite form of ethical and political life; the resurrection of the phoenix from its ashes, of the social Christ from the grave, cannot transpire without disturbing the harmony of its shape; here the absolute does not play purely with itself or with its complementary other. For although the political realisation of the system of ethical life certainly expresses its absolute idea, as Hegel writes, it does so '*distortedly*' (2: TWA, 499). In virtue of this difference – at once bodily deformation and temporal distortion – to which the absolute through its material actuality is exposed, the absolute can only find its unity therein as 'an imitated negative independence, namely as the freedom of the individual' (ibid., 499). The difference between original and imitation, between form and deformation, thus continues to subsist within the drama of the absolute, transforming this tragedy into a mourning-play, into an agonistic encounter in which the victor fails to emerge without losing precisely what was at issue. As long as the deformation of shape and time is still at work within the process of the absolute, then the latter, along with the very part which it has detached from itself, remains entangled in fate, even if it is the Christian community's fate of fatelessness. The sacrificial offering cannot assimilate the power of the other, of time and death, without remainder to the power of the One and still leaves part of that power behind undissolved, though it was to serve as instrument of its incorporation. If the stony weight of objectivity no longer bears upon the wings of the phoenix, then its own ashes do, inhibiting flight, distorting the circle of the absolute's return to itself. The draw and pull of a time which is not purely the power of the concept, not merely a transition to the latter's absolute presence.

Thus the absolute presented in the system of ethical life remains disfigured and torn. But the gash in the dialectically constructed unity runs not merely between political realization of the ethical ideal and the process of the absolute idea, but also therefore through and within the absolute idea itself, which must remain lifeless in part unless it finds an appropriate form of expression. Thus Hegel drew the conclusion which was implied in the Frankfurt system, expressed more cautiously in the 'Natural Law' essay, more bluntly later on: that the absolute cannot find a pure and corresponding form of expression within societies and their history, that it must therefore absolve itself from their temporally distorted process by consciously and independently sacrificing the latter as something separate and distinct from the absolute. This renunciation of everything subservient to the fate of time is to allow the emergence of pure thought as its subject, a thought which can now undistortedly relate to itself. In their withdrawal from this absolute self-relationship, which must first purify itself precisely from this distortion through the philosophical sacrifice, time and materiality still leave traces – for the act of offering these up is not indeed a pure offering in and of itself. Yet although Hegel actually describes this predicament, he cannot systematically expound it, precisely because the supposedly inessential deformation can be represented in the system only *as* deformation, consequently as something which (in part) it is not. The residue of time puts a stroke through the possibility of the system which it grounds – the stroke of the system's *self-inscription*. What is being read is writing – and this operation of reading performed upon the sacrifice of delay and distortion allows the delay of the sacrifice to appear *as* delay. Reading performs the movement of disfiguration, of the imperfect sacrifice, and pursues as nemesis or fate the sacrifice of history at the hands of the philosophical system.

In order to reduce the difference between the various shapes of spirit and its highest shapes, Hegel attempts to reveal the homogeneity of religious cult and political institution, and furthermore of the state, world-history and philosophy. The law which, apparently immutable, connects all of them and repeats itself in all of them, remains that of sacrificial offering, of consumption and of digestion. In the chapter on 'Absolute Knowledge' in the *Phenomenology* Hegel formulates the fundamental reason for the inertia which attaches to the history of spirit: it is because

> *'the self has first to penetrate and to digest the entire riches of its own substance.' (3: TWA, Phen., 590)*

The self-digestion of the absolute assimilating its own shapes presents the exemplary model for the process of nature and history alike. The religions still prior to history proper sought to procure conscious awareness of spiritual self-relation for themselves through the cannibalistic fetish-feast. On the one hand, the sacrificial feast of the Greeks constitutes the recognition of the universal power of nature through a 'useless, purposeless, and therefore unselfish offering' of part of what they themselves were to consume and enjoy – that part indeed which, like the bones, the hide, the fat, cannot be consumed and enjoyed. The inedible residue is the part belonging to the Gods. On the other hand, the act of sacrificial offering is itself an enjoyment of the gifts of nature as food and sustenance, an enjoyment through which the power of the universal is spiritualized and individualized, through which nature is taken up into the fermenting cycle of conscious life, something quite impossible without the sacrifice of nature. Alluding to lines in the *Odyssey* Hegel can write: 'Eating means sacrificing, and sacrificing as such means eating' (17: TWA, *Phil. Rel.*, II, 136 ff.; 14: TWA, *Ästhetik*, 37). Spirit's relation to itself through the other, the sublation of its natural forms through sacrificial offering, can indeed only ever be, as Hegel expresses it, a symbolic one. For in the part which is offered up the totality of finitude is not utterly destroyed, the process signifies only that finitude does not exercise power over spirit (16: TWA, *Phil. Rel.*, I, 225). Inasmuch as the part stands in this way for the whole every sacrificial offering and every operation of consciousness is structured metonymically. This form of rhetorical transposition introduces tensions into the philosophical movement of self-consciousness, where the latter seeks to grasp and incorporate itself not metonymically as a part, but rather in truth as its own totality, tensions which will culminate in the highest form of sacrificial meal there is, in the Christian Eucharist.

In the eucharistic mass, where the spectacle of God's eternal history is performed, the self-mediation of subject with its substance assumes – once again – the form of the consumption of the universal divine individual. In commemoration of the Last Supper the congregation relates to its substance as this is presented to them in the Body of Christ. The agent of mediation, the mediating middle between the subject and its substance, here presents itself in the sacrificial offering, the Host, as an external and perceptible thing of dough. Universal substance, in the middle of its own path towards itself, is transformed into an insubstantial particular. The part no longer contains the whole, is even less than that, because it is supposed to remain substantial presence, to remain isolated on its own account, still unconsumed and independent of consumption. Even in enjoyment this distinction persists, since it is eaten, not with faith as a spiritual body but, as a sensuous body in the collaboration of teeth and organism. Just as the eaters at this feast, which sustains an entire epoch of western history, can be excommunicated from the meal in which they find their substance by the Church, which claims the isolated body of the God as its own possession, so too the body of God is itself something separate, something dead, something extruded from the context of life. The very part of absolute life in which the whole was to be made present is perverted into the extinguished residue of life, remains which will multiply in various other forms, as relics of the cross, the sweat-cloth, the blood-stained head-band. The mediating middle between self and substance, which was to supply their objective unity, has become, hypostatized, a fetish. Just as the witch [*Hexe*], in whom the Middle Ages saw the independent principle of evil personified, transposes good milk into bad by curdling, so too on the other side the priest, exercising his power over the sacred, consecrates the Host and displays the miraculous images of Mary:

> *'(the wonder-working images of Mary are also in their*
> *own way Hosts, inasmuch as they serve to procure the grace*
> *and favour of God's presence).' (12: TWA,* Phil. History,
> *469)*

The imago of the woman, which had already earlier determined Hegel's image of Christ, repeats itself in the connection between the Host of Christ and the image of his mother Mary; but this female feast which both of them present becomes, fetishized, caught up with and infected by the contagious excremental meal of the witch [*Hexe*]. For the sacrifice which substance offers up to itself as subject in the Host is extruded, secreted, from the spiritual context of life to such a degree that it is supposed to remain something absolute even as excrement:

> 'In the Mediaeval Church, in the Catholic Church in general, the Host is also venerated as an external thing, which means that should a mouse eat up the Host, then the mouse and its excrement are to be venerated.' (19: TWA, Hist. Philosophy, II, 538)

This rigorously scholastic conclusion from the Catholic doctrine of the communion, which caused Hegel in 1826 to produce a formal reply to the charge of slandering the Catholic religion (cf. 40: R. Haym, *Hegel und seine Zeit* [Berlin: Gaertner, 1857], 509 ff.; 11: TWA, 68–71), merely manifests the blasphemous perversion which transpires within the divine feast itself, isolated in the form of nature: it falls under the power of animality and transforms itself into excrement. Materialized in the Host, God becomes a digested excrementum that is nonetheless indigestible and inedible; the universe of spirit becomes mouse droppings, its eschatology a scatology. The Catholic mass is the transubstantiation of the mediation of subject and substance, of the absolute, into an absolute excrement which renders all mediation impossible – unless the congregation would like to actualise its self-consciousness in coprophaegia. More than a black mass. *Cena caeni*.

> With this consequence, this contra-sequence, Christianity has not merely fallen back to the level of the Jews. Hegel remarked, as Marx would later do with similar intent ('On the Jewish Question': 60: MEW, I, 374), with a quotation from Voltaire, that it would have been better if their God had instructed them about the immortality of the soul rather than teaching them how to enter the closet

*(aller à la selle) (16: TWA, Phil. Rel., I, 211). More
importantly, the principle of unfreedom and diremption
has also broken its way into the now developed principle of
self-relation and freedom: 'The highest purity of soul is
soiled by the most barbaric wildness, conscious truth is
perverted through lies and selfishness into a means, what is
most repulsive to reason, what is most crude, what is most
filthy, is supplied with religious foundation and support –
this is the most repulsive and disgusting spectacle that has
ever been seen, and one that can only be grasped and in
that sense justified by philosophy.' (12: TWA, Phil.
History, 460)*

At the heart of history the Host, this 'repulsive' and nauseating
excremental mother-meal, leads 'historie', the narrative story of spirit's
historical self-knowledge, back to an incomprehensible residue which
was to participate in that story, a part which was to contain its totality.
The aporia of immediate sense certainty, which is supposed to find its
object in the Godhead objectified in dough and excrement and therefore finds itself thrown back into absolute uncertainty and unintelligibility, can be resolved only by spirit's detaching itself from this its
sensuous fixation, extruding the extrusion, taking leave of what is left.

It is in the medieval crusades that history treads the path which leads
back from the false show of sensuous presence towards the truth of self-
consciousness. Just as the Christian community thinks to grasp its own
actuality in the sensuous *This* of the Host, so too it must also seek the
material presence of his spirit in the spatial 'This' of Christ's presence
as was, in the Holy Land, in the 'footsteps of the saviour', in Christ's
very grave. It is in the relics of the life, and especially the death, of
Christ – 'the sweat-cloth of Christ, the cross of Christ, finally the grave
of Christ became the greatest relics of all'; it is in traces and remains
that the life of the absolute is to be found preserved and be incorporated into the Christian realm as its own property. But just as in the
'eternal history of God' the inversion of the absolute into a bloody
corpse finds itself inverted through the resurrection of the spiritual
body, so too in the empirical history of the medieval world, which
like every other repeats the eternal history once again, the inverted

perspective of the sensuous 'This' finds itself inverted into the spiritual 'This' of self-consciousness.

> *'But it is in the grave that the true point of reversion and inversion lies, it is in the grave that every vanity of the sensuous is destroyed . . . there that ultimate seriousness is found. It is in the negative of the* this, *of the sensuous, that the reversion is accomplished.'* (12: TWA, Phil. History, 471)

In the material trace, the secretion, the relic and the grave, consciousness cannot discover *its* other, but merely an emptiness in which its substance withdraws. Losing its object, consciousness reverts to itself and its own presence.

This historical turning-point, this reversion and revolution, which is played out around the central focus of an empty grave – a stony grave that buries itself and rises again from out of itself as the 'deeper grave of the absolute ideality of all sensuousness' (12: TWA, *Phil. History*, 494) – acquires historical actuality in the Reformation. – And the Reformation teaches us how to eat. – It is true that the Lutheran act of communion retains the Host as a sensuous this, but the consciousness of God's presence and the mediation of substance and subject is attained only insofar as the externality of the Host is not itself consumed externally, but only in and through the spirit. The 'eternal repetion of the life, the suffering and the resurrection of Christ in the members of the Church' (17: TWA, *Phil. Rel.*, II, 327) is accomplished in the sacrament of the Last Supper inasmuch as the congregation offers itself up and consumes itself as the Body of Christ, bodily buries its own body, like the grave buried in the grave, separates itself from what has been separated, and rises again as the unity of substance and subject, as the certainty of the truth in and for itself. Because this food exists only in the enjoyment with which it is consumed, its spiritual character is not fixated upon the external thing, but rather first results from the process of its dissolution within the living organism and its re-membering, its commemorative incorporation, into the corpus of subjectivity. Substance is not the sensuous This, but the *hic* of the ego. Hence the aporetic inedibility of what was destined for consumption is not played out here as it was in the earlier analysis of the love-feast, nor as it was in the Catholic doctrine of transubstantiation. World-history, the world's first course and court of judgement, which finds its first and still subjective conclusion in the Lutheran Reformation, essentially presents itself as a revolution in the order of consumption.

Yet it is not sufficient that consciousness has raised itself to the absolute extremity of self-consciousness and learned in the cultus how to eat; the form of consciousness concentrated upon subjectivity must expand and disseminate itself universally through technological means. In order to be able to appropriate its substance for itself in a universal and ideal manner, the subject must know how to read. If in Hegel's earlier writings the connection between eating and reading had emerged as a metaphor – but what does metaphor signify here and why *this* metaphor rather than another? – then it emerges now from the progress of history, out of a 'need' on the part of spirit.

> 'The new ideas found a principal means of disseminating
> themselves in the recently invented art of printing, which
> like the invention of gunpowder corresponds to the charac-
> ter of the modern age and precisely came to meet people's
> need of relating to one another in an ideal fashion . . . the
> technology is discovered when the need for it emerges.' (12:
> TWA, Phil. History, 490 ff.)

The mechanical reproduction inaugurated through printing and the mechanico-chemical action of firing facilitated by gunpowder correspond to the spirit of the Renaissance and the Reformation. In both technical processes the immediate sensuous presence of the one who writes, the one who kills, is reflected back upon itself and eliminated – written and killed – in order to achieve its effect abstractly and, to a greatly enhanced degree, profanely. The birth of printing and firing from out of the spirit of the Lutheran doctrine of the communion: its own principle is turned against the authority of sensuous presence, the principle of dissolution, and transforms that presence into the authority of an ideal law. In these technical devices the supersession of the sensuous this finds itself objectified in the form of mechanical self-relation. They are at one and the same time the instruments which bring about the collapse of the medieval feudal system and the authority of the Catholic Church.

The printing-press instructs us how to read: it destroys the cultic aura and authority of the original, makes its mechanical reproducibility manifest, and thereby subjects it to the authority of an intrinsically universal subjectivity. Luther's translation of the Bible performs a complementary feat. For Christian doctrine is thereby removed from the trusteeship of the Church, which formerly administered it as its own property in an alien and indeed dead language, is thereby expropriated and entrusted to individual subjects in their own living language, now capable for the first time of relating in this language, as in the communion meal, to their own substance. Like the printing-press, the translation too teaches us how to read: not indeed by dissolving the authority of *one* language and substituting another instead, but by demonstrating the principle of substitutability and repeatability. Translation brings about the dissolution of the fetish of originality. Reading is a reading of the divine word if and only if it simultaneously reads the translatability of the same into the domain of spiritual subjectivity. Through his translation and his doctrine of communion Luther establishes the realm of self-consciousness in its originality, through the unique singularity of the translated book establishes at the same time the unity and objective determinacy of this realm – the realm of the German language.

> 'Luther's translation of the Bible has proved of incalculable value for the German people ... If there is to be a vernacular version for the people, then it is above all necessary that the people can read, something that is less common in the Catholic countries.' (12: TWA, Phil. History, 498)

Like the art of printing and the Luther translation, the reading of this vernacular book must also – although Hegel does not discuss this – correspond to the principle of spiritual self-relation; and as in the Protestant consumption of the communion-meal, so too in the Protestant reading of translated scripture the reader must relate to the divine gift of the written Word not as the lifeless relic of a sensuous this, but as a form of its own inwardness, one produced through the power of subjectivity. On its crusades to the Holy Land of the divine Word this reading has stumbled simply upon the empty grave of the absolute in the letter, has been drawn into an empty space of reading which submits to the objective authority of one particular language; in the multiplication of the corpus Christi into a potentially infinite number of Hosts, this reading has stumbled upon the transition from the ubiquity of the thingly this to the ubiquity of a this as such, of the spiritual universality of the divine logos – upon the subjective principle which underlies the external objectification of God's Word. In the printing-press and its products reading now stands over against this spiritual principle of mechanical reproduction. The machine is the grave into which the empirical grave of spirit vanishes and from which the abstract principle of spirituality rises again; though lifeless, the machine is still the subjective matrix of Holy Writ, the sacred scriptures in which their reader can recognize his own subjectivity. The machine therefore relates to the reader not as heteronomous power, but as the substitution of his own power (cf. 24: *JR*, 216). – If reading, prior to its technological reformation, had remained simply the repetition of the written, then in reading the printed text it must also relate to its own principle, that of repetition. The reading of the printed text also simultaneously reads itself, a machine, as mechanical reproduction. Reading can reflect upon its own abstract principle, that of the understanding, through which it remains fixated within the realm of externality, and can define itself by contrast not merely as mechanical reproduction, but as substantial re-production. This alone would render a speculative reading truly possible, one where the externality of its own operations were transformed – like the externality of bodily eating and drinking in the Lutheran communion-meal – into a spiritual re-membering, one where the remaining objective characteristics, if not eliminated, would at least assume a subordinate role as instrumental functions of universal, subjective self-production.

But just as the participant in the communion-meal must also bodily consume the bread and the wine if he is to enjoy his own universality in a spiritual fashion, so too the reading which reflects upon its own abstractness cannot cease to be a mechanical repetition. Underway as it is towards a speculative reading, which will reproduce the logos, it still remains a machine, a formal iteration which empties the meaning of the logos.

The Protestant reading which Hegel discusses is also a factor in the political realization and expansion of the principle of subjectivity. This reading is a politicum. But although it allows subjective self-consciousness to unfold into objective power, reading does not yet constitute a state. Yet the law which the reversion at the empty grave of Christ, which the printing-press and the translation of scripture, which the reformation of the communion-meal and the revolution of reading all alike observe, is the same law which governs the modern political revolutions as Hegel describes them. The authority of self-consciousness itself is posited against the authority of the king, and the sensuous this of divine right is decapitated in the bodily shape of the king.

> *'Thus in England there arose a Protestant sect which claimed to have been instructed by revelation as to how to govern; in accordance with such deliverances of the Lord they succeeded in fomenting revolt and in decapitating their king.' (16: TWA, Phil. Rel., I, 239)*
>
> *And in France – not in Germany, where 'with regard to the earthly realm everything had already been improved through the Reformation' – in France, where* 'at a single stroke' *'the concept of right and the will which wills itself' made itself felt (12: TWA, Phil. History, 529), this same Protestant principle brought 'the monarch, whose subjective will precisely represented the Catholic religious conscience, to the scaffold'. (ibid., 533)*

The revolution is the decapitation of the this which had been fetishized into something substantial. In its treatment of the this the revolution realizes the tendency towardss particularization and detaches the particular which had accumulated all the wealth of the universal within itself; the revolution expropriates the expropriator of universal consciousness which presents itself as the subject of the latter's substance. Insofar as the king's head, this personified and capital fetish, falls; insofar as the external sun sets in the west, the true concretum of universal self-knowing self-consciousness raises a new head as an inner sun – and it is this which first makes the decapitation, the negation of the negation, into something *revolutionary* and positive. 'The external physical sun rises in the East, and sets in the West: but here on the

other hand the inner sun of self-consciousness rises up and sheds a
higher radiance' (12: TWA, *Phil. History*, 134). This heliophoric revolution, in which the technical, political, religious and philosophical
moments of modernity are focused, takes an epochal political shape in
the French Revolution:

> *'As long as the sun has stood in the firmament and the*
> *planets have revolved around it, it was not recognized*
> *that man places himself upon his head, i.e. upon thought,*
> *and builds actuality in accordance with the latter.*
> *Anaxagoras was the first to claim that nous rules the*
> *world; but it is only now that man has finally come to*
> *recognize that thought should rule spiritual actuality.*
> *This was a magnificent dawning. . . . It was as though we*
> *had now for the first time attained the actual reconcilia-*
> *tion of the world with the divine.'* (12: *TWA*, Phil.
> History, *529*)

With the dialectical re-, the once again and the back again, through
which the process of spirit closes and connects with itself in
Renaissance, Reformation and Revolution, not every remaining trace
of conflict between the false substantiality of the this and the substantial truth of universal self-consciousness has yet been eliminated. This
conflict, born beyond the relics of the Catholic principle into the
heart of the reformed and revolutionized states and their politics, does
not permit the social self-relation, characterized here as a socio-ontological one, to become a universal actuality. The social substantiality
that was to stand secure still remains exposed to the possibility of further revolutions.

> *'The last revolution [Hegel means the July revolution of*
> *1830] was the consequence of a religious conscience which*
> *contradicted the principles of the political constitution,*
> *and yet in accordance with the same constitution it is sup-*
> *posed to be a matter of indifference as to what religious*
> *confession the individual belongs; this collision is still very*
> *far from being resolved.'* (17: *TWA*, Phil. Rel., *II, 245*)

The view, exemplified here in a rather distorted fashion, that the
backwardness of the ideological revolution in relation to the political

one, determines the fraught arena of modern history; that it is 'a false principle that the fetters on freedom and rights can be eliminated without the liberation of conscience, that there can be revolution without a reformation' (12: TWA, *Phil. History*, 535): this insight, emphatically repeated in a prominent place in the *Encyclopaedia* (10: TWA, Enc., III, §552), has eminently significant consequences in the overall context of Hegel's writings. For there it is ethical life which serves as the substance of the state, and religion as the substance of ethical life, which means that the social relations in which self-consciousness is objectified – just as in Hegel's earlier socio-ontological conception – can arise only on the basis of a religion that is centred upon the self-relation of consciousness. As long as the Catholic principle of the substantialization of the external still persists, then the basis of ethical life and the state remains rent, political ethics remains, in part, fetishistically perverted, self-consciousness remains in part unconscious of itself. The revolution in which substance and subject were to have rejoined one another and closed the circle opens out instead into a parabola, and the solar dawn which was to have followed hard upon the night of God-forsakenness, arrives after time, in arrears. Thus the system of philosophy, which claims to be not merely truth in and for itself but 'truth insofar as it comes to life within actuality' (12: TWA, *Phil. History*, 528), must make a delayed appearance too.

Yet none of Hegel's major systematic expositions – and this also includes the *Encyclopaedia of the Philosophical Sciences in Outline* – attempts to conceal the difference between the concept and the actual stage of world-history which is supposed to find its truth in the concept, but cannot yet achieve it. His writings make no pretence about this, but seek rather to accentuate the contradiction in order to resolve it. State, religion and philosophy are, as Hegel writes in the chapter on world-history in the *Encyclopaedia*, in each case particular shapes of absolute truth. Amongst them religion is that particular shape which – like Christ – cannot avoid being distorted on its path through sensibility, cannot avoid being 'corrupted into the oppression of the freedom of spirit and the perversion of political life' (10: TWA, Enc., III, 365). Even if this Christ of a religion, and therefore this Christ of a state, has not yet risen again to absolute ethical life, the principle implicit in both of them nonetheless still possesses enough 'elasticity' from out of its own resources – this is Hegel's utopia – to be able, and to have, to reverse the perverted inversion, to overcome the corruption from out of its own resources. In accordance with the model of Christ's life cited by Hegel himself (ibid.) – and for him the whole of world-history is an *imitatio Christi* – the fate of corrupted religiosity and of anarchic or despotic political power can be fulfilled only in their absolute self-sacrifice, in their destruction. Hegel hints at this literally catastrophic consequence, which could be realized only in further ideological and political revolutions, at the close of his *Lectures on the Philosophy of Religion*. The political realization of the religious community in the state, the actualization of the 'Kingdom of God', appears to have fallen, as Hegel writes, 'into this inner conflict which also seems to be its passing away '.

> [Yet] 'to speak here of passing away would mean . . . ending upon a discordant note. But what help is there? This discordant note is present in actuality. . . . Once all its fundamental supports have silently been withdrawn, the people no longer knows . . . how to help its own innermost impulses. It still stands nearest to that infinite grief; but since love has been perverted into a love and an enjoyment lacking all grief . . . the substantial core of the people can no longer find any satisfaction.' (17: TWA, Phil. Rel., II, 342–3).

Religion, and even the absolute religion which presents itself as a form of absolute truth, remains subject to a mere re-presentation of the parousia, and therefore in its finitude to the logic of decline. And insofar as the state possesses its substance only in religion, it too remains, along with the entire process of world-history, inevitably exposed to perversion, decay and decline, and truth too remains exposed to its fabrication. The philosophy of world-history as the world's court of judgement is a historico-theology of pain and grief whose final satisfaction is still withheld. It is only in this 'ultimately', where religious and political ethics are one and the same in the 'Protestant conscience' (10: TWA, Enc., III, 365), that the subject's painful diremption from its own substance is sublated in sacrifice. This sacrifice is no longer one performed according to the rites of the sensuous this, or to those of mere faith whose fulfilment as the 'Kingdom of God' remains a beyond, but one performed according to the rites of a self-consciousness which consciously knows itself in con-science and thereby liberates itself from all guilt and servitude. This sacrifice, which marks the limit of this 'ultimately', is yet to be performed.

And yet it has already been performed. The not yet is always already there. Like the priest presiding as master of ceremonies over the cultus, the philosopher has secreted the law of this performance in his writings. While the revolutionary struggles of the suffering 'people' still persist, for the philosopher the political dissonance is already resolved into the harmonious consonance of the absolute.

> *'Philosophical cognition has resolved this dissonance for us, and the purpose of these lectures was precisely to reconcile reason with religion. . . . But this reconciliation remains itself only a partial one, without external universality; in this regard philosophy remains a secluded holy sanctum, and her devotees constitute an isolated priesthood which may not consort with the world and must preserve the possession of truth intact. How the temporal, empirical present finds a way out of its conflicts, what shape it will henceforth assume, must be left to this present itself and does not constitute the* immediate *practical matter or concern of philosophy.' (17: TWA, Phil. Rel., II, 343 ff.)*

Philosophy is the final complement, the absolute pleroma of history. But insofar as it is only the law of history, and not also its determinate form, only the absolute form, and not also its particular content, that is fulfilled, it does not solely relate to other forms of absolute truth as a 'separated sanctum', but rather – and this is more significant – the abundant fulfilment as separated relates to its own abundance, the final closing of substance and subject relates to the final closing of subject and substance. The speculative meal which lies inside within the tabernacle of philosophy fails (as yet) to satisfy not merely the historical gathering at the final court and course of judgement – but this court and course, separated from its own concept, is (always already) not yet satisfied by itself.

Between the empirical time of unconcluded history and the concept of time, as it actually realizes itself historically in the 'separated sanctum' of philosophy, there stretches a space-time of transition which is also the space-time of the impossibility of synthetic unity. The separated 'concept of time', or eternity, still finds itself drawn into this between, without on its own part being able to reduce it conceptually, and thus within it relate for the first time purely to itself. The self of time procures the delay of the concept within space-time. – The absolute de-fined, rendered finite and in-finite, through the postponement of history and its close.

The impossibility of closing up the rent exposed in the body of Mother Nature, as already expounded by Hegel at the beginning of his constructive project in the early writings, is repeated here on the highest, logical, level of absolute knowing in Hegel's developed system. This impossibility formed the ground for Hegel's conception of the fetishistic religion of law, and subsequently of the religion of love. Hegel's mature onto-theological philosophy, his philosophy of philosophy, proves no more capable than either of these in realizing the ontological principle through a social synthesis in which relatio and relatum would be one. The impossibility of any unreservedly intact self-relation without remainder, which had seemed settled by the regulated sacrifice of philosophy on its speculative Good Friday, emerges once again in the immediate self-relation of the concept within its philosophical tabernacle. The Host of absolute knowing, its sacrifice in and for itself, withheld from the bite of empirical experience, remains inedible in itself, separated from itself. The pleroma of the perfect sacrifice remains – suspended. The bite of the perfect reader.

The speculative syllogism of philosophy, which is presented not merely in Hegel's *Logic* and his *Encyclopaedia* but also in the earlier and later particular expositions of the system, and in which philosophy grasps itself in passing through all nature and history as its very self, this syllogism remains, precisely because it closes itself, and constitutionally so, unconcluded. Dialectic in difference from dialectic as its own law. The absolute presence of the dialectical-speculative law, insofar as it separates itself – not merely empirically but categorially (9: TWA, Enc., II, §257, Addition) – from the 'temporal, empirical present' which yet constitutes in part its own being, inscribes within itself a delay which makes it into its own absolute anticipation, absolute re-presentation, absolute pre-sence, and consequently makes it incapable of self-recuperation. Hegel's attempt to absolve the re- by erecting the law of speculative dialectic in the 'secluded sanctum' of philosophy introduces time, as absolute delay, into the concept of the absolute spiritual self-presence. It is through this absolute delay that the meal harboured within the philosophical tabernacle always arrives too early, that the flight of the absolute owl arrives only *post festum* and too late, for philosophy to grasp the unity of historical actuality and the ontological law of the same.

> *A topsy-turvy, Till Eulenspiegel of an introduction. Hegel's text can be preceded only by an overture which presents itself as the implicit mirror of the former, a mirror which brings the bird of prey – an owl that grasps the other, though it be a mouse, only as itself – to despair before a mirror-image which projects its self upon a slippery surface that denies all purchase. A mirror-image of the owl which cannot become its image, cannot become its fodder; in which it cannot install a nest, or lay the eggs that would ensure its reproduction. A mirror-play of owls which fails to feed and fatten this absolute knowing – but not to madden.*

Like spirit itself, world-history turns into an absolute threshold for the spirit, a threshold whose beyond, the hysteron, spirit's own self, withdraws.

In this delay, the passing pull of its own time, the absolute reveals itself as self-absolved, as always absolute and empirical at once. Hegel's formulation that the absolute philosophy is a 'separate sanctum' where an 'isolated band of priests' shall protect 'the possession of truth', repeats under an affirmative sign his polemical formulation directed against the Catholic cult of the Host, in which the 'consciousness of what truth is lies in the possession of a priesthood' (19: TWA, *Hist. Philosophy*, II, 538).

If the material shape of truth as property is not repeated here in immediate form, the caenogramm in the hierogramm – , the gesture of separation in the constitution of the absolute is nonetheless repeated within the absolute itself, without the latter being able to grasp *this* absolution or bring it into unity with its concept. The empirical-social or the linguistic lack could indeed be sublated in accordance with the law of speculative dialectics erected within the sanctum of philosophy, but the very position which belongs to this law stands in a relation of difference to the law itself; thus every fulfilment of the law would inevitably have to repeat this difference from itself, the lack would merely be preserved in the same movement through which it was to be sublated. And even if the speculative dialectic, 'separated' as it is, presents the law of separation as the law of the syllogism, it can present it only by repeating the separation and the unification as they are actual in realm of language and society.

The law of repetition is law only as another repetition.

Speculative concretion and its empirical or conceptual articulation are 'one and the same' insofar as the life of the one repeats the death of the other, insofar as they intersect, interpenetrate and complement one another. Not concrete identity, not speculative unity, not ontological synthesis, as Hegel demands, but an identity, unity and synthesis which relate to themselves, to their 'self', as separated, dirempted, as rent; which withdraw themselves, and their 'self'. Unity in difference.

How then to read? How to read a text which itself pre-scribes the law of the sublation of signification into what it signifies, of the sublation of the reproduction of sense into sense itself, and thus the law of speculative reading?

How then to read – the absolute act of reading? The answer to this question, for its part, cannot be a law or maxim, cannot furnish counsel either. There is no ethic, no economy of reading, that would not inevitably transgress the measure it erects, would not inevitably suspend the court of judgement it introduces. Reading reads itself, its 'self', in the experience of the aporias of the absolute, as its merely delayed repetition, as a self-related operation always already in advance of itself and thus always already too late to reflect itself as substance and subject. It could constitute a meta-reading only if it possessed a border, a limit beyond which it alone could continue to read without itself being read. But whatever rules might be read in it, they cannot cease to become the object of another reading with distortions of its own. Where it seizes its ownmost self, takes its very life, it allows it to escape. A veil, it winds between itself and itself, itself a text, and every further reading weaves its own way inside. To read the absolute therefore, to read reading – and this means to read practically, politically, agonistically – is no speculative operation which would lead the absolute back to itself from out of its own externalized forms, no revolution which would restitute the dominating rule of sense, of being, of property and of unity; it is a different operation, one which would transpose the persisting sense of domination sublated into other social forms, the persisting proprietorial economy of being, the ethic of the self and its unity, the historical ontology of its self-actualization.

The revolution, which leads philosophy back to its own proper origin as the conclusive closure of its concept, no longer knows how to contain itself and its circle.

The speculative mass, read before the Host of the absolute in the secret sanctum of a segregated philosophy, cannot – perhaps – be performed after all.

The eucharistic evening meal of the absolute owl, the strix, the witch, is itself the mouse which, seized and strangulated, has all but secreted its own holy offering.

Precisely insofar as it grasps itself as the other of itself and as the self of the other, the clasp of philosophical science almost entirely loses its own grip – once again – upon both other and self, and consequently upon the system which organizes both, and does so without science being able to account for this its autosecretion. – This grip is therefore also no longer merely entirely that of science, but the bite with which it seizes itself as writing. This implies that the system relates to itself, and its particular moments relate to one another, according to a model of reading, implies further that there is no rigorous criterion for distinguishing the writing and its reading. And not indeed because both were one and the same, or might be reduced to one another through the mediations of hermeneutic art. But, on the contrary, because both, text and exegesis alike, represent forms of appropriation and self-appropriation in which the proper withdraws itself, deforms its own structure, fails to remain proper to itself.

Writing and reading are differential operations oriented towardss the self-presentation of their subject, the self-presentation of these operations themselves. In the ideal case – like the speculative reading of the text of absolute knowing – writing and exegesis would converge so perfectly that both should find themselves extinguished in an absolute presence. Yet even in this ultimate limiting case – and this is what constitutes the relatively privileged position of Hegel's text for the systematic investigation and deconstruction of every concept of reading conceived according to the schema of self-presentation in and through the presentation of the other – even in this limiting case, towards which Hegel would seductively lead the interpretation of

his texts, there activates itself in writing and reading a
generative difference, one to which such self-presence, were
it even attainable, would owe its existence.

At this limit there returns – once again – the question con-
cerning the possible presence of writing and the re-presen-
tation of its sense in the act of reading, concerning the
temporality of reading, concerning the temporality of every
text and every reading.

Speculative-dialectical ontology returns to itself. Returns to itself as
its own commencement – as its destination, secures its self-relation in
the only way it can, by attaining once again, in a circular movement of
re-traversal and re-turn, the position from which it originally set out.

The chapter on 'Absolute Knowing' in the *Phenomenology* identifies this return, which was first raised in the interpretation of the
speculative proposition and its reading and has constantly been at
issue since, as a necessity for philosophical science. And in Hegel's
terminology this means a necessity for the *Science of Logic* in which
the concept explicitly grasps itself as concept. This science, which
transcends the *Phenomenology* inasmuch as the *Logic* encloses substance and subject, truth and knowledge, in an immediate unity,
must nonetheless return to the *Phenomenology* since this immediate
self-equality itself is a form of externality which can be represented
only as the nothing of pure being and, in the structure of consciousness, as the sensuous certainty of the immediate this. The 'Logic' is
compelled, by the very necessity which it has conceptually grasped
and affirmed, to introduce a difference – that between consciousness
and being – into its absolute unity.

'Science contains within itself the necessity of externalizing
itself from the form of the pure concept, contains the tran-
sition of the concept into consciousness. *For self-knowing*
spirit, precisely because it grasps its own concept, is the
immediate unity with itself which in its difference is the
certainty of the immediate, *or* sense certainty *– the*
commencement from which we began; this self-releasement
from its own form is the highest freedom and security of its
self-knowledge.' (3: TWA, Phen., 589–590)

This 'self-releasement from its own form' is the gift bestowed by the absolute outcome, by the result of the process of consciousness, upon the forms of pure sensible intuition, the forms of space and time. The necessity of this gift, this process, this releasement, remains to be analysed. Here it is only to be noted that the first chapter of the *Phenomenology* must be read from the perspective of the last, and the whole book from behind as it were. Sense-certainty, simple being and its spatio-temporal determinants are the gifts of absolute self-presencing, and give themselves back again in the progress through the shapes of spirit. The temporal economy of absolute knowing is a circular one. Eternity repeats itself in its own gift of time and recuperates itself once more.

The dialectic of the sensuous This and the immediate self which corresponds to it repeats the dialectic of pure being expounded in the *Logic* and the historico-religious dialectic of the Host and the empty grave. In demonstrating the dialectic of the phenomenological 'This' Hegel appeals to an argument which, on account both of its prominent place – at the commencement of the absolute's return to itself – and its implications for the history of philosophy, is by no means irrelevant to the systematic structure of the dialectic in general. From the standpoint of immediate certainty the question concerning the 'This' in the 'double shape of its being, as the *Now* and the *Here*' can be answered only if a determinate being and a determinate time are indicated and enunciated: '*The Now is night*' or 'The *Here* is for example the *tree*' (3: TWA, *Phen.*, 84 ff.).

> '*In order to test the truth of this sensuous certainty a simple experiment is all that is required. We write this truth down; a truth cannot be lost by writing it down; anymore than it can be lost by our preserving it. When we look again* now, today, *at the written truth, we shall have to say that it has become stale.*' (3: TWA, Phen., 84)

Writing is thus supposed to preserve the truth of the sense-certainty of the Now and demonstrate its purported being as something permanent, persistent and substantial. But in fact writing separates the permanence of the Now from its immediacy, the essence from its mediation. By holding fast to the determinate Now and believing thereby securely to identify its being as such, writing only conducts it into its past, into its untruth, and signifies the non-being of what was originally intended. Inasmuch as writing preserves the determinate Here and thereby attempts to indicate the truth of the latter, it deprives itself of precisely this and permits another, arbitrarily determined, Here to take its place. Inasmuch as *Now, this Now* is written down, then this Now is no longer this one, but another, no longer something which is, but something which is not. Inasmuch as writing preserves the truth of the Now, it loses that truth.

'. . . *a truth cannot be lost by being written down.*'

Hegel's proposition concerning the preservation of truth is, once written down, ambiguous. The truth of the determinate Now and of every possible further modification of the Now is eliminated by its very inscription; but it is eliminated only insofar as the written fixation of the Now can be related to every other possible now, only insofar therefore as the now endures as the universal in that fixation.

This intrication of loss and preservation makes writing, the first argument of the *Phenomenology of Spirit*, into the privileged formula for the dialectical procedure in general: it is in this 'writing down' that Hegel finds inscribed the character of that 'sublation' he mentions a few pages further on:

> '*Sublation here presents its true double meaning* . . . *it is at once a* negating *and a* preserving; *the nothing, as* the nothing of the This, *preserves the immediacy, and is itself sensuous, but it is a universal immediacy.*' (3: TWA, Phen., *94*)

Writing therefore sublates. It sublates the instant, the now-point of time, relinquishes it to its past and bestows it upon its future. Inasmuch as writing reveals the empty determinacy of the instant, it turns its empty, that is, purely negative, abstraction into the universal, 'something permanent and self-sustaining' (3: TWA, *Phen.*, 85). The Now as the universal is the permanently substantial. The universalization of the Now into the Now of time in general, into the 'negative unity of self-external being' as defined by the *Encyclopaedia* (9: TWA, Enc., II, §258), is possible, however, only because writing gives itself over to be read (whether indeed sense-certainty or even perception is

capable of reading remains questionable, for their reading would necessarily limit itself to the proposition '*here* or *now is writing*' and would
have read nothing of what writing was to have held fast) – because the
reading of writing allows comparison with a hypothetical second piece
of writing, in which another Now than the first is held fast. Strictly
speaking, therefore, sublation takes place only through the comparison
between two inscriptions. It is only by virtue of comparison – which
Hegel himself thematizes, though fleetingly, in his analysis (3: TWA,
Phen., 87) – that we can distinguish what is not the same and thus
inconstant in the determinations of the Now from what is the same in
these determinations, that we can distinguish what is sublated from
what is preserved. But it is a condition of the comparison that two
now-points coexist with one another: exist simultaneously. It is the
reading which, even if there is no obvious second inscription at hand,
binds the one inscribed Now with a second one, which grasps both of
them as insubstantial and untrue, which grasps only the universal form
of the Now persisting as the perennial moment.

The contraction of inscripted Nows into a simultaneity, achievable
only by the reading after the event, is the precondition for the sublation of the individual now-points into the universal Now of time in
general. This simultaneity, though constructed after the event, must
therefore precede time in general if the non-simultaneity of its
moments and the persistence of its form is to be intelligible, if a concept of time is to be possible at all. The simultaneity of various now-
points in the reading of writing would therefore allow us first to grasp
the structure of the Now as the (simultaneously) universal continuum
of becoming and as the immediately disappearing now-point, and thus
to initiate the process of sublation, of dialectic and the 'simple history'
of the experience of sense-certainty, and so the experience of consciousness as such (3: TWA, *Phen.*, 90).

The contraction of the various inscripted Nows into a simultaneity is
the condition of the possibility for the experience of time, and thus for
the experience of self-consciousness and the consciousness of objects.
Yet this simultaneity, in order to permit comparison with the non-
simultaneous, must contain not merely the Now as the universal, but
also the Now which has immediately disappeared in this simultaneity,

the Now which is therefore non-simultaneous not merely with any succeeding Now, but with itself. The Now does not remain (itself), yet in
order to be written and preserved, to become universal, as Now; in
order to be able to disappear as the determinate Now of sense-certainty,
this Now must remain (itself), must be simultaneous with itself and
the other Now which follows. In order to be able to sublate itself and
become the Now of time as such, whose succession excludes all simultaneity, the Now must remain, and in simultaneity with itself. Prior to
the time which excludes the simultaneity of the now-points, every Now
must be simultaneous with itself and first demonstrate its non-simultaneity through this impossible simultaneity. The impossibility of
remaining (the same), explicitly formulated in the formal-dialectical
determination of the Now in Hegel's Jena Philosophy of Nature ('The
System of the Sun'): 'the Now is immediately the opposite of itself, the
negating of itself' (22: *Hegels Jenenser Logik, Metaphysik und
Naturphilosophie*, ed. G. Lasson [Leipzig: Meiner Verlag, 1923], 203) –
this impossibility of positive self-equality can itself be identified only
from the standpoint of the possibility of such equality and simultaneity; the temporal process itself can be identified only by virtue of the
spatial simultanization of various now-points in writing, of the literally
duplicitous writing and the reading to which it is subjected. The ever
unsimultaneous now-points and the Now of time in general – namely
the abstract form of subjectivity, of the I=I which reveals itself as the
truth of time – are therefore grounded in the reading of the spatially
simultaneous inscriptions of the now-points themselves. The possibility of time, consciousness and self-consciousness are grounded in the
simultaneity of the now-points in the spatial domain of writing and the
complementary temporalization of spatial inscription produced in the
simultaneity of reading.

But if the determination of the Now as an immediate self-negating,
an intrinsic disappearing, which excludes any possible co-presence with
itself, is to preserve its validity, then it must literally extend itself into
the spatialization of now-points in writing. The abstract externality of
time in space, the only site for any potential fixation of simultaneity,
does indeed impose the primacy of its universality upon the now-
points sublated within it, but as particular Nows, whose negation is

first produced by this universality, they still cannot be simultaneous therein. Like the immediate co-presence of the Now with itself, their spatial co-presence, the condition of possibility for their abstraction, would only paralyse time and emasculate any process of consciousness even before it began. Even the process of the absolute, which releases itself into time and is supposed to return to itself in this movement, would be petrified. The same holds for space of the consciousness which reads. If the reading is successfully to accomplish its comparative operation, the inscription of the past Now must be simultaneous with the inscription of another, equally past, Now, which means that various contents of consciousness must coexist in consciousness. But since pure co-presence is not a possibility for consciousness either, such simultaneous equalization would be conceivable only by virtue of a retention which, as delay, no longer corresponds to the concept of the pure self-withdrawal of each and every Now.

It is always the presupposition of a possible spatial simultaneity which decides over the impossibility of simultaneity, the impossibility of the selfsameness, of the self, of the Now, over the necessity of immediate self-negation; always a temporal simultaneity, that must remain impossible, which decides over the possibility of a spatial simultaneity. It is upon this reciprocal presupposition of the possibility and impossibility of persisting permanence that the concepts of space and time in general are grounded, and with them the concept of the I which is supposed to be able to relate simultaneously to itself in its experience as a self. The simultaneity is possible insofar as it is impossible, impossible insofar as it is possible. The site of this impossible possibility of simultaneity is the writing which delays the disappearance of now-points, and the reading which accomplishes the simultaneous equalisation of spatially differentiated now-points through a complementary delay. Thus writing and reading alike constitute the privileged instruments for the sublation and self-relation of the concept only insofar as both evade the order of the concept of time.

The dialectic of sense-certainty – which passes into the self-certainty of the self which experiences itself as universal, into the self-consciousness which grasps itself as such, and into the absolute – cannot survive without this impossible possibility of reading and writing. The dialectic must itself pass over this *a priori* aporetic possibility of the impossible, since it cannot think that impossibility which (simultaneously) withdraws the foundations for the entire conceptual and categorial system, for the entire path of spirit towards itself. The path of the absolute dialectic is only possible insofar as each step, and even the last, passes over the structure of the path itself.

> *The always already inscripted and delaying character of simultaneity falls subject to repression, in accordance with the tradition of semiotic theory since antiquity, namely that of Aristotle. In a short piece –* 'Ousia *and* Gammē. Note on a Note from 'Being and Time' *in* Margins of Philosophy *(33: tr. Alan Bass [Brighton: Harvester, 1982]) – Jacques Derrida has analysed the fundamental features of this tradition, which still remain operative even in Heidegger's critique of 'vulgar temporality', and has exposed the aporias of the metaphysical concept of time defined by the exclusion of simultaneity, of the* ama *in the Aristotelian definition of the* nun. *The* ama *is precisely what the now-points – and that already means the graphic inscriptions of the* Now, *as well as the continuous line under whose image the process of time is traditionally figured and which necessarily implies the graphic fixation of this process – what the now-points are incapable of becoming if they are not to freeze into the immobility of the* nunc stans *and thereby arrest time itself (28: Aristotle's* Physics, *tr. W. Charlton [Oxford: Clarendon, 1970], 218a). But the* ama *is also the very simultaneity which decides the impossibility of temporal stasis insofar as it is posited as possible in* spatial *simultaneity. The simultaneity (*hama*) is the intrication (*hamma*) of possibility and impossibility which the metaphysics of time cannot dissolve and cannot grasp, because this metaphysics itself is caught up in the coils of this knot.*

The paradigm of writing and reading is not the only one which Hegel employs for the demonstration of the immediate 'self'-negation of the sensuous this but it does contain the programmatic model for all the others. Thus the gesture of pointing, and its underlying semiotic concept which relates both to the Now and to the Here, possesses the structure of writing, and the understanding of the same that of reading. Insofar as the indicated and the designated presents itself through the semiotic gesture as a complex of various Heres and various Nows, which permit the particular Heres and Nows to appear as their result and thus as immediately universal, then the universal remains dependent upon the retention of the always already eliminated particular, the possibility of truth and semantic sense remains tied to the enduring persistence of the untrue, heterogeneous, sensuous moment, the continuum and unity of space and time remain bound to the stasis of particular places and various times. 'The *pointing out* is itself the movement which expresses what the Now is in truth; namely a result, or plurality of Nows grasped together; and the pointing out is the experience that Now is the *universal*' (3: TWA, *Phen.*, 89). But the Nows can be synthetically grasped as the one and universal Now only if the conceptual grip which grasps them also grasps their occasional particularity in each case and thus grasps what the universal *not yet* is, and what the immediate particular already *no longer* is. The sign grasps a spatial or temporal point only when determined by difference with regard to all other possible points and by the impossible retention of every particular This. The unity and universality of the This, the meaning of time – and of being – in general can be affirmed only at the cost of an almost total restriction of difference which determines the designated object, the sign and its truth; can be affirmed only through the elimination of the particular which first facilitated the emergence of the complex from which the universal is derived. The universal truth of the sign is produced through the recession of fleeting particularities, whose truth it was supposed to be, and which themselves escape all truth.

> *The determination of spatial and temporal points as results already anticipates, in the phenomenological domain, the transition to the concretum which presents*

itself in the philosophy of nature as the mediated unity of space and time: as place and motion. The mutual implication of spatial and temporal determinants, which first facilitates their definition in terms of specific quantities, is here defined by Hegel as a temporal circulation in the medium of space. For if the three-dimensional character of time refuses the existence of one dimension without the others and produces each dimension out of the other two, then each one must be capable of returning to itself from out of the others. The circle delineates the form of temporal process: 'This return of the line is the circular one; it is the now, before, and after, closing and connecting up with itself; it is the indifference of these dimensions, in which the before *is just as much an* after *as the* after *is a* before. *This is the first necessary paralysis of these dimensions posited in space. Circular motion is the spatial or subsistent unity of the dimensions of time.' (9: TWA, Enc., II, §261, Addition)*

Writing, a Gorgon, paralyses time into the shape of space.

If time can only be thought under the form of its spatial paralysis, if every now, thought and paralysed as now, is always already its future, and its future always already its past, then it is not merely the identity of the respective now-points which is dissolved – for the fourth dimension of space has always already been introduced into the three-dimensionality of time, a paralysis prior to any possible time, and – since this pará, this externality of space, also presupposes the paralytic contraction to the temporal point – a paralysis prior to any possible space-time, an original retention as the condition of space, time, continuum of motion, or determinacy of place. This 'original retention' is not the retention of an origin already conceived in terms of self-presence, which draws everything deriving from it into its power and thus contains it, but signifies rather the retention of a difference which first constitutes the origin and its functioning, a difference which every system of

> *arche and telos, every system of presence and circular self-*
> *return, must eliminate as an impossibility.*
>
> *The paralysed space-time is only the concretum of dura-*
> *tion, the* matter *(cf. 9: TWA, Enc., II, §261) which is*
> *destined to pass over into spirit.*

The This in the 'double shape of its being, as *Now* and as *Here*' (3: TWA, *Phen.*, 84) is therefore always already determined by the sign of writing and the reading of the same. Space and time are designated elements (These) which do not reveal themselves independently of their being pointed out, independently of the sign. The designatum of the process of writing is first constituted by this process and its repetition. Time and space are constructions of writing, of a language grasped in terms of writing. But they draw their universality from the iterability of the linguistic sign through which every possible This always already co-designates another one, from the otherness of the sign's identical demonstration, itself sprung from retention. Thus the unique singularity of the linguistic operation which designates the This is separated from itself through the reproducibility which permits it to endure and relate to another This, and reveals itself as universal. In this demonstrative iteration and alteration permeate one another in such a way that the particular This becomes a word for the most universal, for the concept of universality itself. This This is This in general; this Now is all Nows; this Here all Heres, this I is all possible I's, the truth and the concept of the I.

> '. . . *we do not say what we mean in this sense-certainty.*
> *As we see, it is language which is the more truthful here;*
> *therein we ourselves immediately refute our own meaning,*
> *and since the universal is the truth of sense-certainty and*
> *language merely expresses this truth, it is utterly impossible*
> *for us to say the sensuous being which we mean*' (3: TWA,
> *Phen., 85). And further: 'Language possesses the divine*
> *nature . . . of inverting our intended meaning immedi-*
> *ately, of transforming it into something else, and thus pre-*
> *venting it from* coming to utterance *at all.' (ibid., 92)*

Insofar as the linguistic sign, the *monstrativum*, signifies what it signifies, then it also already signifies something else, something other in which it first concludes and closes with itself. *This*, as identical, extinguishes its own identity and only re-acquires it in the circular movement through the paralysed selfsameness of *this* other as the universal. The process of writing, in which the particular Now has always already passed away and has thereby lost its truth, nevertheless re-acquires this truth precisely by virtue of this passing away, in which what was meant now signifies something different. The concept of time is bound to a difference which reveals itself in the process of designation, to the negation of its particular signification through its universal one. If it is this difference which decides upon the untruth of every sensuous This, then it is also through this difference that the thought of the truth of the *This in general* can be produced at all. The differential sign places itself in difference; its very sign-character, in which its sensuous determinateness remains virulent, must be eliminated; and the only thing which remains over from that character as pure persistence is the certainty of the power of the universal over the particular.

The self-relation of time and the sign can be realized only through this withdrawal of its own process, through the elimination of its own trace. This elimination, whose agent is reading, must be so complete that it destroys every relation to an empirical factum, every certainty of sensuous being and its truth. So radical that even the written articulation of *this* thought must also have fallen victim to elimination through reading, if it is to be grasped in its truth:

> 'They mean this *bit of paper on which I am writing* – or rather have written – this; but what they mean is not what they say. . . . In the actual attempt to say it, it would therefore crumble away; those who started to describe it would not be able to complete the description, but would be compelled to leave it to others, who would themselves finally have to admit to speaking about something which is not. . . . Consequently, what is called the unutterable is nothing else than the untrue, the irrational, what is merely meant.' (3: TWA, Phen., 92)

This, which Hegel himself has written, would therefore be the unutterable, the untrue and the irrational itself. And the untrue would even be this system of absolute truth in its totality, insofar as it expounds itself as a This. The system can be grasped as true only by a reading whose operations allow the external determinateness of the system and its claims, allow everything to which we could relate as to a This – to crumble away. And it is only inasmuch as *this* 'Phenomenology of Spirit', only inasmuch as *this* system crumbles away, that the Phenomenology, the System, can arise, as read. But the system still remains a This, albeit an ideal one, from which the possibility of its alteration into another This can never be removed.

In the act of writing down, the inscription of now-points, the inscription which expresses the untruth of these now-points and the inscription of the system, there also always emerges the Untrue – 'The Now is night' – and also the Untruth of Truth – This is the truth of the This, namely that it crumbles away – and is preserved. Inasmuch as sense-certainty reads the inscription of the this, it reads something already intrinsically crumbled away, something stale, something which is not, and therefore fails to read what was meant. Every written inscription is, in this strict sense, unreadable. But insofar as reading reads the nothing of inscription, fails to read the This, it reads the truth of the This. The unreadable in writing is read, and this reading even constitutes the condition of the possibility of every reading which reproduces the signification of the inscripted sign. But along with the unreadable in writing, what is still or already readable in it must also be read: that Now, Here and This which proves persistently enduring in comparison with every other This, which – inasmuch as it disappears, unreadably, as *this* This – persists, readably, as a This in general. It is because the remains of what crumbled away remain that the unreadable is already and still readable, that writing is the transition from the immediate non-being of the sensuous to the being of consciousness.

At once readable and unreadable, writing is the form into which absolute knowing releases itself, the form of spirit's absolute self-expenditure, and at once the form through which spirit returns to itself. Insofar as the system as book – as *Phenomenology*, *Logic*, *Encyclopaedia*, etc. – abandons itself to decay in the shape of the sensuous This and all its restrictions and becomes unreadable in its inscription, it has also procured for itself – readable, though scarcely so, as remains – the surest affirmation of its permanent existence. The self-expenditure of spirit in writing, mediated by the 'scarcely' of such readability, passes over into the circle of its universal reappropriation. Absolute knowing allows its own inscription to fall away and sublates what was universal in it, the negativity of its self-relation. The fall of sublation into time and writing is, scarcely read, the sublation of the fall into infinite knowing.

As always with Hegel when there is talk of reading, eating too – once again – is never far away. Heavily freighted with allusions to the Christian sacrificial feast, and to philosophy's sacrificial feast at the particular shapes of consciousness, there is a reference in the series of arguments against sense-certainty to 'the mystery of the eating of bread and the drinking of wine' and to animal consumption as ways of sublating of sensuous being.

> *'In this respect we can tell those who assert the truth and certainty of the reality of sensuous objects that they should return to the most elementary school of wisdom, namely the ancient Eleusinian Mysteries of Ceres and Bacchus, and that they have still to learn the secret meaning of the eating of bread and the drinking of wine. For he who is initiated into these mysteries not only comes to doubt the being of sensuous things, but to despair of it; in part he brings about the nothingness of such things himself in his dealings with them, and in part he sees them reduce themselves to nothingness. Even the animals are not shut out from this wisdom but, on the contrary, show themselves to be most profoundly initiated into it; for they do not just stand idly before sensuous things as if these possessed intrinsic being, but, despairing of their reality, and completely assured of their nothingness, they fall to without ceremony and eat them up. And all Nature, like the animals, celebrates these open mysteries which teach the truth about sensuous things.' (3: TWA, Phen., 91)*

This meal, celebrated by nature and cult alike, presents, like writing, like reading, the dialectical process of being and the time of being.

Consumption, like inscription, is sublation. And indeed not merely
sublation in the sense that the being of sensuous things would be
utterly destroyed, but also in the complementary sense that what resists
destruction, as something already itself caught up in the movement of
negativity, is also preserved in higher form in the process of animal life.
This celebration of consumption also draws the other, already mentioned forms of dialectical process into the same framework: writing
and reading are both operations which immediately destroy given
being and preserve the universal they thereby produce from that
destruction. Reading and writing are, like nature and cult, ontopha-
geous and chronophageous. The Here and Now of sensuous being are
transformed through eating into essential being, transformed through
the biting grasp of the concept into time in general. As bread and wine
or as the inscription of now-points, being presents itself as retentional
trace, one which is not merely cancelled and written off, but obliterated and written out by a reading which always also functions as consumption. The This crumbles away, decays, ferments, in the process of
digestive assimilation. The Now becomes duration.

> *But duration is the universal of the now-points, although*
> *it is not already their sublation into eternity. Duration is*
> *not time as it exists eternally as itself in its very concept.*
> *Consequently, duration is only something relative, some-*
> *thing which remains inevitably bound to the natural tem-*
> *poral process as long as it is not yet reflected into itself to*
> *become its own eternal concept. Thus the duration of what*
> *is natural and without process stands between the natural*
> *process of time and the pure procession of the concept of*
> *time, which, unlike duration, 'is not itself in time'. But*
> *duration draws both these its extremities – the time of*
> *nature and the concept of time – into its own pernicious*
> *middle. The relative universalization of the now-points is*
> *already a result of the process of sensuous perception; and*
> *in the Addition to §258 of the* Encyclopaedia *(9: TWA,*
> *Enc., II) Hegel observes that the 'law of time' does indeed,*
> *'on the side of phenomenal appearance', enter into time,*
> *where it does not 'lose' itself, however, but rather finds*

itself 'returned' to a processless quiescence which itself is not 'a part of the process, and is not in process'. Nevertheless, this conclusion remains problematic to the extent that the whole cannot cease to appear entirely within its phenomenally appearing part, and the part can be returned to the whole only insofar as the former already intrinsically allows the processlessness of the whole – even relatively, and consequently only as retention and duration – to actualize itself within it. Thus the transition from the time of nature to the concept of time would be tied to an irreflexive duration and the aporias of a pre-reflexive simultaneity. Eternity would find itself 'affected' by the false and delusive appearance of temporal duration. This conclusion confers a certain weight upon the resigned tone at the end of Hegel's exposition of duration in the Encyclopaedia, *a weight that also even bears strongly down upon the 'eternal concept' of time itself: 'It is mediocrity which endures and finally governs the world. Thought also displays this mediocrity, with which it afflicts the world around it, eliminates spiritual vitality and transforms it into mere habit, and thus it goes on. It endures precisely because it rests upon untruth, never acquires its proper right, fails to honour the concept, fails to present the truth as its immanent process.' (9: TWA, Enc., II, §258, Addition; 51)*

Just as the operations of writing, reading and eating present themselves in context, in a temporal text – and the question concerning the time of reading could find a provisional response in the expression 'reading is temporalization' – so on the other hand time presents itself only as the most universal form of this reading and eating which leads objective things over into their truth. 'Time is nothing but the abstraction of consuming', according to the definition in the Addition to §258 of the *Encyclopaedia* (9: TWA, Enc., II); and in the main text of the same section Hegel reclaims the ancient myth of Chronos devouring his children as the immemorial expression of the dialectic of time:

> *'But it is not in time that everything arises and passes*
> *away, but rather time itself is this* becoming, *this arising*
> *and passing away, the* existing process of abstraction, *the*
> Chronos *who gives birth to everything and destroys his*
> *own offspring.'*

Hegel's formal-dialectical interpretation of Chronos here is not concerned with providing a historical interpretation of the relevant myth
or with distinguishing it from other – and historical – structures of
temporality, – unlike the expositions in the *Aesthetics* and the
Philosophy of Religion, where Chronos (he too a Negro) is placed as 'the
unhistorical might of time' at the threshold of the history of spiritual
subjectivity and of the law of ethical life. Hegel is concerned rather
with a critique of Kant's interpretation of time as the pure form of sensible intuition. Against this position Hegel insists upon the objective
character of time as the form of negativity which is itself at work
within all the shapes of finitude. Chronos is the 'existing process of
abstraction', the permanent withdrawal which consumes as food precisely what he himself – now a maternal figure – bestows and 'gives
birth to'. Chronos only ever bestows and ravens down himself in the
shape of his children (until, through feminine cunning, he swallows a
stone instead of his son): a gargantuan process of destruction and self-
generation which is driven on by the power of the concept.

Time – Meal-time, TempOrality

In his analysis of the Kantian conception of time, against which the
myth of Chronos is evoked as dialectical counter-image, Hegel
maliciously emphasizes these oral aspects. In his *Lectures on the History
of Philosophy* this is what Hegel says concerning the pure forms of sensible intuition, concerning space and time:

> *'The matter is pictured in the following way: first of all,*
> *there are things in themselves outside of us, but still with-*
> *out space and time; now consciousness comes along, which*
> *already possesses space and time within itself as the possi-*
> *bility of experience, just as it also possesses mouth and teeth*
> *for eating with as the conditions of eating anything. The*
> *things which are eaten possess neither mouth nor teeth,*
> *and consciousness subjects space and time upon them, just*

> *as it subjects things to eating; just as consciousness places*
> *things between the mouth and its teeth, so it places them*
> *in space and time.' (20: TWA,* Hist. Philosophy, *III,*
> *341)*

For Kant space and time are not themselves empirical data at all, but rather the condition of all empirical experience, of that *a-priori* enframing which takes shape as the original-synthetic unity of apperception. This spatio-temporal framework of pure self-intuition structures the world of sensibility as a unity which permits that world to be incorporated into the system of experience as such. The framing structure of space and time – the oral body-image which pre-forms all knowledge – is the *a-priori* form of identity; more precisely, of i-Dentity. As such, it is the object of a 'transcendental aesthetic'. Insofar as Hegel, who cites this term in his structural analysis of the Kantian concept of space and time, reads this aesthetic, *à la lettre,* as a transcenDental one, he inevitably arrives at his own characterization of the pure forms of sensible intuition: they are not in fact structured, as their name suggests, according to the model of diffuse somatic sensation, but rather after the analogy of oral incorporation. It is the mouth of space and the teeth of time which prepare the world of appearance to be grasped in the identity of knowledge.

The structure which Hegel exposes with such a denunciatory gesture in Kant's concept of space and time is very much the same as that which underlies his own concept of time. Hegel's chronology distinguishes itself from Kant's insofar as the former does not regard time as the formal condition of experience which violently subjects its objects to the biting grip of temporal apperception by contraction of the transcendental frame. For Hegel time is the process in which the objects consume themselves as natural objects, even before all culture and all sublimation into knowledge, and through consuming themselves in this way sublate their natural form into the form of spiritual subjectivity. Temporality is not a transcendental presupposition, produced by the cognitive apparatus of the subject, but an organism in which the Idea translates itself into finitude, in which the finite becomes objective to itself, in which this its finitude is transcended and returns itself in the process of its negativity, its own dis-identification, back into the

Idea. Temporality is the disi-dentification of the infinite into the finite, of the finite into the infinite.

Thus time not only swallows up its children, and thereby derivative forms of itself, but must – following the cyclical economy of the concept, presenting itself as the gift bestowed by the same – also consume itself and re-imburse the concept. By seizing itself as time, seizing itself as the self of time, time grasps itself as the concept. The absolutization of time frees it from its derivative forms, from itself as a form of finite spirit, as well as from its external existence in the forms of historical time, and turns it into the absolute, related to itself in the thinking of time. The chapter on 'Absolute Knowing' in the *Phenomenology of Spirit* argues that: '*Time* is the *concept* itself that *is there* and which presents itself to consciousness as empty intuition; for this reason, spirit necessarily appears in time and it appears in time just so long as it has not *seized* its pure concept, i.e. has not annulled time. It is the *external*, intuited pure self which is not *seized* by the self, the merely intuited concept; when this latter grasps itself, it cancels its time-form, comprehends this intuiting, and is a comprehended and comprehending intuiting. Time, therefore, appears as the fate and necessity of spirit that is not yet complete within itself' (3: TWA, *Phen.*, 584 ff.). What is always already at work in time, its conceptual grasp, its grip, its bite, seizes itself in the thinking of time and thereby cancels itself. The 'unity of thought and time', in which thought and time experience their pure self-presence, experience their eternity as the absolute present, is produced according to the same oral schema through which time consumes its own derivative forms. Self-consciousness still remains subjected to the 'fate' of time until in the course of its history

> '*self-consciousness has thereby wrested from consciousness the whole substance, and has sucked into itself the whole structure of the essentialities of substance.*' (3: TWA, Phen., 584)

Thus time as concept sucks itself in as the external substance of mere consciousness, becomes the whole filled and fulfilled with itself, becomes the subject which as self-knowing self-consciousness is at one with itself as its own substance, becomes absolute. The drawing pull of time draws itself in, giving suck to itself, draws its circle together in the universal point of the self-conscious present, and, a biting which bites itself, a sucking which suckles itself, becomes absolute knowing as the pure self-relation of its relata: the search for absolute knowing, presenting itself as the course and path of history, has found itself – and comes to a close.

But the search not merely closes, it also presents its own closing. However strictly the presentation of absolute knowing in the completed 'System of Science' is distinguished from the mere representation of the same in the domain of religion – for Science is the truth of religion, presentation the truth of representation – the concept nonetheless necessarily retains in this presentation its connection with a derivative form of temporality. It is true that spirit remains 'in time' only 'for as long as it has not *seized* its pure concept', but even once seized, the concept, as time relating purely to itself, must nevertheless still appear in time. What is already eternity is still time. Or what is still eternity is once again the time which is not yet eternity itself. The temporal conjunctions and temporal adverbs, through which Science as the self of time determines itself, reveal as much: 'Only when the objective presentation is complete is it at the same time the reflection of substance or the process in which substance becomes self. Consequently, until spirit has completed itself *in itself*, until it has completed itself as world-spirit, it cannot attain its consummation as *self-conscious* spirit. Therefore, the content of religion proclaims earlier in time than does Science, what *spirit is*, but only Science is its true knowledge of itself' (3: TWA, *Phen.*, 585–586). Thus the very self of time must, in its own presentation, situate itself in a time which has not yet attained its self, must still remain in the time which it annuls, must in this annulled time still and once again preserve the trace of that unannulled time, as remnant.

For what can it mean to speak of time itself, the concept of time, the drawing pull of time, the suck of time? Nothing but the drawing pull which withdraws itself, the sucking which sucks in itself. Yet if it withdraws itself, then the concept of self-consciousness, which knows itself, no longer exists for self-consciousness, remains a mere in-itself and thus is not yet itself. If it is pure self-withdrawal, then it cannot be fully presented and therefore fails to exist as such. In its presentation it finds itself paralysed, in its inscription arrested. Ex-posed in presentation, in the stasis of its own movement, the draw and pull of time withdraws itself. But it does so in such a way that, even there where this presentation assumes the form of a circle which contracts into the universal point of the present, it nevertheless remains, as a process of withdrawal, nevertheless still permits the possibility of grasping this withdrawal, the possibility of a further drawing, a further sucking, the possibility of providing a reading of its graphic trace. The withdrawal of time must generate its presentation as a free gift in order, though withdrawn, to remain itself. The cyclical economy of time's self can only reappropriate its gift, the time of nature and of history, at the cost of this free gift which is not exhausted in that economy. The dialectic of giving away and taking back, of infinitude and finitude, the circuit of which prescribes the form of the entire process, depends therefore upon a form inadequate to it, upon the graphically fixed circle which contracts the self of time and time itself, the concept and the self of the concept, and in this contraction sustains both of them, at once derivative with respect to both and yet the retention of both. Thus the self-withdrawal of time, as presented and paralysed in the dynamic process of writing, is the condition of possibility and the condition of impossibility for the dialectical economy of the self. That is why the presentation can possess the form of systematic Science which as logic exhibits the 'pure spirits' of appearing or phenomenal knowledge; but that is also the reason why the presentation of Science, explicitly described by Hegel as an 'objective presentation' (3: TWA, *Phen.*, 585), must still retain the 'not yet' of natural or historical time even in the presence of the self of time, must still in this way connect the latter to the difference from the self-conscious self, to withdrawal and to subsequentiality.

The fact that the process tarries alongside by itself in its ex-position and presentation, is drawn into itself as a still unfulfilled self, leads Science as the logic of appearing spirit into a repetition of that aporia in which the now-point, co-present to itself as its own other, inevitably found itself entangled at the beginning of the history of consciousness. Absolute knowing is the site of the impossible possibility, once again, of a pure self-relation, of a self-withdrawal, of time with respect to an absolute present. Since this present must be held back and presented, in order to become present, those remains of the process which offer themselves up to a different form of suction other than that of the self remain suspended – a state of backwardness by virtue of which the absolute must give itself the form of writing and, having returned to its beginning, must abandon itself to the reading of sense-certainty, to a biting and a sucking other than its own. The remains of time, which presentation must keep open for its self-relation, mark a heterogeneous moment in the absolutized movement of spirit's self-appropriation, mark the externality in the absolute interiorization of re-collection [*Er-innerung*], and thus the necessity of securing – once again – this heterogeneity for itself, of repeating spirit's passage towards itself. The concept accommodates itself to this necessity in 'releasing itself from the form of its own self' (3: TWA, *Phen.*, 590). The gift of time is but the gift of that remaining trace of time which could not, for the sake of its self-presentation in its concept, be consumed, and is given as gift only with the thought of being taken back again. But just as absolute knowing in its 'immediate equality with itself' (ibid.) is not entirely complete, neither can it give itself over entirely to nature nor can it return entirely from the latter back to itself. There always remains a remainder – though sublated – which continues to sustain difference within its totality. The passage of spirit only ever exists as the repetition of its own distance from itself.

What cannot be recuperated once again in the internalizing recollection of the concept must be repeated. What remains unrepeatable is repeated. It is by virtue of this impossibility harboured by the absolute itself that the latter, in liberating itself from the fate of time, falls under the fate of having to abandon itself to time once again and ever again, of having to turn back as absolute knowing to sense-certainty and the unconscious process of nature. The fullness of time goes empty away, the uttermost extremity is broken off, the contraction expands; the concept of the concept, the concept of time, the absolute grapheme – since it writes itself, cancels itself and preserves its cancelled self in writing – sublates itself. Sublates and abandons itself to a writing which decays, whose truth as immediately determinate has always already turned stale; to a reading which is not its own, which grasps not its eternity but merely its duration; to a suction which is no longer entirely the return of time into its self and not yet entirely the repetition of its self. The reading of the concept finds itself transposed into the space of this difference, this rupture in the circle of absolute knowing's self-repetition – transposed between the fullness of time, which only allows us to speak of the present, of the sense and being of time, and its own pure disappearance, between this fullness and itself, between the fulfilled sense and the sense-certainty which sees itself immediately confronted with its emptiness and untruth. Reading is that operation which regulates the dialectical transition of the 'no longer' into the 'not yet' of the immediate self-relation of spirit, into its re-petition; reading is the simultanizing process which transpires between the suction of abstract disappearance and the immediate self-relation of time in the form of delay, a form inadequate to both.

> *Without delay there is no time, and not the reverse. The circle of time, through which past and future come together and every now is its own past and as such its own future, can only be closed by virtue of a restriction upon its immediate self-negation, upon that which was to define it as time – by virtue of the arresting of transience, of the advancing process of what is yet to come, of the tarrying with the present.* Mora *makes time. Ex-pectation constitutes the present (cf. 3: TWA, Phen., 434). What determines the structure of the present, though it does not in this way precede it as its condition, should have disappeared in that time which is characterized by its fleetingness, by its fluidity. In fact this condition, as the irrecuperably prior character of retention, inscribes itself, along with the historical world characterized by duration, into the pure process of time as a hindrance, thereby rendering it inert. 'Inert' because the shapes of spirit, which are also shapes of a time which is not yet entirely at home with itself, have still to be digested in the passage of history, and because they prove extremely hard to digest (ibid., 446). They impede the running flow of immediate disappearance, turn it turgid and meandering, make its moving*

currents sluggish. Through such retardation the various tempi of historical duration are inscribed into the single time of circular withdrawal. The time which consumes itself and its shapes finds it hard to digest itself, in part even in the absolute, finds itself in part quite indigestible. As historical time it is characterized by the same delay which constitutes its structural presupposition.

If now this absolute reading possesses the function of properly maintaining the circulation between the self of time and its natural form, between time as the presentation of the absolute and time as the form of its representation, the function of organizing and articulating this circulation and thus securing the absolute for the first time, of being the absolute itself – then it can accomplish this only by repeating in itself those characteristic features with which Hegel defines the absolute. Accordingly, the process of reading cannot be regarded, as it traditionally is, as an uninhibited and unimpeded progress under the guiding thread of the writing which is read, as a process of linear succession, or indeed hardly as a process at all. For the latter excludes, ex definitione, *the possibility of its coming to a halt, a standstill, and recognizes a tarrying only in the form of the process itself, as the eternity of its dialectical continuum. By contrast that inertial reading which advances towards and thereby postpones – and infinitely – the absolute would appear a lamed and crippled one, delaying every present manifestation of sense, even of its own, restraining every metaphorical transition, reserving judgement upon every conclusion, a reading which can, at times, move so slowly that it reads backwards, reads against the grain. A reading which lies in wait. And if it springs, fleetingly or in direct assault, it does so only to tarry and to digest its quarry all the more peaceably. It is decayed, and furthers decay. A ferment. But since it is always supposed to be its own concept which it consumes, it also, like time, eludes itself: for the eternity of time reading*

> *always comes too late because it is – in advance of itself –*
> *always already there. It is something more than mere*
> *'reading', an animal for example, a hare, a hedgehog, or*
> *Zeno's tortoise, and though it were Achilles, it still cannot*
> *catch up with itself.*

Reading is the articulated structure [*Fuge*] which alone could close
and conclude the circle of self-appropriating knowledge, yet, wavering
as it does between the lack which first produces its suctorial movement
and a plenitude of sense, between an externality over against knowledge and the interiorization of that externality, between its impossibility and its actuality, this reading opens up itself and its circle,
interminably and without conclusion. Absolute knowing finds itself
inserted within the interstices of this structure.

But what does it signify to say that the sucking motion of reading is
a mode of the self-relation of the absolute? Why does the cyclical figure
of time and spirit repeatedly and preferably present itself, besides the
form of inscription, with the metaphorics of orality: of consuming,
devouring, suckling and digesting? Why, in addition, the form of the
circle in which the passage of spirit itself forms an *os*? That the passage
of spirit must present itself as such requires no further commentary,
but why must it do so in metaphorical form, and why in the form of
this particular metaphorics? And why is it that the more obviously
scoptic operation of reading is presented as an oral one, and thought
presented likewise?

> *Responding to the proposition that philosophy originally*
> *owes its existence to experience, Hegel remarks in the*
> *Introduction to the* Encyclopaedia *(8: TWA, Enc., I,*
> *§12): 'With just as much truth, however, we may be said*
> *to owe eating to the means of nourishment, so long as there*
> *is no eating to be had without the latter. And indeed if we*
> *take this view, eating is certainly represented as ungrateful;*
> *it devours that to which it owes its existence. Thinking,*
> *upon this view of the matter, is equally ungrateful.'*

And why is it that the processes of reading, thinking and philoso-
phizing find themselves presented according to the model of organic

metabolism not only by Hegel, but also by those other theoreticians who have been most scrupulously attentive to the physiology of spirit, among them Novalis and Nietzsche?

> *Novalis: 'Everywhere, as it seems to me, there lies a gram-*
> *matical mysticism at the root of things – one which could*
> *most easily excite our original wonderment concerning*
> language *and* writing. *(Even today primitive peoples*
> *regard writing as a kind of sorcery.)*
> *This tendency towards the wonderful and the mysterious is*
> *nothing but a striving – towards non-sensuous – spiri-*
> *tual stimulus. Mysteries are means of nourishment –*
> *potential forms of excitation. Explanations are mysteries*
> *which have been* digested.' *(72: III, 267)*
> *'The philosopher lives off problems in the way a man lives*
> *off food. An insoluble problem is indigestible food.'*
> *And concerning anorexia philosophica: 'One philosophizes*
> *precisely because one lives. Should the time ever come*
> *when we were capable of living without the given means*
> *of nourishment, then we should also come so far as to*
> *philosophize without given problems, – if it is not the*
> *case that some have already reached that point.' (72: II,*
> *565)*
> *And Nietzsche, who identified the German spirit as a*
> *form of indigestion and diagnosed its origin in 'disturbed*
> *entrails' (66:* Ecce Homo, *in Werke, 1083), provides a*
> *prelude to the appearance of Zarathustra: 'For verily, my*
> *brothers, the spirit is a stomach!' (ibid., 452)*

What is at issue here is the body of spirit, the incarnation of spirit in a living organism, the privileged organ and the privileged organic system in which spirit remains closest to itself, in which it finds its way back to itself with greatest ease. At issue also the body of the word in which the spirit incarnates itself, in which meaning seeks its 'expression'. But the question must also be posed the other way around: how does the body attain to spirit, and at what privileged site does this transpire? How – once again – does representation successfully pass over into presentation? In the 'Introduction' to the *Encyclopaedia* (8: TWA,

Enc., I, §3) Hegel describes this problem in terms of the '*unintelligibility*' of philosophy; and he explains this through the difficulty which
customary consciousness encounters in habituating itself to the 'uncus-
tomary nature' of philosophy: of moving in the realm of pure thought
and liberating the same from all admixture with the material of sensible
intuitions, feelings and pictorial representations. Such representations
possess no certain index for their abstract meaning. They can be
regarded, as Hegel asserts, 'only as *metaphors* of thoughts and concepts'.
These representations thereby assume the same status with regard to
the language of philosophy, as does religion which dwells in the
domain of mere representation with regard to the philosophy which
first completes its truth. The content of both is one and the same, but
the difference of form is *toto coelo*, like that between Gods and men:

> '. . . but just as Homer says of certain things that they have
> two names, one name in the language of the Gods, and
> another in the language of toiling mortals, so also for this
> content there are two languages, the one of feeling, of rep-
> resentation and thought confined to the understanding . . .
> the other that of the concrete concept.' (8: TWA, Enc., I,
> 24)

The task of speculative presentation is to translate the finite language
of representation into the infinite language of the concept, to conduct
metaphor back to its original and proper meaning and thus to render
religion truthful and philosophy intelligible. But this transition between
both languages, between both spheres of spirit, between signifying
intent and signification, between sensibility and sense, would remain a
purely arbitrary and external movement if philosophy were incapable of
presenting this transition in the sphere of the sensuous and of representation itself. And the fact that this transition finds its privileged site in
language, that the difference between the proper and the improper is
expounded as a difference between two differing languages, is not unre-
lated to the body that also stands in question here: for language proceeds after all through the mouth. And since 'the metaphorical'
dimension finds its 'principal application . . . in linguistic expression',
Hegel demonstrates this form of transition in his 'Lectures on
Aesthetics' exclusively with reference to linguistic metaphors.

In accordance with the traditional metaphorological schema, the original and 'proper meaning' of Hegel's conception relates first to an 'entirely sensuous content' and is subsequently 'exchanged for a spiritual meaning' (13: TWA, *Ästhetik*, I, 518). This exchange is connected with the process in which the sensuous itself is 'worn down', thereby loses its original plasticity, and finally through sensuous utilization itself becomes something unsensuous. The coinage of the word, worn down through constant use, becomes the representative of the universal equivalent that is the concept. To illustrate this process Hegel uses an example that is more than simply an example: with the genesis of the concept of the concept out of the sensuous meaning of the words '*fassen, begreifen*': 'to grasp' and 'to comprehend'.

> '*When we take 'grasping' something in the spiritual sense, for example, it never occurs to us in any connection to think about the act of sensuous clasping with the hand.*'
> *(13: TWA,* Ästhetik, *I, 518)*

The process of the sensuous is thus actually the process in which the concept comes to itself. Yet the sensuous, sublated into sense through well-worn usage as it is, must remain so harmless, so little virulent, that even the difference between the sensuous and its spiritual meaning is no longer perceptible. The sensuous has disappeared in its sense; what initially was nothing but an improper sensuous sign, has now become the proper and authentic expression of its own process, has been appropriated to the truth of its being. The act of conceptual comprehension, of grasping, destroys its own sensuousness and grips itself firmly and securely as its own concept: an ontological semiotic, a dialectical semontology.

But who is it that suggests that we should take 'grasping' something in the spiritual sense, for example? At least in the passage where Hegel cites this word, both of its meanings are in fact virulent, and even if only because Hegel himself expresses the original, sensuous meaning of the word precisely in order to negate it. Insofar as Hegel attempts to restrain the meaning of the concept, he permits it rather – the law of contrasequence – to expand. The sense of the sensuous, its telos in the spiritual, still therefore retains a trace of sensuousness which fails to attain its destined spiritual sense. And if it is the very 'sense and purpose of metaphorical diction in general' to display the 'power and might of spirit' over nature 'by dwelling upon different things and binding and building the twofold into a single unity' (13: TWA, *Ästhetik*, I, 520 ff.), then this act of constructing a single sense, the single sense of the concept, which thereby secures itself in this its teleological path, always reveals an open seam, a crack or fissure, which fails to disappear without trace into the unity, into the sense, into the being of the concept. A fissure in the edifice which may well allow 'us', in grasping the conceptual grasp of the concept, in one connection or the other 'to think about the act of sensuous clasping with the hand'. This semontology, impotent to affirm the natural meaning entirely as its own spiritual meaning and thus to sublate the former into its full and total meaning, disseminates itself.

The metaphor of spirit in the sphere of representation, the translation and transference of its proper and authentic meaning into the improper language of sensuous intuition, cannot therefore successfully be carried over and carried out without loss or residue. But this transition of spirit to its other and its return into itself, presented here in the analysis of metaphor as linguistic form, is not merely the specialist object of a regional aesthetic theory, and this metaphor of metaphors designates the relationship of philosophy to its own self-presentation in language and in those various forms – like religion, art and the state – in which spirit only ever finds a deficient mode of expression. Consequently, the self-relation of the absolute is also afflicted throughout with this fissure which exposes it to its own superseded forms and therefore to a sphere which restricts its own sense and its own presence. If now this metaphorology constitutes more than a regional theory belonging to one specific level of the system, but rather simultaneously presents the general theory of every transition and of the constitutive process of the entire system itself, then an analysis of the philosophical system as such is possible only insofar as it analyses the rhetorical dimension of the same. Furthermore, every particular metaphor – if, as Hegel demands, it represents more than merely decorative ornament for the presentation of science – marks the fissure through which it is connected to the specific level to which it refers. Consequently, again, the metaphorics of consuming, of sucking, of digesting, which structures the entire corpus of Hegel's texts just as much as the metaphorics of grasping and generating does, institutes a connection between the absolute and the form of nature as its self-alienation, a connection through which, on the one hand, the absolute loses its own sense and omnipotence, but through which, on the other, it can return to itself, as if by a canal, through the open mouth. The oral and genital metaphorics, that is, the metaphorics of *regeneration*, places the totality in relation to a particular part of the system and makes it possible, if not without certain restrictions, to read the whole in the part.

Access to the body of speculative philosophy will – perhaps – disclose itself along the tortuous pathway – it will not be the last – of the animal organism and the analysis Hegel dedicates to the subject in the *Encyclopaedia* in the sections on morphology, assimilation and the reproductive process. This is the circuitous detour which the system of the absolute itself takes in the process of its self-presentation in order to demonstrate the intrinsic speculative unity of nature and spirit.

> *In our reading of these paragraphs from the* Encyclopaedia, *together with their notes and additions, concerning the animal organism and its processes of assimilation and reproduction, we shall also be prepared to read – as in all of the readings here presented – something concerning the relationship between the concept and itself in the form of other-being, the relationship between the concept of time and the time of nature, the relation between a reading and its text. And indeed precisely that relation, that suction and that bite, under whose image the concept re-incorporates its alienated shape, its external and literal natural form, into itself as absolute, and thereby – once again – sublates the natural form of its absolute self-relation, the bite and the suction itself. In this* pars pro toto *we are to read the concept sublating itself in this its own reading and eating, the reading cancelling itself in this its own – repeated – reading.*

The body of the absolute is – and this in the first place – a body of bodies. It is a differentiated body and presents an entire hierarchy of differentiations, not merely in the more developed animal organism itself, but also in the relationship which obtains between the organisms themselves. 'The most rudimentary of creatures' - for even here the three characteristic features of animal life, namely sensibility, irritability and reproduction, are already to be found – 'the most rudimentary of creatures consist of nothing but an intestinal canal' (9: TWA, Enc., II, §354; 454).

> *Just such an intestinal canal is for example, the Medusas – the Gorgon is not so far away – the Hydras, the Vorticella and the Polyps. Hegel cites Treviranus: 'The sac-like receptacle which comprises most of the polyp's body opens and receives the prey, which is changed almost as soon as it is swallowed up; it is transformed into a homogeneous mass, and continually loses volume in the process; finally, the mouth of the Polyp opens again, and part of the ingested food is evacuated by the same path, through the same orifice by which it originally entered the stomach of the Hydra's stomach. . . . Furthermore, the Polyp is also capable of digesting by means of its own outer surface. It can be turned inside out' - like a glove, as Hegel himself adds – 'so that the inside surface of the stomach becomes an outer covering, and yet the phenomena described still transpire as before.' (9: TWA, Enc., II, 485 ff.)*

Although the stomach and the intestinal canal even in more developed creatures consist – like a glove – of nothing but an external membrane turned inside out, or rather outside in, the digestive tract as a whole is nevertheless differentiated hierarchically into various branches, namely the mouth, the gullet, the stomach and the intestines. What we could call the dialectic of the membrane still remains intact even within this differentiation of the digestive tract into the various specific organs. For the skin or membrane, the border-line which separates the individual organism off from its external world and thus defines it as a singular being, does not for all that simply turn the organism into a self-contained sphere whose inside could be wholly separated from what is external; on the contrary, the outer skin forms the inner space of the organism in such a way that the skin reverses upon itself from within, and thus constitutes the entire organism as a complex unity of skins and membranes, of cutaneous folds and sacks, of ossified membranes in hair and nails, claws, bones and teeth – constitutes the inside itself as the complexly unified border-line over against an external environment. For the organism the inside is nothing other than the outside. The organism itself is simply this border-line which relates to itself as its own other.

As its own threshold, however, the digestive tract of the animal body relates to itself as to something inorganic, at least insofar as this contradictory unity is realized only in an objective form. This externality, which is posited in the organism simply as a moment, must therefore, if it is to become an externality *for* the latter, be released from the organism and opposed to it as an object.

> '*The standpoint of living being is precisely this act of scission [Ur-teil] in which the sun and everything else is ejected from itself in this way.*' (9: TWA, Enc., II, §357, Addition 1)

The objectivity of nature is thus in each case nothing but the ejection of the individual organism, nature but the expansion of the idea of life concentrated within the organism. The individual living being relates to this its inorganic ejection as something which belongs to it as its own, something which it now lacks. It *contracts*. – It *tenses*. It tenses itself against its other. This contraction, this tension, which permits nothing to remain external or indifferent to itself, is the pain of lack, is the need which triggers the instinctual drive to re-appropriate what now opposes the organism, alienated from the latter though its own, as an alien power – in the process of hunger and thirst. Hunger and thirst are forms of negative self-relation; they represent not merely experiences of general lack in the absence of something entirely other, not merely the feeling of lacking something alien, but rather the determinate feeling, mediated as it is through the 'senses of opposition' (those of smell and of taste) and the 'senses of ideality' (those of sight and hearing), that what is lacked is something which belongs intrinsically to the organism. Sensibility, the 'theoretical process' of the senses as a whole, presents itself here as the sensuous but 'non-objective unity (of the organism) with the object', as an 'immediate unity of being and what belongs to it' (9: TWA, Enc., II, §358 and Addition).

> *'The lack in the chair, if it only possesses three legs, is in us.' (9: TWA, Enc., II, §359, Addition)*

But if we ourselves lack such a leg, a fourth one, then, insofar as we sensibly perceive and know about it, this ceases merely to be a fact any longer. The limiting lack in the seat is sublated through the theoretical process of the senses – these differentiated membranes of the skin, of the digestive tract; it is appropriated as *our* lack and the negative is determined and defined for us as *our* negation. What was ejected returns to the inside through the circle of the senses; the gap is filled and the organism closes in upon itself.

> *'[A]nimal desire is the idealism of objective being, in accordance with which the latter is not something alien.'*
> *(9: TWA, Enc., II, §359, Addition)*

Amongst the forms of the negative self-relation of desire it is the 'senses of opposition', namely those of smell and of taste, which are less 'idealistic' insofar as they are immediately directed towardss a self-dissolving corporeality; while it is the senses of ideality, namely those of sight and hearing, which are properly 'idealistic' insofar as they allow corporeal being to subsist indifferently or to vanish in the act of perception. Hegel also describes taste and smell as the 'practical senses' since their object is 'the real being of things for another, one through which they are consumed' (9: TWA, Enc., II, §358, Addition). All of the senses thus possess a more or less immediate relation to the dissolution of objective being, that is, to the constant re-appropriation of the border-line or limit ejected by the organism from itself in its act of primal partition or separation [*Ur-teil*]. The sensory relation in question is a relation to that death of objective being through which the latter is reintegrated within the animal organism. – And it is within the voice as the 'active sense of hearing' that the circulation of organism and its desire transpires with the least resistance of all. This 'active sense of hearing' is the site for the pure economy of organic being and for the idea of life which is incarnated there. It is through this sense that all expiring life immediately flows back into itself, hears, even as it speaks, its own ideality, thus perceives and sublates itself.

'Every creature finds voice for itself in the throes of violent death, and utters itself as a sublated self.' (9: TWA, Enc., II, §358, Addition)

The voice is the highest point and extremity of animal negativity. That movement which occurs in plants merely as the process of secretion (for they allow their rind to decay and their leaves to fall), and which characterizes the individual animal organism as the free motion in space, finds itself idealized in voice as the most unobjectifiable mode of expression that is possible. The voice is the ideal movement of corporeal being in space, the death of such being insofar as it is immediately perceived as tone and thus returns within the living body; this is the form in which the externality of corporeal space negates its very self and brings itself into the abstract unity of self-feeling. As the pure self-affection of the organism the voice is not itself determined and defined in temporal terms, it *is* rather the privileged form of animal time as such.

'The organism is itself time, that which is self-moving. It contracts into its own simple time, posits itself as sublated space, subsistence, and moves in and of itself. It is simple time as subject, the externally unmovable, or rather the simple unity of time and space. It is the power, the subject of the same; it is not they which are a power over it.' (24: JR, 175 ff.)

Insofar as the 'active sense of hearing' properly belongs to the 'theoretical process', the time which has there been transformed into subject still remains quite abstract, however:

'This subjectivity for itself is, quite abstractly considered, the pure process of time, which constitutes vibration and tone in the concrete body as self-realizing time.' (9: TWA, Enc., II, §351, Addition)

It is on account of this abstractness and insubstantiality, through which articulated desire there relates immediately to itself, through which the organism presents itself as a process of negativity, that the voice enjoys a particularly close and intimate relationship to thought itself. The self-relation of the digestive tract, as it contracts its own materiality into the pure inwardness of voice, is even what is 'closest of all to thought'.

> 'The voice is the closest of all to thought; for here pure sub-
> jectivity becomes objective, not as a particular actuality, as
> a condition, state or sensation, but rather in the abstract
> element of space and time.' (9: TWA, Enc., II, §351,
> Addition)

The voice, and the apparatus of hearing which belongs to it, the
mouth and the complementary vocalization of its expression, in short
the entire 'active sense of hearing' constitutes the privileged site,
appointed and articulated by the organism itself, for the self-
appropriation of life. Here arche and telos are united, decisively closed
together in organic being, to form the circle through which such being
opens for itself a path to the logos. The externality of the voice can disappear 'with regard to itself' and thereby find itself, along the pathway
of the ear, sublimated, idealized, re-collected and in-ternalized. The act
of self-perception is the privileged form of self-appropriation, is indeed
the organic schema of internalizing re-collection. If the field of signification stands under the governing sign of semontology, then the field
of the somatic stands under the sign of phonontology. The phenomenon of 'sense', whether it be *determined* [*bestimmt*] as sensuous or as
spiritual sense, possesses a specific *vocation* in each case; a vocation
which is fulfilled through the process of internalizing its own externality. Sense, being, what is one and what is ownmost: the logos here
describes the smallest possible circle from itself to itself, the path upon
which it loses least of all and experiences the least possible material
impediment – the path of the voice from mouth to ear. This economic
character of the 'active sense of hearing' turns voice into the schema for
the circular economy of the self-appropriation of the absolute in the
sphere of nature, the schema of the transition from nature to spirit.
This dialectical ontology, this organology, is structured phonocentric-
ally.

This self-perception is the purest form of self-enjoyment – Hegel
offers the example of bird-song – and the purest form of self-consumption. The mouth forms the jointure, the articulated organic structure,
the 'metaphorical' transition between the self-relation of the logos and
its presentation as a process of self-consumption. The sucking draw of
breath is thus the sensuous truth of the self-relation of the logos. The

'active sense of hearing', the sucking mouth, enjoys more than one specific location in the system of spirit, for this 'itself', grasped in its very truth, is what systematizes body and spirit, what joins them together and articulates their unity.

In §401 of the *Encyclopaedia* (10: TWA, Enc., III), where the systematizing dialectic of internalizing re-collection and external embodiment is developed, Hegel briefly sketches the twofold function of the mouth for the process of ingestion and vocalization. The voice, he writes, receives its 'ultimate articulation' through the mouth,

> *which possesses the twofold function, on the one hand, of initiating the immediate transformation of food within the shape of the living animal organism, and on the other, in contrast with this internalizing of the external, of accomplishing that objectification of subjectivity which transpires through voice.'* (10: TWA, Enc., III, §401, Addition, 117)

Hegel proceeds to investigate the complexity of the mouth more comprehensively in his analysis of animal form and shape. He explains the fact that there is a corporeal complex of functions here at all rather summarily – for this problem still causes 'considerable difficulties' for his speculative approach – by claiming that 'the soul which corporeally determines itself is present in these soul-like nodes, although it is not possible to pursue the specific connection of bodily functions in detail here'.

> *'Thus the mouth, for example, belongs to a particular system, that of sensitivity, insofar as the tongue, the organ of the sense of taste, finds itself there as a moment of the theoretical process; furthermore the mouth possesses teeth, which belong to the bodily extremities insofar as they are destined for grasping things externally'* [thus it is not merely the hand, but the teeth as well which grasp, to facilitate the bite of the concept] *and for masticating things; in addition, the mouth also serves as the organ for the voice and speech; and other related sensations, that of thirst for example, are also found here; laughing, and kissing as well, similarly transpire with the mouth, which*

> *therefore combines within itself the expression of many dif-*
> *ferent sensations. Another example is furnished by the eye,*
> *the organ of sight, which also sheds tears, just as even ani-*
> *mals weep.' (9: TWA, Enc., II, §355, Addition; 456)*

There are also other examples of such 'soul-like nodes' – and we shall have a third one to consider in due course – but the mouth is not prop- erly merely one example amongst others, not even, as Hegel himself punningly elucidates the significance of the German word '*Beispiel*', a merely external and exemplary by-play. For it is the mouth itself, by virtue of voice also the closest of all to thought, which defines and lays down the logic of connection here: the mouth is the model, the exam- ple of examples, the speculative example, which determines the struc- ture and functioning of all other possible examples and secures the systematic interconnection of organs as an order of the logos in accor- dance with the oral schema of the body.

> *When it appears as a metaphor of the spiritual, the activ-*
> *ity of the mouth is far more than a merely external anal-*
> *ogy for the process of conceptual grasping, but rather*
> *represents the organizing device for articulating the inner*
> *relation of nature and Idea. The metaphor of the mouth*
> *effectively functions as a paradigm for any and every pos-*
> *sible dialectical transition from the materially real to the*
> *ideal, from the ideal in itself, the sphere of the in itself*
> *generally, into the sphere of the for itself, as the metaphor-*
> *ical schema which structures all forms of inferential clo-*
> *sure and conclusion, and especially that of speculative*
> *closure.*
>
> *As the schema of all metaphors, the paradigm of all transi-*
> *tion from the other which is posited by the concept into the*
> *sphere of the selfsame which proves homogeneous with it,*
> *the oral metaphor enframes the speculative process as a*
> *whole – the dialectic is determined in and through the*
> *rhetoric of the speculative metaphor, the metaphor of the*
> *speculative mouth. As eating, reading has already been*
> *grasped in accordance with the rhetoric of the speculative*
> *mouth, of the logos, in concordance with the measure of*

> *the economy of phoné. In the performance of this transi-*
> *tion from sensuous eating to conceptual grasping, from the*
> *somatic to the semantic process, along with the devalua-*
> *tion of purely formal mediation which this implies, a*
> *transition executed in accordance with the organizing*
> *example of mouth and ear, with the model of self-*
> *perception, something nevertheless interrupts the schema of*
> *the logos, slips out of this framework and shatters its econ-*
> *omy and its species of rhetoric.*

In the mouth, over and beyond its 'theoretical' function as the sense of taste, the process of digestion turns practical. For in the mouth, after the mechanical accomplishment of assimilating what the senses have already determined as their own, there commences that further incorporation which does not permit the object to subsist as something alien, but rather robs it of all specific independence of its own, and which operates in the first instance through saliva, and then through the 'pancreatic juice'

> *'from the great gland or pancreas below the stomach'*

and further through the bile, which 'plays the principal role' here as the being-for-self of the animal organism precisely because it ignites on contact with the food, which was externally introduced into the system (9: TWA, Enc., II, §365, Addition; 490):

> *Hegel's mother 'died in 1783 of a bilious fever, from*
> *which his father, his sister (Christiane) and Hegel himself*
> *also suffered badly at the same time'. The memory of his*
> *mother remained sacred for Hegel. On 20 September*
> *1825 he still wrote to Christiane from Berlin: 'Today is*
> *the anniversary of the death of our mother, a day I always*
> *hold in remembrance' (73: Ros., 4)*

– and finally transmutes the food and transforms it into identity with the organism itself. Over against the physiologists of his time Hegel lays the greatest emphasis upon the claim that the digestive process cannot be completely understood as one that is purely mechanical or chemical in nature. For unlike any merely mechanical or chemical connections and combinations, what is accomplished through the process of digestion represents a 'living and absolute unity' of outer and inner, of food and organism. The '*gradual character*' of the chemical process is broken in the act of organic feeding (9: TWA, Enc., II, §345, Note) and all externality is here *substantially* transformed.

Once the gall has biliously ignited against the inorganic which finds itself within the organic – and for Hegel the gall-bladder is just as much the outer corporeal manifestation of anger as anger is the internalization of gall – and once the food-substances have been dissolved, fermented and prepared, they can enter the circulation of the 'universal substance', the blood. Insofar as it brings all the parts of the organism into an inner dynamic unity, the blood constitutes 'the living subject as such' (9: TWA, Enc., II, §345, Addition; 449). The blood is substance and subject in so strict a sense that it can be described as the being of movement itself, 'the unmoved mover' as Hegel says with an allusion to Aristotelian metaphysics:

> '*νοῦς is the essence of the world, that is, the universal, the simple or onefold which is the unity of opposed moments, and is consequently the* unmoved *one which nonetheless moves other things. This is the* blood. *It is the subject, which initiates movement much as the* will *does.*' *(24:* JR, *152)*

But it is not merely as the synthesis of the organic and the inorganic, not merely as the organization of bodily parts into the totality of the organism, not merely as the combination of subsisting bodily shape with its vital power, that blood constitutes a unity of opposed moments. For above all blood is a unity of mover and moved. Blood is moved by nothing outside itself, and it moves nothing outside itself. As the pure self-mediation of substance and subject, as the 'immediate expression of the concept, which one can see here with one's very eyes as it were' (9: TWA, Enc., II, §354, Addition; 449), the blood is also conceived in accordance with the oral schema of the body. 'Just as all food-substances are transformed into blood, the blood itself is also bestowed in turn, from which everything derives its sustenance' (ibid.). Once the digestion of the external is completed, the process is continued as the inner self-digestion of the organism. Mediated through the blood as the universal process of digestion, each and every part of the body feeds and lives off every other one. 'Every member draws upon the other for itself, inasmuch as each secerns the animal lymph, which is distributed to the vessels only to return to the blood, and each renews itself from this secretion. The process of shaping is therefore conditioned by the consumption of these formations' (ibid., §356, Addition; 460 ff.). Blood is the cyclical movement of bodily parts consuming themselves in their otherness and thereby digesting themselves as a totality, is the materially configured suction of self-relation as such.

> *'Blood is this absolute thirst, this agitated unrest both within itself and in opposition to itself; blood is hungry for animation, craves differentiation. More precisely, this digestion is at the same time a mediated process with the air . . . as its satiation, i.e. that the blood resembles other forms of digestion by perpetually appeasing its hunger or thirst (however we wish to put it), and thereby achieving being-for-self by negating its otherness.' (9: TWA, Enc., II, §362, Addition; 477 ff.)*

The self-consumption, the self-production, of the digestive tract which has taken on circular form as the passage of blood through the entire organism transpires according to the mechanism of suction, as a continuous sequence of contractions and expansions, as a process of pulsation. Blood itself is the subject and object of this oscillating movement, the 'leaping point' of the organism through which the

> *'contraction of the arteries coincides with the relaxation of the ventricles of the heart'* (9: TWA, Enc., II, §354, Addition; 450). It is the 'peristaltic movement *in general'* (ibid., 448) *through which the universal fluidity is condensed into the specific fluid of subsisting organic shape, and emerges by means of the secretion of 'animal lymph', through which the body*

opens itself to this immanent movement and thereby returns to circulation. This *'peristaltic movement'* in which the speculative dialectic of the digestive tract realizes itself is also time – the second determinant besides the process of self-consumption which brings the circulation of the blood into connection with the oral schema of the body. The peristaltic character of the blood is – like the resonance of voice – an 'absolute quivering within itself'. Whether it is the quivering of the

vocal cords, of the eardrum or the veins, this quivering, because the
organism relates therein purely to itself, is time.

> 'The blood *is the result, the external organism which*
> *returns in itself to itself through itself.* ... *Blood as the*
> *axial movement revolving and racing around itself, this*
> *absolute quivering within itself is the individual life of the*
> *whole, in which nothing remains separated – it is animal*
> *time.' (9: TWA, Enc., II, §354, Addition; 447)*

Voice and blood – both alike are time. The temporality of the blood
is distinguished from that of the 'active sense of hearing' insofar as one
is the temporality which belongs to practical self-digestion and the
other the more abstract temporality which belongs to theoretical sensibility. In both cases time is the self-relation of the digestive tract which,
related to its other, expands and contracts once more into its simple
onefold self by returning from its externality – a peristaltic-circular
process between the pure movement of consumption and its presentation as bodily shape. The temporality of the circulation of the blood is
thus the *Logos* or *Nous* in its organic concretion, the spatio-temporal
continuum which has been unconsciously sublated.

The opposition between inner and outer, between the organic and
the inorganic, between shape and motion, is thus sublated through
transubstantiation into the universal process of the blood, in which
substance and subject each culminate in the other. The process of
digestion has revealed itself as the natural form of re-collection, of
sublimation, of spiritualization, while in this natural form spirit has
revealed itself as the power over nature. But –But since, already in
relation to the system of the theoretical senses through which the
objects are destined for consumption and as it were predigested, the
essentially inorganic moment in the process of assimilation has not
been considered at all with respect to its own determinate being, but
solely in accordance with its relationship to the organism, with its
immanent teleology, and thus with its concept, which defines it as
something already immaterial, organic, and therefore spiritual (cf. 24:
JR, 119); since 'eating and drinking . . . turns inorganic things into
what they are in themselves' (9: TWA, Enc., II, §365, Addition; 485),

then the mediated process of digestion, accomplished mechanically by the action of the teeth and chemically by the bile and the 'pancreatic juice', appears to be 'superfluous'. However appropriately the structure of the organism may be designed to facilitate the gradual identification of the merely objective with organic life, 'these elaborate procedures of digestion are nonetheless equally superfluous' (24: *JR*, 120). Hegel introduces principally two examples to illustrate this immanent surplus of organically differentiated, mediated mediation, over and above the immediate mediation accomplished within the inorganic itself.

> '*It is well-known to those who catch Thrushes and Fieldfares, for example, that if the birds are very thin, they will fatten up considerably after exposure to mist even within the space of a few hours – a transformation of moisture which transpires* without any further secretion or passage through the separate moments of the process of assimilation.' *(24:* JR, *120)*
>
> [*And further*] '*The* faeces *reveal, particularly in children, who assimilate a greater amount of matter than other individuals, that the greater part of the food usually remains unchanged in state and is mixed principally with* animal *substances, with* bile, *phosphorus and the like, and that the principal activity of the organism consists in overcoming and ridding itself of these its own products.*' *(9: TWA, Enc., II, §365, Remark)*

Consequently, the circuitous detour through the specialized process of assimilation, through superfluity, is not forcibly subjected to any external form of purposiveness, like that of nourishment as the material reproduction of the individual; for all of that can be accomplished, as Hegel demonstrates with reference to an entire series of physiological experiments, in a direct manner by means of the respiratory organs or the cutaneous membrane itself. The differentiation of the organic machinery of mediation and the differentiation of the animal species in their entirety obeys on the contrary an inner teleology, and one of sub-jectivity. Insofar as the organism exposes itself, superfluously, to the inorganic which is already in itself organic, exposes itself – once again – to an externality which is in itself already appropriated by the organism, the latter transforms itself into something external and must now relate to itself as an object and as the negation of its subjectivity. Thus it is not the objective thing, the food itself, which is digested, but rather the external relationship to it. What the organism digests is the process of digestion itself.

'The animal deceives itself, therefore, when it turns against ... its means of nourishment'; ' its relationship to the same [is] untrue'. Indeed, its relationship is so untrue that with this turn towardss externality, this 'false direction', the animal actually risks its own destruction.

> 'Through this struggle with the external the organic threatens precisely to lose itself; it gives something away to the inorganic.' (9: TWA, Enc., II, §365, Addition; 490–1)

This danger of mediated mediation, of external exposure, of giving something away, of overtaxing itself, something which threatens to become an unappropriable loss and thus to interrupt the organic circling of the *Logos*, the cycle of temporality – both that of the blood and that of the voice – and the circulation of truth between spirit and nature; this excess of self-relation, in every sense a life-threatening one, encounters – nausea.

> It is nausea that is in question here. Nausea. [Ekel]

The nausea of the organism – and Hegel speaks of nausea because the organism is determined by the corporeal schema of the mouth, the throat and the digestive tract – is directed therefore not in opposition to its food, but in opposition to its opposition to food; nausea is directed against the bile, which 'plays the principal function' in the process of superfluous mediation, against the excess of the developed digestive tract, against the surplus of traction.

> If Hegel's application of the concept of nausea differs from customary usage, insofar as for him it is not essentially directed in opposition to an object but rather to this opposition itself, it does correspond to that usage inasmuch as the impulse behind the latter is also provoked by an encounter with excess. This nauseous disgust or 'Ekel' (fastidium, taedium, nausea) – described in Grimm's

*German Dictionary as 'one of the most striking words
in our language' – arises, as Adelung writes in his
Grammatisch-kritisches Wörterbuch der hochdeutschen Mundart (26: Leipzig: 1793), 'not merely in
the presence of certain things which are repellent to our
sense of taste and smell, but also from an excess of satiation, for it is also quite possible to eat oneself sick in such a
way that one experiences a nauseous feeling of disgust in
the presence of any kinds of food . . . In such cases nausea
expresses a profound degree of sensuous disgust. According
to yet another figure, one also employs this word to describe
a profound degree of spiritual or psychological disgust, of
extreme reluctance or opposition. . . . In Nieders the word
appears as 'Ekern', and in Pictorius as 'Erkung', which
is also accompanied by the adjectival form "erklich"
instead of "ekelig" and the verb "erkeln" in the sense of
producing a sense of nausea. The impulse to vomit is
indeed the primary meaning of the word 'Ekel', and it
can fittingly be regarded as a case of onomatopoeia. Yet it
can also be included within that numerous family of the
word 'Eg" or 'Eck', signifying corner or edge, where it
would then express the pressing and stabbing sensation
which is experienced in the stomach in cases of nausea.'
(ibid., 1782)*

In the experience of nausea the organism, as Hegel understands it,
revolts. It revolts not merely against an excess which it has itself produced, but rather against the self-misconception through which it is
produced, against that lack of self-consciousness which prevents it from
recognizing the intrinsically organic within the inorganic, against that
being-for-self which the bile unleashes upon the substances externally
posited within the organism, precisely in order to appropriate for itself
once again what is already its own. In nausea the organism is directed
against itself – and indeed against itself as something in excess of itself,
against its untrue repetition. Not against the sustenance, but against
sustaining this once-more in which it threatens to lose itself. Hegel's
nausea, his '*Ekel*' , against his gall, his '*Galle*' – KL against GL:

*'Insofar as the organism separates itself from itself in this
way, it disgusts and nauseates itself, because it no longer
enjoyed control over itself; this is what the organism does
when it expels its struggle, the bile which it has excreted,
from itself.' (9: TWA, Enc., II, §365, Addition; 492)*

The nausea of the organism – the natural form of the *Logos* – is
directed against the struggle with the organically inorganic to which it
has been exposed; directed also against the externality immanent to the
form of the organism itself, against that organism which is not that of
the Logos, against the organism which is an immanent but false repetition of the organism. This immanent doubling, which commences
with the process of the bile, finally emerges on the 'last level of animality' in 'real production', as excretion. For this is the act 'in which the
animal doubles itself in extruding itself from itself' (ibid.). Nausea separates the organism from itself, because the organic self here is other
than it is in truth: a piece of excrement; and because thought itself,
where its truth is grasped, is intrinsically connected with an organ the
composition of which is comparable with that of excrement. Thus it is
no arbitrary metaphor when life is described as the '*Ur-teil*' or 'primal
act of scission', in which the organism 'ejects the sun and everything
else out of itself', and turns everything, even the central focus of a
system, into an eject; for Hegel this is an experimentally confirmed
truth:

*'The ingredients of the urine [as Hegel quotes] are encoun-
tered again pre-eminently in the bones. Several of the substances involved also constitute ingredients of the hair,
others constitute ingredients of the muscles and the brain.'
(ibid., 493)*

No one will conclude from this, nor will anyone really deny, that it
is the excrement which thinks, thinks itself, thinks itself as thought,
and by thinking in this way, constitutes the absolute as excrement. Yet
it is only the brain, and not the hair or the urine, which is capable of
thinking. The excrement *is* not, since it possesses no independent subsistence or identity; as excrement, something extruded by the organism, it can neither know nor itself be known. It is the same as the
organism which excretes it, it is the organism itself, but it is

simultaneously only its inorganic repetition, its immanent spectral double in which it becomes unrecognizable to itself, in which it threatens to lose itself.

> *'The abstract expulsion of itself from itself, by means of which the animal makes itself external to itself, is the act of excretion, the conclusion of the process of assimilation. Insofar as it merely makes itself into something external, this is an inorganic, an abstract otherness, in which the animal does not possess its identity.' (ibid., 492)*

The object of nauseous disgust here is something which properly *is* not in the fullest sense: not something which simply is not, for being suffers no disturbance whatsoever from its negative mode, but rather something which is less or more than nothing, which cannot ever be properly identified, something other which, although it is the organism itself, is not *its being*, but is an abstract other. The organism cannot recognize itself in this other, even though it is its 'own' product – an irreversible repetition of the organic *Logos*, one which cannot be repeated by the *Logos*, one through which the *Logos* can neither return to itself nor conclude by closing its own circle. What is nauseous is what proves indigestible for the *Logos*, what interrupts and breaks the self-relation or circle of the organic, the schema of somontology, and is brokenly brought up by the organism as a result.

But what provokes nauseous disgust also breaks the circle of orality, the body articulated according to the measure of the *Logos*, the circulation of the blood, of the voice, of signification, the cycle of time. But for the indigestible, for the assimilated matter, or for the bile – one of the meanings of the term 'Ekel' – to erupt, to be brought up through the mouth, would already mean returning the nauseous to the circle of the *Logos*, to the analogy of orality; would already signify. And the very *word* 'eklig', nauseous – if it is indeed, as Adelung suggests, onomatopoeic and therefore literally brought up in being brought forth – already finds itself placed in the mouth, passes through 'the active sense of hearing', and, once perceived, is identified and digested within the circle of subjectivity proper to the organism, within the sphere of signification. The nausea, whether brought forth or brought up, is no longer nauseous. The work of nausea and of the system of orality with which it is bound up consists precisely in transforming what remains indigestible into something digestible, of catching the remainder which was not absorbed into the self-relation of the organism, that which drops away, and of reintegrating it within its schema.

Yet the disgusting object, extruded by the logical organism, is nonetheless not without effect upon the central axis around which the organism turns. For in the act of retching the mouth itself – and this is the third 'spiritual nodal point' which is in question here – is rendered analogous to the organs of excretion, the anus and the urethra, and to the genitalia; the organ of the *Logos* and of consumption analogous to the organs of excretion and reproduction.

> 'The organs of excretion and the genitalia, the highest and lowest moments of animal organization, are intimately connected with one another in the case of many animals' – fascinated by this particular connection, Hegel already notes in his Phenomenology that the relationship between the consciousness and the unconscious in the domain of pictorial representation is 'the same combination of high and low which nature naively expresses in the living being through combining the organ of its highest perfection, the organ of generation, – with the organ of urination' (3: TWA, Phen., 262); and Heine supplies a similar formulation on the basis of his personal discussions with Hegel: 'just as language and kissing on the one side, and eating, drinking and spitting on the other, are connected in the organ of the mouth'. (9: TWA, Enc., II, §365, Addition; 492)

In the act of nausea the oral schema of the body which underlies and sustains the system of spirit comes into contact with and finds itself affected by other schemata, namely these that are anal, urethral, or genital. The schema of orality, of the *Logos*, is not destroyed in the encounter with the nauseous – even if the latter is expressed and brought up through the mouth – but insofar as its framework, at once transcendental and empirical, as the power of the concept therefore, is expressed, expectorated and brought up, then it ceases to be purely self-contained and opens itself up to the excremental function, relates to itself as an other which is no longer its 'own', finds itself disfigured. It still remains, in its disfigurement, the framework in which the self-relation of spirit presents itself.

> *Just as Heidegger elevated 'Care' to the status of an existential category, so too Sartre, the fundamental ontologist of decision, did the same with the phenomenon of nausea. From the perspective of 'existential psychoanalysis' projected by Sartre in his* Being and Nothingness, *nausea represents the transcendentalizing figure of being-for-self in which consciousness 'ex-ists' its contingency, its corporeality, its being-for-others. It is only against the background of this transcendental configuration of the nauseous that the phenomenon of nausea, always particular in each case, 'discloses itself' as the empirical experience of alienation. Nausea is the transcendental schema of existential ontology. It marks the irruption of that being-for-another which is constitutive for the self-relation of human existence, and which reduces itself, as pure contingency, to the nothingness of a being. Sartre's aggressive reversal of the synthetic logic of all traditional ontologies actually culminates, with its hypostasis of the Wholly Other, in the restoration of that logic. It is not merely that what is repudiated – or also what is accepted – is 'the being of this being itself'; the repudiation, the nausea itself, is the nauseous as non-thetic ex-istence, the repulsion is just this being as the being of the Other, or Nothingness (75:* Being and Nothingness *[London: Methuen, 1969], 439 ff.). This betrays an anal-sadistic complicity with nauseously clinging being, a complicity which grounds Sartre's entire philosophical 'project' and permits only an economy of appropriation, irrespective of whether the position of the contingent Other is negated or accepted. Which is why the for-itself of consciousness cannot mistake [fail to grasp] its own, its lack, namely the meaning of being. The nauseous represents a possible meaning of being for consciousness*

(ibid.), nausea and decision the condition of the possibility
of this me-ontological meaning.

If the gastric system has given something away by turning against
the inorganic natural substance of its food; if it is indeed disfigured
beneath the pressure of the nauseous which it expels, the impulse of
nausea itself is nonetheless the very thing that most securely restitutes
the integrity of the organism, and of its meaning. Even more than
shame, which is mentioned once again in this connection, and more
than anger, both of which repel any immediate threat to the identity of
the organism, nausea is apotropaic. It is the organism's apotrope
directed against the externality and untruth of the organism itself. It is
only through this its nausea that the organism becomes an organism,
that the body, which misrecognizes itself as a purely natural thing,
becomes the incarnation of spirit. For it is only through the process
which is initiated by nausea that the body liberates itself from its objectivity, digests its digestion, corrects that external purposiveness that
leads nowhere into a true internal teleology, that the body, precisely by
isolating and extruding its own inorganic organism, permits life as pure
relation to self to supplant any relation to otherness. A negation of the
negation, nausea moves the organism to return into itself; is itself the
movement of self-reflection in organismic subjectivity, the conclusive
act of closure through which life grasps itself as immediately self-identi-
cal (9: TWA, Enc., II, §365 and the Remark). Nausea expels the mediated being-for-self of the organism, sets it over against the organism,
and allows the latter to recognize its being-for-self even in reflection
upon its objectified and reified in-itself. Nausea is unconscious self-
recognition, a non-conceptual conceptual grasp of the organic self,
which reproduces life as being in and for itself through the 'real production' of an external being-for-self in the process of excrementation.
In this concluding act of closure, which in excluding the false from
itself thereby asserts its power over what is excluded, thereby transforms excrementation into the incrementation of its own self-relation,
nausea would consequently have to represent the affirmative negation
of the negation, the law of the dialectical self-relation of life. The peristaltic movement of nausea, of the digestion of digestion, now resti-
tuted, produces that '*peristaltic movement* in general' (ibid., 448) which

presents the organic presence of the *Logos* in and as the circulation of the blood.

If the organism is the metaphor of the absolute, then nausea, as the movement which produces the self-relation of the organism, is its absolute metaphor, the metaphor through which the absolute closes conclusively in upon itself. If the gastric system is the articulated structure, the jointure through which the natural form of the Idea is connected up with its conceptual form, then nausea is the aperture in this jointure, that which properly secures the inner consistency of the organic system and its synthetic functioning, the consistency therefore of the entire system of the absolute and of its self-relation. The result of this nausea is the pleroma, 'the satiation, the self-feeling which now experiences total satisfaction over against its previous feeling of lack' (ibid., 493).

Nausea would represent the schema of speculative dialectic.

> *A false proposition, a false conclusion, a premature conclusion, an impossible, or at least a highly problematic, at any rate a disgusting and nauseating, proposition, one which not merely distorts the consequences of the dialectical method but also distorts and exposes to ridicule the very method itself, and the entire logical, historical and political system which is based upon it – a proposition which cannot be too hastily refused, rejected, and ejected, in order to facilitate the return of a meaningful analysis. It must be cast out, because it introduces the movement of nausea, and the affective complex associated with it, into the meta-empirical, meta-psychological sphere of pure spiritual formations, into the Logic itself; must be expelled, even though there are good reasons which support this proposition. For 'the standpoint of living being is precisely this act of primal scission which ejects the sun and everything else from out of itself' (9: TWA, Enc., II, §357, Addition), which so to speak spews forth Nature itself, this Son of God, which reproduces itself in this Other insofar as this eject once more ejects its own externality, its own relation to the external, which returns itself to the standpoint of pure life through repeating its own operation.*

The process of nausea is the process of sacrificial offering.
Seized by nausea, Absolute Knowing and its Philosopher
disgorge.
The structure of the self-presencing and self-presenting
word: ontological litEructure.
This eruction, which comprehends itself, and whose con-
cept comprehends itself only through the process of dis-
gorgement, answers to the double desire for absolute
difference and for a pure presence realized in this differ-
ence – for a hysterical presence.
Disgorgement, extrusion, expectoration, ejection. Yet what
has been disgorged and extruded, this spittle and these
egesta, hardly lend themselves unconditionally to this
desire for absolute self-relation. Indeed, they resist the
drawing power of spirit's internalizing re-collection so
strongly that the entire realm of nature, as Hegel observes
in §575 of the Encyclopaedia *(10: TWA, Enc., III),*
relates itself asymmetrically to the axis of the absolute. And
if, within the architecture of the system, that in which
spirit cannot recognize itself without loss or remainder is
relegated to inferior status, then nausea, the most extreme
impulse of defensive rejection, relates to that from which it
cannot return to itself as from its Other. Nausea produces
only an abstract Other which cannot become a moment of
its own concrete self-relation.

Thus nausea does not represent the schema of speculative dialectic
after all. But it does designate the quantitative extreme by which the
progress of the dialectical method is defined. This limit of the dialectic,
marked by nausea inasmuch as its object presents what properly
belongs to the living being solely in an abstract and formal manner, is
certainly itself a dialectical figure. But it is one in which *the* dialectical
figure, that of the self-relation of identity within *its* Other, is not present in its entirety, and therefore as one which the movement of the
concept is incapable of controlling and appropriating as its own.
Nausea at once belongs and fails to belong to the speculative dialectic
and its onto-theological economy, allows the organism of the Logos to

return to itself and yet must irreversibly externalize and alienate a part of that organism, supports the logical-oral schema of the body and simultaneously unsettles it.

There is no dialectical relationship between nausea and dialectic, but only one of complicity. Just as nausea marks the outer limit of the dialectical process, that indispensable but always problematic relationship to an abstract Other in which the schema of self-relation appears only in a deformed fashion, so nausea nonetheless remains an operation which restitutes the progress of spirit towardss itself, restitutes the logical organism and its economy. Nausea provides the dialectic with the means of transcending nausea itself and accomplishing the transition to something else. But insofar as nausea, itself something nauseating, is merely excluded from the process of the absolute, is incapable of being brought full circle into concrete coalescence with the living process of the organism, then a moment of nausea still persists even in the pure self-relation to which it advances.

> *There is a double dialectic at work in the speculative system of dialectics, one member of which mimetically, as it were, duplicates and subverts the other. Apart from Jacques Derrida in* Glas *(32: Paris: Galilée, 1974), no one has struggled more relentlessly than Theodor W. Adorno to reveal the mechanism of this immanent doubling of the dialectic. In his study 'Skoteinos, or How to Read' Adorno describes it as follows: 'From the perspective of the reader's understanding, what is unintelligible in Hegel is the wound left by identity thinking itself. Hegel's dialectical philosophy becomes entangled in a dialectic which his philosophy cannot account for, whose resolution exceeds the all-embracing power of his own thought. To pursue its failure is vain. The truth of the irresolvably non-identical manifests itself within the system, according to the law of the latter, precisely as error, as unresolved in another sense, as its own untruth; and nothing untrue can be fully comprehended.' (27:* Drei Studien zu Hegel, *[Frankfurt: Suhrkamp, 1969], 164)*

Yet if that other dialectic, to which the systematic dialectic is subjected, presents itself for Adorno as that of the 'non-identical itself', whose 'content' still 'remains' separated from its 'concept' (ibid.), then Adorno substantializes its negativity. Insofar as he declares the unintelligible and unpresentable element, that which is untrue according to the law of the system, to be the truth of the non-identical, Adorno places the relationship between these competing dialectics under the power of the ontological, and perpetuates modo negativo *its domination. It belongs to the dialectic of this critique of Hegel, that what it critically destroys is resurrected once again within the critique itself. It is not the 'non-identical itself' and its truth which is at issue here, but the self-repelling movement through which the system of negativity itself is first constituted – but in such a way that, contrary to its own claims, nothing substantial, no truth, can be left firmly standing, can be interpreted as a criterion of critical judgement either for or against the system.*

With the allergic sensitivity so characteristic of him, Adorno himself drew attention to the mechanism of repulsion with which the system of capitalist production reacts to whatever fails to correspond to its own law of equivalence, something which penetrates right into the reading and interpretation of texts: 'The tabu reaches right down into the idiosyncratic market demand that all trace of the human be eliminated from the product, that the latter itself be nothing but a pure in-itself. The fetish-character of the commodity is not merely a veil, it is an imperative. Congealed labour, once recognized as that of human beings, is rejected with nauseous disgust.' (ibid., 143)

After Hegel has dealt with the process of abstract and formal excre-tion, he proceeds to discuss the next and higher stage of self-reproduc-tion, that of the formative or constructive instinct [*Bildungstrieb*]. The difference between this, also described as a productive instinct

[*Kunsttrieb*] that constitutes an animalistic-physiological prelude to the self-conscious aesthetic productions of the human being, and the process of excretion consists in the fact that the former transforms the extruded externalized bodily substances – the secretions of the spider, the honey of the bee – into instruments of the organism itself and thereby turns them into external organs. In this case it is not nausea which drives on the process of excretion, but rather the need for self-relation in the sphere of externality.

> *'The other aspect consists in the animal's secreting certain formations from itself, something which is motivated not by nauseous disgust, in order to be rid of such things; on the contrary, the excrementa, once externalized, are shaped and formed to satisfy the animal's needs.' (9: TWA, Enc., II, §365, Addition; 494)*

With the progressive advance of spirit the nauseous finds itself pushed aside. The nauseous turns against this opposition to Otherness, without itself producing an affirmative relationship to the externalized moment of excrement; thus it is the nauseous itself, a repetition of a false orientation towardss externality and of an untrue self-relation, rather than this excrement which presents the most nauseating spectacle as far as the movement of the absolute is concerned. Yet the sublation of this most nauseating of phenomena, this disgust, can never entirely succeed, for its negation, like all negation which is supposed to restitute the economy of the Logos, is forced to repeat – once again – the formal and abstract extrusion of the nauseous. There is eructation at work even in the absolution of the absolute itself. There remains a relationship to what has been expelled, to that repetition of itself which is already no longer or is not yet entirely true, in which therefore spirit can see itself only as deformed, rather than knowing and recognizing its own truth. A relationship from which it cannot withdraw, precisely because it is constituted in and through it.

> *From the perspective of nausea, then, what can it mean to read Hegel? For the act of reading, which was supposed to be an eating, an incorporation, an assimilation of the text identical with the way in which Absolute Knowing ravins up its natural and historical forms into an absolute*

synthesis and compression, has shown itself to be a self-mis-understanding of the theoretical and practical relationship to the text. A reader who still seeks to appropriate the text on the premise that it can substantially be distinguished from the reader's own thought, that even an organic system would relate as something inorganic to the concept effectively at work within itself, such a reader has failed to understand that this concept is already realized in itself within the text, that the concept has already read the text in its entirety. The belief that we could experience something substantially new through the reading is, according to Hegel's formulation in the Introduction to the lectures on the philosophy of religion, 'just as absurd, as if we attempted to endow a dog with spirit by encouraging it to chew on printed matter' (16: TWA, Phil. Rel., 13). Thus it is the act of reading, this sucking and consuming operation itself, which inevitably arouses nauseous disgust in a reading on the way to the absolute, and which must be brought up. Reading is, like eating, a dangerous excess. The digestive process of reading and the mechanical operations of the understanding that belong to it are indigestible for the organism of reason and the immediate self-perception of the reader.

Just as eating would prove inedible, so reading itself would be illegible.

What is illegible, and defined as illegible, has already been read and inwardly re-collected within the order of the Logos; what is read – the reading as a process of appropriation integrated into the Logos through mediation, proves superfluous, indigestible, unreadable.

It is only on the basis of the pure legibility of the self that the legibility and illegibility of reading can be decided. Naturally, this criterion cannot be discovered by returning to a quite unmediated form of self-perception; for although, as in the case of the fieldfares, this would certainly establish the power of the subject over the external

*world and thus a relation of appropriation without risk,
it would merely be accomplished non-reflexively, and not
explicitly as such a relation, something which would
result in the loss of reflection-into-self, the criterion of
subjectivity. It is only through the* mediated *act of closure
therefore that a criterion of legibility or illegibility can
possibly be discovered; and consequently there is no pure
criterion to be discovered. For if the nauseous disgust has
directed itself against the mediated process of appropriation and extruded the mechanical-reproductive reading
from the logical organism of self-relation, then this reading, this excrement, stands over against it as something
nauseous, as an abstract Other in which the* Logos *fails
to recognize itself. This blind stain upon self-relation in
otherness forcibly inflicts a delay, a distortion, on the self-
reflection of the* Logos, *something which does not indeed
destroy it altogether, but disfigures it enough to disparage
all further unconditional talk of the conclusive closure of
subjectivity here. Even there where the organic* Logos
*turns away from nausea and grasps itself as such, it is
'conceptually caught up in the imminent threat of loss'. In
truth it does not lose itself –* true *loss would already be
made good through the truth of the* Logos *– but the
process of nausea, like the mediated process of appropriation which it rejects, is caught up in imminent threat of
losing itself to something heterogeneous, something which
promises no gain, something in which the absolute
inevitably escapes its own grasp. The* Logos *loses itself –
almost.*

*This scarcely accomplished feat of self-relation is all the
more disturbing because the object to be repulsed, to which
it owes its existence, transfers its abstract otherness to the
organic concretion of the* Logos *through a kind of repulsive infection. If one wished to see reflection-into-self, the
for-itself of digestion in itself, as the only reading which is
devoid of dangerous excess, of a circuitous or misleading*

detour, which presents instead the dialectical return of sense and signification to itself, then one would nevertheless have to concede that such sense and signification are possible only by means of precisely this detour, and thus necessarily remain infected with the abstract otherness of the nauseous. If there arises no homogeneous continuum of reflection between what is understood in itself and its actualization as what is understood for itself in a reading which reads itself and its history in the Other, then neither is that reading already entirely submerged in an infinite lack of reflection-into-self, in a sheer absence of being-for-self. If it were, nothing would prove easier for it than to erect, within the non-reflexive and unmediatable abyss of the formal process, the insignia of a universal mediation which is thus only apparently suppressed in its irreducible alterity; nothing easier than to erect, in the absence of every concrete relation, whether it be historical, semantic or affective, the figure of a presence which is all the more powerful and none the less aporetic. Yet the process of reading – if we can still speak unconditionally of a process here – bears the mark of that, albeit transitory, non-reflexivity; and the transition from the in-itself of the structure of signification, abstractly always already read, to the for-itself of the comprehending and self-organizing reading, this transition finds itself disfigured in this process through that, albeit momentary, immediacy of abstract otherness. The unfulfilled period of time and sense, which seems only – and necessarily seems – to close conclusively upon itself in the transformation of the in-itself into the for-itself, this period of time and sense affects that contented self-relation in the other, introduces a difference into the self-presencing movement of the for-itself, thus also into the presence of the in-itself which is first produced by this movement, and consequently into the schema of being in and for itself – a difference which, since its exemplification is neither substantial nor subjective, does not indeed persist, yet can be

*read in every figure of synthesis to which it contracts, read
as its own disfigurement.*

*Such a speculative-dialectical reading of a sense alienated
from itself in external signs, a reading which has 'itself'
inadvertently provided its own signature, is anything but a
hermeneutic parousia of the text or the effective history
mediated through it, a parousia produced by the comprehending subject's immersing itself in an interconnected
context which should, like a mirror, reflect back, in the
mode of re-presentation, the subject's own subjectivity, as
the refulgent configuration of the latter homogeneous with
itself in this its medium; but nor does such a reading
exemplify the process of a phenomenological negativity
which, through an unending correction of the self-understanding of the reading subject, might successfully measure
up, if only ever approximately, to the text and its own history that is sedimented there; both of these — the
re-presencing reading modelled on a hermeneutic of self-
consciousness oriented to speculative effective history, and
the negativity in the act of reading that is grounded in a
'reception-theoretical' manner — are governed, either consciously or covertly, by the* a priori *of a* single *movement: a
reproduction of sense which homogenizes subject and
object with one another, a process of disjunction which
removes what still clings externally and distortingly to
sense, an act of consolidation for what was supposed to
have preserved itself from the process of disfigurement, to
have maintained itself and thus to have demonstrated its
truth, for the historically invariant figure of a subjectivity
appropriating its own history for itself. The alterity which
was formerly restrained, the untrue mediation which was
formerly devalued in the process of its exclusion, forces its
way back into every such reproduction of somontological
self-relation from behind, and affects the dialectical self-
relation when it relates itself to an otherness that exceeds
its truth.*

Reading cannot come to a conclusive close. No text is exhaustively read, or is one with itself in its interpretation; no readers, even if they relate to themselves as to a case of inscription, can attain a self-presenting presence of any kind whatsoever in and through their own text. There is no lego, ergo sum *through which Being or a meaning of Being could be grounded in a reading conceived on the model of an act of consciousness; there is no* lego me legere *which could serve as a reflexive-hermeneutic basis for a self-securing subjectivity. The self-relation involved in the reading of the other, and in the reading of reading – and there is no hermeneutic which does not implicitly claim to read itself reading – is fractured, because reading, in order to become an understanding and moreover a grasping of sense (namely its own), must separate itself from itself as a purely external, formal and abstract process of mediation that is 'in itself' superfluous, although the comprehending and comprehended reading itself cannot dispense with this necessary superfluity of the formal for-itself. Thus the unity towardss which it advances can only be an impure unity, the satisfaction it enjoys in the concrete for-itself of the in-itself can only be a defective satisfaction; it fails to grasp (itself), though only just.*

It proves impossible to separate the legibility from the illegibility (of reading). Reading moves within the awkward space of interference between speculative dialectic and nausea. It is never entirely one with itself, always plays, and gets played, in two different registers.

As reading, this immanent doubling thoroughly permeates its subject and object alike, permeates the self-relation of the Logos, *whose concept seeks conclusively to close itself up with its natural form in the articulated structure of the gastric system. The schema of orality, which guarantees the synthetic power of the* Logos, *the schema of analogy between spirit and nature, necessary as it is not merely for the elucidation but for the self-reproduction of the concept,*

is disfigured. If the schema of orality, the self-analogy of the
Logos *in the speculative mouth, must suffer distortion for*
necessary internal and structural reasons, then the
metaphor of eating which serves for reading, the specific
rhetorical character which is determinative for reading
itself, also finds itself subjected to this process of implicit
corruption. The metaphoric trope, that of the one which
relates itself to itself in the other, in which the relata and
their relation were supposed to be united; the systematic
economy involved in the circuit of the voice, the circula-
tion of sense; the figure of a reading through which its for-
mal operation was supposed to be substantialized, firmly
secured within the framework of speculative self-relation:
all of this now finds itself subverted by another trope,
another economy, another figure, in fact fails to find itself
once more. The economy of self-relation is interrupted by a
surplus generated by its own process of concretion, and the
metaphorical transition is immanently interrupted by the
false trails of an irreducibly external allegory – reading is
an alloy fabricated out of dialectic and allegory. Every
philologico-philosophical oper-ation – every philology and
every philosophy – finds itself bound, as an instance of
philia, to the concept of hospitality and shelter, implicitly
subjected to a quite specific economy; must open itself, a
limine, *as here, where it seeks to grasp its meaning, its self,*
to a tropography of reading, of the Logos, *of Being, of the*
subject, one which traces an economy, an an-economy, of
loss.

'There are portraits, as it has been well put, which display a nauseating resemblance to their sitters' (13: TWA, *Ästhetik*, I, 67).

'Jacobi's opinion concerning knowledge in general actually comes
true here: the capricious old Nuremberg game is played out over and
over again, until all its moves, all its possible twists and turns become
nauseatingly familiar to us' (2: TWA, 253).

[N]o idea of rational cognition ever emerges here except that which
is repeated *ad nauseam*' (2: TWA, 219).

This is a nauseating because mechanical repetition, an unproductive reproduction, simultaneously all too similar to the original. But the degradation of philosophical seriousness to a platitude in which thought is simultaneously repeated and reduced to a play on words without meaning or reason is equally nauseating (2: TWA, 176). In his review concerning 'An Outbreak of Popular Enthusiasm upon the final Demise of Philosophy' Hegel pours his scorn upon one 'Reverend Professor Salad': 'How the vigorous Bavarian mentality must be nauseated by these asthenic salads and sententious sermonizings through which a crusading Berlin Enlightenment of the shallowest kind is to be advertised and introduced into Bavaria as an example of moral and humane Illumination.' And Hegel regales Krug, who had challenged speculative philosophy to deduce his pen, with the equally gastronomic allegory of a nauseating 'brew': 'One merely has to imagine a jug [*einen Krug*]' – one with no handles to grasp – 'in which Rheinholdian water, stale Kantian beer, that Enlightenment syrup so popular in Berlin, and various similar ingredients, are all thrown together by sheer chance like so many "facts of consciousness"; the said Krug-Jug is the great Synthetic container of these latter, i.e. = Ego' (ibid., 202 ff.). Here 'everything gets mixed up with everything else, like mouse droppings and coriander' (ibid., 201).

> Nausea turns against the depraved production of sense which arises through the repetition of the latter. Nausea does not function here as a psychological term for some affect which could unconditionally be reduced to specific aspects of Hegel's own life-history, which could thereby be distinguished from the intellectual sphere. If the organic process and its psychical correlates in the 'soul-like nodes' are not merely endowed with empirical existence, if on the contrary they, and especially the gastric system, the mouth and its various expressions, perform an ontological function which systematically regulates nature and Idea, then the affect of nausea also represents more than a merely marginal moment in the metabolism of spirit, represents rather an ontological nausea, a speculative affect which arises with immanent necessity from the dialectical structure of

the self-relation of meaning. Nausea is the internally, structurally necessary effect of the interpretation of meaning as the progressive self-appropriation of its own truth, as the extrusion of anything which is incapable of assuming a concrete relation to its self. As the dangerous and purely paraspeculative repetition of the self-affecting of meaning, nausea simultaneously marks the immanent limit of that meaning.

And precisely as such repetition, as Nietzsche will point out, nausea also marks the implicit limit of the entire history of metaphysics.

It is nausea (Ekel) that is in question here. And Hegel. – The intersection between the contingent empirical name of the philosopher of speculative dialectics and the name of that movement which – amongst other things – designates the outer limits of his system, an intersection which cannot claim the sanction of philosophical necessity, nonetheless marks the trace of that externality within the system itself which the latter strives to exclude with all the means of mediation at its disposal. This intersection shatters the structure of the name itself, the name which, according to Hegel's claim in the Encyclopaedia, *embodies representation in its simplicity (10: TWA, Enc., III, §459, Remark). That unambiguous clarity, that meaning in its very unity, however mediated, which characterizes the substantive, the word, and in particular the proper name, must disintegrate under the pressure of such contingency. But what takes its place is not merely semantic ambiguity or an unlimited proliferation of meaning; insofar as the specific meaning of the name in each case – and even today 'Hegel' in Swabian dialect means a fop, simpleton, or fool, a useless thing, a dead-end, 'hegelig' means senseless and irrational, and 'Hegelkitt' means a mad-house – insofar as this name and its phonetic metonyms introduce in every case an identical meaning into each of the others, and therefore,* stricto sensu, *no one meaning exists without*

> *the other, then every possible meaning must be thrown up,*
> *if only through the nauseous movement of revulsion from*
> *the selfsame. The meaning of the name is not merely mul-*
> *tiplied, it is simultaneously de-identified and denied the*
> *capacity to renew itself synthetically once again within a*
> *comprehensible context. Every specific and determinate*
> *meaning remains itself only in the disfiguring repetition of*
> *the others. And if it is true that we think in names (ibid.,*
> *§462), then any thought which refers to Hegel and the*
> *speculative dialectic would find itself inflicted with nausea.*
> *Where Hegel writes, there also always writes the knife, the*
> *witch, the madman, the vomit and the angel. . . . How*
> *are we to read 'Hegel'?*

There is always a remainder which is not entirely absorbed in the
movement of the same, something whose superfluous or insufficient
being, whose more or less, nonetheless sickens the circle of the same
with nausea. And the circle of time likewise. The organic temporality
which is constantly restored through the excretion of the material
object and its digestion, through the movement of nausea, this too is
choked with nausea. The organism, the concept of time in its reality,
divides itself internally in two through the process of self-digestion.
'The final product of digestion is the chyle, which is the same as the
animal lymph into which the organism . . . transforms whatever offers
itself up to it or whatever it finds for itself' (9: TWA, Enc., II, §365,
Addition; 489). As something that is 'already pre-digested', this
'entirely *homogeneous* animal lymph, the mother's milk' constitutes the
appropriate nourishment for children, themselves secretions in which
the genus has actualized itself, even though it proves 'indigestible for
hardier natures' (ibid., §373, Remark). The result of the organism, the
organism itself, arouses nausea in itself whenever the latter presents
itself to the organism as its own secretion. It is the very law of the
dialectic that the circular reappropriation of the selfsame, for which the
totality of the organism and the totality of the system is designed,
remains unaccomplished. To suckle at its own breast, to eat its own
cadaver, to consume itself as its own result, this represents at once the

telos of the dialectical operations of the corporeal system and the unsurpassable limit of that system. The totality becomes the parasitical eczema of itself in its immanent process of doubling. The circle of time can only conclusively be closed in the organism, can only be transformed into time itself, into its concept, where it overcomes the nausea at its own past, extruded from itself, which now approaches it as the future. Like the organism, time too must accomplish what it cannot accomplish: to digest once again what has already been digested, in order to have digested itself utterly and to have enlivened everything other, everything dead and done with, into utter presence.

> *What is in question here is no longer the formal relation to otherness. As far as the latter is concerned Novalis, less delicately than Hegel, had already asked himself: 'Could we not say that the means of nourishment themselves also eat* the one who eats them?' (72: III, 99). *And further: 'Could someone maintain themselves if they were to eat their own excrement?' (ibid., 270).*
>
> *What is in question is a superfluity that is not merely indigestible, the milk in which the body finds its own substance repeated, which nonetheless transforms itself into a secretion for the body almost like all the others. Another version of the* Logos *as milk, that process of sucking in, of coming up again, of redigesting, of the perceiving, writing and reading of the divine word – and this too is in question when Hegel speaks of the body – is provided by St Augustine in his* Enarrationes in Psalmos. *Augustine's reading of Psalm 144.9 is a hymn to the Eucharist, reads itself as a Mass which celebrates the parousia of the Godhead:* 'Memoriam abundantiae suavitatis tuae eructabunt. O epulas felices! Quid manducabant qui sic eructabunt? *Memoriam abundantiae suavitatis tuae. . . . Haec memoria eius (Dei) super nos, quia non nos oblitus est, praedicanda est, enarranda est; et quia valde dulcis est, manducanda et eructanda est. Sic manduca, ut eructes; sic accipe, ut des. Manducas, cum discis; eructas, cum doces; manducas, cum audis; eructas, cum praedicas: hoc tamen*

> *eructas quod manducasti. Denique ille audissimus epula-*
> *tor Iohannes apostolus, cui non sufficiebat ipsa mensa*
> *Domini, nisi discumberet super pectus Domini, et de*
> *arcano eius biberet divina secreta, quid eructavit?* In prin-
> cipio erat Verbum, et Verbum erat apud deum.
> Memoriam *ergo* abundantiae suavitatis tuae eructa-
> bunt.' *(31:* Corpus Christianorum*: series Latina, XL*
> *[Turnhout: 1956], 2094)*

The repetition of digestion which is what the self is, this remanduca-
tion, creates difficulties for Hegel, the philosopher of absolute self-
appropriation, of the repetition of the self in its other.

> *'Si Sacerdos evomat eucharistiam, si species integrae*
> *appareant, reverenter sumantur, nisi nausea fiat: tunc*
> *enim species consecratae caute separentur, et in aliquo loco*
> *sacro reponantur, donec corrumpantur, et postea in sacrar-*
> *ium projiciantur. Quod si species non appareant, combu-*
> *ratur vomitus, et cineres in sacrarium mittantur.' (64:*
> Missale Romanum *[Ratisbon: 1953], 'De defectibus in*
> *celebratione Missarum occurrentibus', 43)*

If the mediating system of digestion already constitutes a 'superfluity' for a body into whose organism everything in itself has already
been transformed, so too the fourfold stomach which the food must
traverse in ruminants, in fourfold fashion. Hegel's consternation here
can be read off from an unanswered question he penned in the margin
of the *Jenaer Realphilosophie*: 'a double stomach – do ruminant animals
possess a pancreas?' (24: *JR*, 150). But whoever eats, whoever reads,
also ruminates, manducates in one manner or another. For such an
eater, such a reader, the doubling of digestion in itself and digestion for
itself, of preliminary understanding and understanding proper, of text
and reading, does not simply close, conclusively, to form a synthesizing
trias and a dialectical-hermeneutic circle. With the nauseous movement in which reading turns against its 'own' operation the triadic-
circular figure opens out into a fourfold one.

> *This is not then the last of four chapters, but rather – as*
> *with an animal: a llama, a goat or a cow – the last of four*
> *stomachs.*

Or the last of four passages, four courses. Like the courses
of a meal, the fecula, and the recourses of a method.
The canals, the tracts, through which Hegel's food must
pass; the pathways and movements which permeate that
food; the enzymes, the etyma, which dissolve it; the seg-
ments, the secretions, which once mandicated, ruminated,
offer themselves up to other things as a meal. . . .

If absolute knowing reads itself this way, as it must, and – as the
Preface to the *Phenomenology* decrees – repeatedly must, then it is
always already its own pre-digested secretion, this utterly homogeneous
milk of spirit which is simultaneously heterogeneous; and with this
milk the trias of the absolute must spit out itself, transform itself into
abstract externality in the form of inscription, that amalgam of digestion and digestibles extruded in the process of nausea. Spirit can only
recognize something repellent, rather than itself, in this inscription of
the absolute, already read as it is, in this fourfold into which the trias
has externalized itself. Spirit can indeed restore its dialectical unity and
relate to itself all the more intensively through this repulsion. But what
remains for spirit itself is only its purely formal doubling in a shape
which has been sloughed off. Thus the absolute does return to itself,
though not without distortion or delay, but something else also returns
to this abstract otherness, to the absolute in its paralysed form as
inscription, something other which the absolute is not, but can only
imitate. Another reader, another reading, which is the spectral double
of the absolute reading, one which has perhaps failed to read the text of
the absolute 'itself' properly; a reading which is not its reading, which
can perhaps hardly be cognized or recognized. A reading that arrives
from a future that remains its past, and one that nonetheless fails conclusively to close the circle of absolute presence with the absolute or
with its 'self'.

Nietzsche's reading, for example.

Hegel – once again – reads. But Nietzsche also reads Hegel.

When Hegel, at the close of the first part of his history of philosophy, writes – and we are now familiar with the connections between
proximity and alimentation, with the allegories of the table of the Lord

and the crumbs thereof, with the priest in his secluded sanctuary, with the peculiar and intimate interrelation of the reading, writing and transcribing of the original text:

> *'The philosophers are . . . closer to the Lord than those who feed upon the crumbs of the spirit; they read or write his decrees in their original form and are obliged to transcribe them first-hand. The philosophers are the* μύσται, *who have been heaved into the inmost sanctuary and involved in all the proceedings; whereas other people have their own special interests: this dominion here, this wealth there, or this particular girl.' (20: TWA,* Hist. Philosophy, *489)*

– then Nietzsche, calling Hegel a superstitious venerator of the actual, a priest of mythological ideas, and inviting him to consider his wounded knee, continues with the appropriate respect and the appropriate mirth as follows:

> *'Hegel has already taught us once that "whenever the spirit has heaved forwards, then we philosophers are involved as well": our time has also heaved forward, towards an ironical attitude about itself.' (66: Werke, I, 263, 267)*

and asks the question whether the apocalyptic view of the 'world-process' which presents history as something concluded and the future simply 'as the musical coda of a world-historical rondo, or indeed as something properly superfluous' (ibid., 263), whether such a view is not the phantasmagoria of one who 'insists on suffering as intensely as possible from the indigestibility of life' and yearns to harvest the 'nausea at everything in being', the precious grapes from the vineyards of the Lord (ibid., 268 ff.). For Nietzsche nausea, along with Hegel and his epigones, stands at the end of this conception of history. The history of metaphysics, as it culminates in Hegel's philosophy, is a history of nausea over finitude; and nausea is the symptom of decadence *par excellence*. Nietzsche, himself a decadent and familiar with nausea, himself a 'spectral double' rather than a *single* person, never reacts to the latter without ambiguity (*'Apart from the fact that I am a* décadent, *I am also the very opposite.'* And: *'To express the matter enigmatically, as my father I have already died, and as my mother I still live and grow old.'* [66: *Werke*, II, 1072/1070]). For Nietzsche, on the one hand, it is true that amongst all the Germans Hegel perhaps possesses the most *esprit*, and the further virtue of concealing this happy advantage as shamefully as a young woman – Hegel, the 'old man', a young woman! – beneath the veils of his convoluted style (ibid., I, 1141); but on the other hand, Hegel proves a disgusting taste, the taste of an ontology oriented to infinitude and meaning (ibid., II, 924); on the one hand, nausea represents 'that dangerous *dyspepsia*' of the *décadent* who is disgusted by his own history, his superficiality, his nothingness – that 'after-table nausea' which threatens to destroy precisely the self-executioner, the analyst of ontological ideologies (ibid., II, 748); but on the other hand, it is nausea itself which redeems him from nausea. The decadent, the Platonic dialectician, the castrated Christian, and even the 'free spirit' – Hegel has nothing to say against himself, for whatever charge he brings against himself is determined by nausea against his finitude, his meaninglessness, his false appearance, and ergo represents nothing but a consequence, a contra-sequence: the repetition of the nausea which already grounds his principles, those of being, subject, truth. Yet it is precisely this nothing, this hardly anything, which the dialectician has to say; precisely this repetition of his own that role turns him into a player, a tragical parodist of himself – turns ontology into its nameless counterplay, negation into the affirmation of negation, turns Nietzsche the decadent, whose gastric system has given way to mucous retching (ibid., 1070), into the author of *Zarathustra*, and Hegel into Nietzsche. The dialectical ontology is always already caught up in the concept, caught up in loss: always already about to be repeated parodistically by 'itself'. Always already and yet still to be – ever again –

Incipit Zarathustra.

But if nausea – even the most sublimated nausea – is always still in play, if repetition – even as the law of repetition – displaces all identities, then who is reading here? And who is reading whom? Is it 'Hegel' reading Hegel, or Hegel reading 'Hegel'; does Hegel read Nietzsche, or 'Nietzsche' read Nietzsche, or Hegel, or Zarathustra – or is it 'Zarathustra' who reads 'Nietzsche' reading 'Hegel'? Or is it 'I' – or I – who, already read by them, reads them both together? But this question concerning the subject of the reading stands in question itself, posed as it is from the perspective of the *Logos*, for which all undecidabilities and delusive appearances prove repellent – from the perspective of nausea.

> *The hammer reads.*

> '*. . . To pose questions here for once with the hammer and, perhaps, to hear in answer that celebrated hollow tone which speaks of swollen entrails – what a delight for one who even has ears behind his ears.*' *(66:* Werke, *II, 941)*

In the Preface to the *Genealogy of Morals* – which indeed presents itself as the 'interpretation' of an aphorism from Zarathustra – Nietzsche formulates a challenge to 'Reading as *Art*'; that is, he formulates an image of an artistic reading that is more than purely philological or purely philosophical, an image that itself requires reference to *Zarathustra* in turn for its interpretation. Nietzsche writes:

> '*Of course, in order to practise reading as* art *in this way, one thing above all is needful, something which we have utterly forgotten how to do, especially these days – and that is why the 'readability' of my writings will have to wait a long time yet – for that one will almost have to be a cow, and certainly* not *a 'modern man': rumination.*' *(66:* Werke, *II, 770)*

But the cow is not a cow and rumination not yet rumination. In the fourth and final part of *Zarathustra* – nausea and rumination hover between the third and the fourth part – Zarathustra encounters one of those 'higher human beings', the deliberate beggar, a preacher on the mount who preaches not of angels and children, but of cows. But if his sermon to the cows, the only creatures which know no nausea, repeats the sermon of that other preacher on the mount –

> '*Unless we turn again, like the cows, we shall not enter the Kingdom of Heaven. For one thing indeed we should learn of them: how to ruminate, to chew over the cud.*
> *And verily, even if a man should gain the whole world yet fail to learn this one thing, this rumination, then what should it profit him! He would never feel free of tribulation.*
> *– his great tribulation: which today is called nausea.*' *(66:* Werke, *II, 506)*

and if he includes Zarathustra in his gospel:

> *'This is the man without nausea, this is Zarathustra him-*
> *self, the overcomer of mighty nausea.' (ibid., 507)*
> *'You yourself are good, and better even than a cow, O*
> *Zarathustra!' (ibid., 509)*

then it is still nausea that repulses him from nausea and that vouchsafes to him, the higher human being who is not yet the overman, the idea of rumination, the idea of a reading which is not nauseated by the finitude, the delusory appearance, the tardiness of writing. Zarathustra, who also suffers himself like those higher human beings from a 'mighty nausea' (ibid., 532), expresses this dialectic of nausea; against those who posit a world beyond this world, he objects:

> *'There is wisdom in the thought that there is much in this*
> *world which smells foul: nausea itself creates pinions and*
> *powers suggestive of new springs! Even in what is best*
> *something provokes nausea; and the best is still something*
> *which must be overcome!' (66: Werke, II, 451)*

But Zarathustra, who would advance beyond this nausea at nausea, is not merely cow and more than cow; he is also the animal, the little snake, that sucks in its nausea over itself, this 'remnant of God' that is conscience – a blood-sucking leech, the 'mighty leech of conscience'.

> *Nor does Hegel lack his leech.*
>
> Hegel – brutalized – is a leech.

>> To read 'Hegel' so that the H, with which he some-
>> times signed himself, is drawn off, drawn into the
>> German '*Egel*', the leech.

>> To write an *Egel*/Leech which fastens its bite on
>> Hegel, and even to imitate the peristaltic contrac-
>> tions of its sphincteral tract.

>> Or to write a Hegel, a blood-sucking leech that even
>> sucks up into itself the nausea which it repels and
>> provokes.

> *And indeed Hegel strives – in a passage to which Nietzsche*
> *alludes in the* Gay Science *(66: Werke, II, 226) and on*
> *account of which he proclaims Hegel as the necessary fore-*
> *runner of Darwin – in his discussion of the species, to pro-*

vide in two detailed pages a decisive answer to the question: to which of the two principal groups into which zoologists divide the animal realm does the leech actually belong? To animals with blood (ἔναιμα) or to those without blood (ἄναιμα)? (9: TWA, Enc., II, §368, Addition; 508 ff.) The classification of the leech proves so difficult because the 'impotence of nature' is incapable of presenting the logical forms in their purity and succeeds in realizing only the 'traces of the conceptual determination'. Consequently, the lines of transition between the individual genera and species are fluid ones, representing monstrosities and hybrids, and prove to be 'something repellent', like the amphibian creatures which belong partly on the earth and partly in the water. But this classification is precisely so important because, along with the impotence of nature, the power and potency of the concept itself are also found in question. For 'that impotence of nature sets limits to philosophy' (ibid., §250, Remark). Philosophy itself proves incapable of doing more than merely revealing the traces of the concept within the unconscious body of nature.

The leech sets limits on Hegel's philosophy.

Thus Zarathustra, the leech, sucks up the nausea into himself. He sucks it up into himself in order to liberate the others, to whom he himself also still belongs, from himself and from themselves. The leech still remains, nauseating creature as it is, an animal for repelling nausea—

But ruminating signifies – if it still signifies at all – not merely the spitting-out of what is nauseous, but also its repeated eating. Reading signifies – if it still signifies at all – not merely transubstantiating the meaning of what is written into oneself, not merely spitting out again the externality and meaninglessness of the inscripted sign and its transformation in order to preserve the purity of the self from the dangerously nauseous operation of another reading; it also signifies, before its repetition, before the nauseous, avoiding nausea at nausea itself. Even the nausea which leads beyond nausea, repels and repeats the latter, must be affirmed. Even the repetition, even the return, which as the 'return even of the smallest thing' is what provokes the greatest nausea, the 'mighty nausea' (66: *Werke*, II, 465), must be taken up again, must be ruminated once again.

When Zarathustra proclaims his 'abyssal thought', the thought of the Eternal Return of the Same, of the smallest thing, he faints and loses consciousness with a threefold cry of 'nausea, nausea, nausea'. Only after another seven days, upon the Sunday as it were of this advocate of return, does he recover consciousness; he then falls silent and, as a convalescent, allows his creatures with their mechanically repetitive movements, the circling eagle and the self-coiling snake, to speak instead, allows his most abyssal experience to be falsified as a 'Lyre-Song' that has been played continuously ever since by his philosophical interpreters. Zarathustra allows this to happen and endures his creatures without disgust. Inasmuch as this experience could barely penetrate beyond the threshold of consciousness, inasmuch as the eternal return already find itself miscarried in its repetition, then the convalescent is equally incapable of clearly presenting this idea to himself or to others in the language of truth – for words are merely deluding bridges over the abyss of this 'abyssal thought'. What he says –

> '– and how that monstrous creature crawled down into my gullet and began to choke me! But I bit its head off and spat it out of me.' (66: Werke, II, 463)

– does not refer to what he has experienced before or during his loss of consciousness, or to this simply as a repetition of the riddle he had formerly posed to his companions at sea. In this 'sight and riddle' – *riddle of reading* – in which dream and idea, memory of remotest childhood and anticipation of the future are all coiled up together, it is a shepherd who finds that a monstrous creature has crawled into his gullet, and the monstrous creature is a snake, the animal of Zarathustra, the sign and symbol of the eternal return of the same.

> *'Have I ever beheld so much nauseous disgust and pale terror in a* single *countenance? Had he fallen asleep? For the snake had crawled into his gullet there – there fastened its bite upon him.*

. . . .

'Off with its head! Go to and bite!' – thus it shrieked from
me, my terror, my hatred, my nauseous disgust, my com-
passion, all that is good and evil within myself cried out
with a single shriek—

. . . .

But the shepherd bit, as my shriek had counselled him; bit
with a ferocious bite! Far away he spat out the head of the
snake – and leapt up.' (66: Werke, *II, 410)*

But the riddle is a double one, and so devised that each of its two
parts illuminates the other in turn. For in the first part Zarathustra presents his dwarf, in order to free himself from the latter, with the doctrine of eternal return in the form of a parable: that two paths lead
away from the gateway at which both of them pause, each of which
vouchsafes eternity, past and future, that everything which has already
once travelled the one path has also travelled the other, that every
future has already transpired, every past shall be repeated once again,
and the present moment, taking itself in tow, shall return eternally.

'They contradict one another, these two paths; they come
into collision with one another, head on – and it is here,
at this gateway, that they converge. The name of the gate-
way is inscribed above it: "the moment".' (66: Werke, *II,*
408)

Up to this point the riddle with which Zarathustra presents the
dwarf appears to be neither more nor less than the utter repetition of
the ontological concept of time, as it was first comprehensively formulated by Aristotle and finally developed by Hegel into the system of
speculative dialectics. And indeed the dwarf murmurs contemptuously:
'Time itself is a circle.' But the gateway of temporality, at which the
two paths of past and future, the future that is past and the past that is
to come, converge with one another in the present moment as the *ama*,
and at which – since the 'moment' is paralysed in the inscription of its
name and in the spatial figure of the gateway – both paths have always
already converged with one another and always will have done, so that
every now is an again and every here is a there – at this gateway of the
inscription of the moment the past and the future do not converge
merely, but also contradict one another and 'come into collision', head

on. The moment is the head of the snake of eternal return, and there where its colossal kephallography, crawling through all times, coils and closes with itself, it collides with itself, head on, and thus repulses its head. Inscription itself, inscription of the moment which always repeats itself, crawls into its own gullet, bites itself, and bites its own head off: the moment, the present. This is where the apparent repetition of the dialectic-ontological doctrine separates itself from the cyclical structure of time which is oriented towards the *parousia* of its pure selfhood in an absolute presence, for the return of the same disidentifies itself at the very place – at every conceivable place – where it contracts itself into the utterly fulfilled now-point. If ontological time is phallic and kephallic, the time of return, which transposes and repeats the former, is at once, in its *ama*, akephallic, is a woman. The return of the same facilitates and decapitates the repetition of the same.

The time of a reading. The reading of time. The snake of the eternal return of the same bites its own head off, the creature that provokes the greatest nauseous disgust crawls into its own gullet, nauseates itself, bites and spits its head out. But its bite is always already too early and too late to grasp itself. Before the bite of the moment, before the reading of this name, it must already have bitten infinitely often, and when it does bite, what it finds between its teeth is not its authentic aboriginal self, not the substrate of time, but merely something Other, the devalued repetition of its self. The repetition cuts through the circle of time. But the incision into repetition repeats the return, the opening closes up. The decapitation erects the head of eternity and the moment; the castration, absolute apotrope, repeats the position of the nauseous creature. But moment and eternity, the return and the bite ('Whither now has gone the dwarf? The gateway? The spider?' [66: *Werke*, II, 409]) are not identical with themselves; they are, within a context of riddles and parables, at once distorted – it is not the snake which bites the head off, but the shepherd, not the shepherd, but Zarathustra, not Zarathustra, but his riddling figure. Nor is the bite identical with itself, it does not bites itself but bites a bite which is always already past or is still to come, and does so *as* a past and future bite. It ruminates 'itself' – the nausea 'its self' and the repulsion of nausea 'itself' – always already and always once again.

reading – to chew the cue, the cut . . .

Reading, if it is reading the inscription of the moment as in Zarathustra's riddle, repulses inscription, as the *caput mortuum* of the present. The snake of inscription nauseates the reader upon whose gullet it fastens its bite; the very reader bites and spits out the snake. Yet what the reader bites and what bites the reader is always already bitten and always still remains to be bitten, and consequently the reader bites, like the head of the snake, the incision which separates the snake from the reader and the snake from its head.

. . . argument of the gorge . . .

What gets spat out has already been and always will have been regurgitated in the reader's mouth. The reader is a cow that ruminates what it has brought up: as something other than it is. Which means that, as ruminating, reading is indeed the condition of the reproduction of authentic signification, but simultaneously also the condition of its impossibility. If the signification, the presence of an inscription is not simply reproduced in returning, in ruminating, then the operation of the bite is not identically repeated in the process either. Reading names a generative separation which never conclusively coincides with itself in fulfilled co-presence at any site of self-encounter. A separation which always produces a surplus, inaugurates a difference, leaves open a remnant, another reading: thus Nietzsche – or Zarathustra – who performs reading as a *cow*, as an *art*, reads himself – or Hegel – reading nausea.

Yet the allegory of a reading, presented by Zarathustra in the riddle of the eternal return of the same, is no more true than it is an allegory of truth. The doctrine of the return – the doctrine of an *a-priori* iterative reading – must, once it is read – read by its 'self' – forfeit its head. And when Zarathustra's disciples perceive that this is no binding truth which, with a nauseous disgust, would exclude all others, perceive that even a truth that holds cannot be held on to, they can begin to celebrate not indeed a dialectical but a mulish mass in which the mule [*Esel*] bleats its everlasting E–A.

> 'Nausea *then retreats before these higher human beings. . . . They pour out their hearts, happy hours return to them once more, they celebrate and ruminate once again – they become* thankful.' *(66: Werke, II, 546)*

These 'higher human beings' learn the speaking with which 'mankind (dances) over all things' (66: *Werke*, II, 463) – and dance with this their mass even over the return of the same. Whatever has been said concerning this return – whether it be that of Zarathustra or that of his creatures or of here and now – cannot contain their truth. The return of the same in language – and Zarathustra's animals, his interpreters, sing of the latter as the 'House of Being' (ibid.) – obeys an economy identical only in appearance with that of the circular reappropriation of the concept. Wherever this return coils and closes itself up in language, there it also bites; wherever it shows itself, there it withdraws, and even withdraws from its withdrawal. Wherever it gives without reserve, there it has already taken and persisted in its silence: Thus spake Zarathustra. As his language in everything gives too little, in everything gives too much, always mistakes the boundary of his own property, though but slightly, then this language must, Zarathustra must, and he too simply in the expectation of a sign, not merely take and ruminate like a cow, but also be an udder and give: 'That I might one day be ripe and ready on that great midday . . . like . . . an udder swelling with milk' (ibid., 460, 468). Zarathustra, the manliest one of all, is – for as the contradiction between past and future, reader and read is sublated, so too that between the sexes – at once a woman who walks heavy with the future; yet is not woman enough to yearn for this future that he bears, to yearn for it as his woman: a wife whose 'truth' always withdraws beneath a net of deception and shame; udders which have always already (not yet) suckled; milk which never escapes the danger of turning sour. Zarathustra's language.

> 'Language speaks as the uttering of silence.' *Zarathustra also reads Heidegger – just as Heidegger reads Trakl:*
> *(Pain has petrified the threshold.*
> *There gleams in purest clarity*
> *Upon the table bread and wine.)*
> *'Language speaks as the uttering of silence' – a silent uddering – the Christian communion feast, the last supper, at the breast of mother language once again. 'In sounding, whether it be speech or writing, the silent quiet is broken.' (41:* Unterwegs zur Sprache *[Pfüllingen: Neske (1959) 1971], 30 ff.)*

The language in which Zarathustra displays and distorts himself and his teaching would therefore be a woman who seeks to seduce herself as another woman – or as something other than a woman. Insofar as this language, in accordance with the doctrine of eternal return, represents a deconstructive, and that also means a parodistic, repetition of every other philosophy, then it equally reads every other philosophy and the totality of philosophy, which is presented in Hegel's speculative dialectic as absolute truth, as a woman. Absolute 'truth a woman' (66: *Werke*, II, 565). But a woman who, as Nietzsche says about Hegel (ibid., I, 1140), veils herself out of anxiety and shame, a 'rattlesnake' who disguises herself as a man. A man is not one who presents himself as the opposite of woman, but one who wears his manliness, like a woman, as a mask. One gender is 'itself' only insofar as it actualizes the sexual difference within itself, the play of transformation which no longer possesses a central signification. Now if it is the case in Nietzsche's theoretical practice, designed as it is to de-essentialize the ontological hypostasis of presence and its dichotomous forms of past and future, of masculinity and femininity, and thus to deconstruct logocentrism and phallocentrism, that the strategic priority of feminity is readily understandable, it nonetheless still remains problematic whether Hegel's dialectical philosophy, repeated and subverted by this practice as it is, does in fact privilege the phallus, problematic how the sign of the phallus can constitute as it were the veil which conceals the femininity at work within his philosophy.

The various forms of self-excretion, which together represent 'the final stage of animality' prior to the transition into spirit, are subjected to the process of 'abstract formal repulsion' and the formative and constructive instincts and culminate in the reproduction of the species (9: TWA, Enc., II, §365; Addition; 492). Even the seed, even the child, are excrementa. But in the child it is not the individual self that finds itself externalized in thingly form but the species itself, albeit as purely negative identity, which as the unity of the different sexes, as the species in-itself, is their product. In every individual human being which is differentiated as male or female the unity of man and woman is still present. In the male the original anatomical identity of the sexes in the embryo develops into external and distinct sexual organs, whereas in the female the moment of indifference, the 'undeveloped unity', still persists. If 'in the woman the clitoris . . . is unactivated feeling in general', then in the man the penis is 'the active feeling, the swelling heart'. The analogy Hegel draws between the testicles and the 'active brain' (24: *JR*, 165), one common enough in the 'romantic' philosophers of nature ('The brain resembles the testes' [72: Novalis, III, 444]), serves to make the priority of man over woman perfectly clear: if *he* has developed into the active subjectivity of the concept, into external actuality and being-for-self, then the woman, the material element of his subjectivity in the reproductive process, remains passively enclosed within her own interiority in the dimension of substance, of mere being in itself.

The unity of man and woman, the unity of difference and unity, which is actualized in every individual being of the species, cannot therefore, as Derrida has pointed out in *Glas*, be other than asymmetrical. In this unity the masculine moment, that of difference and negativity, is dominant in every respect. But it is a consequence of this latent hierarchialization that the species is fulfilled in-itself only through the individuals and their immanent sexual relation with one another, and finally therefore that the process of the genus must issue in an unending, or 'bad', infinity (9: TWA, Enc., II, §370). The disproportion between masculine and feminine sexuality renders individuals and the species itself mortal and turns the process of the genus into one of disease. Disease – defined by Hegel as a '*disproportion between being and its own self*' (ibid., §371, Addition; 521) – signifies the following: on the one hand difference exceeds indifference, masculine sexuality exceeds feminine sexuality, while on the other the material moment of mere being, the feminine character of the individual organism, falls short of its masculine subjectivity. The individual, in whom both sexual characteristics are latently present, is the disease of the species because its femininity is the disease of the organism. Or, expressed the other way around: because femininity already realizes the unity and therefore the species, though only in-itself, as an individual being, the disease of the individual is its own species itself. Thus the organism – 'coupling and mating with itself as it were' (ibid.) – is already 'diseased by nature' (ibid., §375, Addition); 'thus every individual is itself the unity of both sexes. But this is its death' (ibid.).

Death is a woman. For, as the femininity intrinsic to every living individual, she persists as it were in the state of nature, of a purely immediate life. A life that does not emerge from out of itself; a unity that does not separate itself off from itself; an in-itself that does not become for-itself; being that is not self – she is simultaneously the negation, but the abstract, non-self-sustaining, negation of her 'self' and 'her' other, of masculinity. What is most utterly interior is the absolutely external. In this its femininity the organism enjoys its unproductive, aneconomical dialectic of life and death. Hence the distribution of that unity of unity and difference, attaining concrete form only in the species, into two different sexes must find its limit when both sexes are represented in every single individual. And the femininity economized in bisexuality also retains its fatal power and potency.

The fact that possibility and actuality, substance and subject, cannot conclusively come together in the individual organism must be ascribed to the enfolded undeveloped self-relation of femininity, which although already a unity is not yet for itself, and therefore reveals itself as a regression in comparison with the masculine sexual character. The lesser completion of the woman opens up the organism, which could only intrinsically survive as the absolute synthesis of the latter, to disease.

> *'The organism can be stimulated over and beyond the bounds of its possibility because, being equally the total unity of possibility and actuality (of substance and self), it exists totally under one form or the other.' (9: TWA, Enc., II, §371, Addition; 522)*

Insofar as the masculine actuality of the organism constitutionally represents an excess while the feminine possibility always represents a difference, insofar as possibility and actuality can never fully coincide with one another in the finite individual, then the actuality of the for-itself must exceed the possibility of the organic in-itself, femininity must remain in part an unrealizable potency, and masculinity in part an impossible actuality. Thus the organism of the logos, always already phallocentrically organized, in which sexual difference is inscribed in the form of an impossible actuality, must penetrate the disease of the inorganic, the feminine, the natural genus. For the phallogocentric organism of the self and of self-digestion – 'the process of digestion itself is the *self*' (24: *JR*, 171) – the feminine is the absolutely indigestible. And thus it is the female diseases which Hegel names in expounding the relationship between disease and sexual difference: symbolic pregnancies.

> *'It is equally true that the activity of the gall-bladder can turn virulent and produce gall-stones, for example. If the stomach is overburdened ... [t]his isolation can reach the point where other creatures are produced within the entrails ... [r]ing-worms.' (9: TWA, Enc., II, §371, Addition; 522)*

This disease of sexual difference, of the feminine withdrawal into itself – how is it to be healed? And in the first place, how can the empirical diseases be healed if the sublation of sexual difference, which is the condition of their possibility, proves to be impossible even in the realm of organic life? For Hegel, who postulates a strict connection between the brain and the process of digestion (24: *JR*, 162, 163; Remark 4), and therefore between masculine reflexivity and the self-relation of the organism, disease is defined as the dysfunction of the gastric system, which presents itself on the level of the concept as the system of the phallogocentric organism. If the feminine here assumes the position of the inorganic, indigestible for the masculine system to which it constitutionally belongs, then its contagious potency, its abstract negation, must be negated in turn, must be 'sublated, digested' (9: TWA, Enc., II, §372, Addition; 527). The feminine indifference towards the external, towards the different, must be digested because this indifference, turned in upon itself, possesses its negativity within itself and obstructs the developed closure of the organism. Disease – and each and every one is a feminine disease – is almost always diagnosed by Hegel as a kind of hypochondria:

> *'every disease (but especially every acute one) is a hypochondria of the organism, in which the latter loathes the external world which nauseates it, because, confined to*

> *itself, the organism possesses its own negative within its*
> *very self.' (9: TWA, Enc., II, §373, Addition; 532)*

Against the intrinsically indigestible – thus Hegel's recommended homeopathic therapy – the indigestible; against inorganic indifference the inorganic; against femininity the feminine: against poison poison. A 'fixed self' has particularized itself against the organism which relates itself to itself through difference, has confined the organism to dealing with this externality immanent to itself, the gall-stone, the ring-worm. Now if this indigestible particularity, which as immanent externality indeed remains feminine, though it displays phallic characteristics, is to be *posited* as something external, and extruded as such, this very externality, this phallically feminine secretion homogeneous with the diseased substance, must itself be prescribed as the remedy which will mobilize the activity of the organism against the external world.

It is of course quite true that Hegel cannot accept this concrete medication, which results from his own homeopathic considerations, without certain reservations. Nonetheless, it does result with the strictest rigour from the very dialectic of sexual difference, disease and homeopathy, and simultaneously reveals the phantasmatic characteristics harboured within this dialectic.

> *'Here our experience with chicken-droppings is as valuable*
> *as that with the various officinal plants; for in order to*
> *produce nausea-inducing medications one formerly turned*
> *to human urine, chicken-droppings, and peacock-drop-*
> *pings.' (9: TWA, Enc., II, §373, Addition; 532 ff.)*

In and of itself the diseased, the effeminated, body is incapable of mediated reflection-into-self and the nausea connected with it. The dose of its immanent externality, its false because intrinsically unconcluded masculinity, must be administered in doubled form to the female body in order to stimulate its nausea, the excretion of the alien body lodged alone within it. The diseased organism is copraphageous. The phallic kybalon of the woman (the peacock-dropping) is the medicine, nauseous and indigestible, which provokes its secretion, initiates self-digestion, re-establishes the self-closure of the organism and the relative unity of masculine and feminine sexual characteristics, of unity and difference. The gift of the phallic kybalon is a feminine gift, which

would release us from the diseased dominance of the feminine, a gift
that gives nothing and is given merely to be negated. It functions – like
all nourishment, even the mother's milk, and the process of digestion
itself – as a vomitive. The purely inorganic, the feminine, becomes
what it is, becomes an indifferent excrement; but the convalescent
emerges from the process of disease, as if from a sexual act, as a new-
born unity of man and woman, as individuated genus.

> *Thus the disease in which the organism 'couples as it were
> with itself' and the process of healing present, like the
> meal, a sexual scene.*
>
> *And the scene of the reading. – This too is a meal, in
> which the eater, if only by the mechanism of digestion,
> comes upon an indigestible moment that isolates itself over
> against the organic circulation of self-relation. The read-
> ing transforms the reader into a passive recipient, into the
> 'material element' of the subjectivity of the text, and the
> reader himself becomes a hypochondriac woman obsessed
> with herself, pregnant with something like a gall-stone or
> a ring-worm. The reader is diseased. He has isolated the
> sexless character of the infant, in which the negative iden-
> tity of the genus is actual, as an inorganic moment within
> himself, as a text indelibly inscribed within his memory, a
> text to which he cannot relate as to himself, a closed text
> whose circle he cannot conclusively close. If the suckling
> infant obtains the feeling of unity with the other, the 'feel-
> ing of the genus' (9: TWA, Enc., II, §368, Addition; 514)
> through its mother's milk, so too for the reader – also a
> suckling infant – the milk of writing, the grammamma,
> solidifies as an indigestible alien body which obstructs the
> circulation between the individual and its species.*
>
> *Whatever the shape which writing now assumes for the
> reader – the penis of differentiating understanding devel-
> oped into full subjectivity, the seed of a semontological
> process which results in the form of a child, the milk
> through which it experiences its unity with itself as species,
> the species which reproduces itself individually here in the*

child – all these synthetic shapes of its self-constitution find themselves reversed and translated into forms of disjunction, prove to be themselves secretions. The masculine text, active as subject of the reader's substance – the text of the father who penetrates the reader as his wife or child – the son is also a daughter – itself becomes an indifferent feminine substance, which is not lacking masculine features of its own, becomes the imaginary feminine phallus, which is supposed to stimulate merely the nausea of the reader and cure him of his femininity. Scene of disease, scene of a reading – a homosexual, an incestuous, a fetishistic, at any rate a 'perverted' sexual act. An act whose final conclusion, the successful reunification of both characteristic sexual genders, is never consummated, which remains an unrealizable possibility and this impossible actuality at one and the same time. An act in which the entire system of production of self and being is immanently suspended. – The text – the penis, the seed, the child, the faeces, the father; but also the mother, the breast, the milk, the child, her phallus, the faeces, and her veil as well; and the reader – the son, even more the daughter, the father, the mother, the breast at which the text draws nourishment, the penis which penetrates that text, the seed, which produces its meaning, its name, but also the faeces, which indigestibly inhere in the pure shape of the text, the corpse which resists the text, just as the corpse of the text resists the reader and can only be excluded unproductively, with neither cognition nor recognition, as an abstract duplication of the living being and its reproduction: this 'Phenomenology' of reading, a rigorous fugue *which results from Hegel's metaphor of reading and sexual relations alike as an act of eating, has remained concealed within the texts of philosophy until Nietzsche precisely because it displaces the system and the logic of self-consciousness, of its teleological history and its ethics, and only since Freud and the psychoanalytic theory of the unconscious has it first become susceptible to*

theoretical articulation. In an essay which has been gener-
ally neglected, and indeed totally ignored by the academic
hermeneutics of re-presentation, namely 'Some unconscious
factors in reading', James Strachey employed analytical
material concerning reading-habits and reading-inhibi-
tions to expose certain dominant traits involved in the
unconscious interpretation of reading. However problem-
atic the concept of symbol which serves for his interpreta-
tive schema may be, however limited his concept of sexual
difference may also be – his conclusions prove extremely
illuminating nonetheless:
'According to Freud, the book stands for a woman, and it
will now be seen that this by no means contradicts Ernest
Jones's interpretation of printed matter as faeces. For if the
book symbolizes the mother, its author must be the father;
and the printed words, the author's thoughts, fertilizing
and precious, yet defiling the virgin page, must be the
father's penis or faeces within the mother. And now comes
the reader, the son, hungry, voracious, destructive and
defiling in his turn, eager to force his way into his mother,
to find out what is inside her, to tear his father's traces out
of her, to devour them, to make them his own, and to be
fertilized by them himself.' (82: International Journal of
Psycho-analysis, *XL [London: 1930], 330 ff.)*
Speculative dialectics and psychoanalysis ground their
attempts to structure the scene of reading upon a logic of
substitution, or, more precisely, upon a mechanism of
metaphor-ization which regulates the respective transfor-
mations of the individual figures in this scene: of the
reader into 'author' who violates the maternal book, and
further into this maternal book, this belly; and just as the
act of reading counts as an impregnation by the fatherly
text, as a reception, it counts equally as a castrating act
perpetrated upon a phallic mother. . . . The circulation of
metaphors between the shapes of the familial trias,
between book, writer and reader, discovers its ground and

its limit in the fact that while each shape irrecuperably precedes every other, not one is so completely itself as to avoid wishing to be another.

In his Fragment on an Analysis of Hysteria *(35: GW, V [1905]) Sigmund Freud – the name Sig*mund *was hardly without its consequences – described a case in the aetiology of which the act of reading plays a significant role. His patient suffers principally from certain ailments of the oral system (that is why Freud calls her Do*ra*): attacks of anorexia, aphonia, dysnoea and vomiting. Analysis of the case reveals that these disturbances are based upon a fellatio-phantasy on Dora's part, but further that this fellatio-phantasy – and Dora's hysteria is motivated by her 'gunaikophile' tendencies – itself simply represents a substitute for sucking at the breast of a much-loved, but also competing, woman. It should also be added that a similar fellatio-phantasy and her own ambivalence towards the image of the phallic woman may well have been activated in virulent form through her reading. Concerning Dora's hysterical vomiting Freud remarks: 'The sensation of nausea appears indeed originally to be the reaction to the smell (and later also to the sight) of excrement. But the genitalia and especially the male member can call to mind the excremental functions, because the organ in question, quite apart from its sexual function, also serves that of urination' (35: GW, V, 189 ff.) – Hegel's 'soul-like nodes'. But the fellatio-phantasy which provokes Dora's nausea must arise precisely because 'the actual sexual object, the penis' stands in for 'the original nipple and the finger which substitutes for it'. 'Thus this utterly repellent and perverse phantasy of sucking at the penis has the most harmless of origins; it represents the elaboration of what we could call a pre-historic impression of sucking at the mother's or the nurse's breast, something which is usually reactivated through contact with breast-fed children. In most cases' – Freud remarks – 'the udder of the cow has* *served as a suitable intermediary image between nipple and penis.' (ibid., 212)*

Milking Hegel

Freud's remedy for the hysterical nausea, which conceals the wish for impregnation by the text – a tissue of secretions from the phallic mother – lies in its controlled repetition, working through it during the period of cure, while Hegel's remedy – once again – lies in the intensified repetition of nausea. But if the psychoanalytic operation is, in an extremely Nietzschean sense, a reading, a ruminating, the repetition and totalization of nausea operated by Hegel's dialectical-homeopathic therapy are supposed on the other hand to 'sublate' nausea. Indeed the entire process of the genus is nothing but a retention, negation and sublimation of nausea: for the nauseous element in the individual organism remains, in the natural form of the genus, the particularized finitude of the latter, the individual as parasite upon the totality it actualizes within itself, so that the strongest medicine, the most potent vomitive, for that natural death in itself already realized in the genus is – death. 'The animal dies. Death of the animal [is the] genesis of consciousness' (24: *JR*, 164). And it is only with this consciousness, which recognizes the death of animality as manifestation of its own power, that thought first constitutes itself as the 'element homogeneous with the genus' (10: TWA, Enc., III, §396, Addition; 76) in which the unity of the universal and the particular is truly actualized as such. But this death to which nature is subjected by its own concept, this death in which the animal perceives its own voice and awakens to conscious awareness, is not an abstract, sensuous dying, but a dying of sensibility in which the possibility of the conscious is preserved. Abstract death, like the abstract otherness of digestion and the nauseous, is extruded, and what is retained of the power of the Other is only what intensifies the power of the One. The transition from nature into spirit, the process in which nature and spirit alike each descends into itself, remains delineated by the hysterical 'feminine' gesture of nausea. Even the structure of consciousness, of reflection-into-self and syllogistic self-closure, even the function of language and its ontological self-comprehension, thus even spirit which recognizes itself as spirit, the absolute itself, can be read equally as a theoretical and a therapeutic process, as a self-expectoration in which, here confronted with themselves, the finite and therefore restricted forms of the concept extrude themselves only to re-unite conclusively with one another through this process of, so to speak, spiritualized excretion, to form a unity of finite and infinite, of relatio and relata. Even insofar as unity recognizes itself as the process of difference and transforms negativity into something positive, even in this unity of self-recognition and self-knowledge, this synthesis of substance and subject, nausea is still at work. And with it, therefore, the hostile affect directed towards what is abstract in the self and its substance, what cannot be recognized by the self as the selfsame, as its own, what inevitably remains beyond the reach of consciousness even for absolute knowing. But if this nauseous and, *strictu sensu*, unconscious element is not merely the object of spirit, that is, if nausea constitutes in part spirit's immanent relation to itself, then the process of absolute knowing is possible only by virtue of a further relation which undermines the ground of this self-relation. The repulsion of the abstract Other serves to deposit within the absolute something quite heterogeneous to it, to divide its path in two, into a speculative-dialectical one and another, quasi-dialectical one that is bereft of any ontological foundation. The system of dialectics is not aporetic, but diporetic. Even sublated, the in-itself of the universal, the feminine disease of immediate indifference, works its way within the absolute, and it is this which even impels the absolute, thereby distinguishing itself from itself, to posit its own difference. Without this relic of the feminine lodged within the absolute it would be unnecessary for 'science', upon attaining the ultimate unity between the knowing self and its objective self-presentation, to heave itself back into the form of sensuous consciousness (3: TWA, *Phen.*, 589–590). Only with this 'act of self-releasement from the form of its own self' has spirit finally extruded that residuum of immediacy which necessarily inheres in it, and opposed the latter to itself – precisely in order to return to it – as the natural time of sensuous consciousness. What impels the circling concept to restrict itself, to enter into the particular cycles of appearing knowledge, and thereby alone to find concrete form for itself as a circle of circles, is therefore pre-

cisely what characterized the position of the feminine in the process of
the genus: the undeveloped, still enfolded, in-itself of the universal,
abstract unity. Even sublated, the negativity of this unity is always only
caught out in the conceptual act of having sublated itself, always only
about to perform this sublation. The very process of sublation – with
and against Hegel's intention – sublates itself; splits in two, into one
part which stands and another part which, repeating the former, falls.
Thus the imago of a woman peers – one more time – through the veil
of the absolute, the imago of a Maria, perhaps, who brings a new
Christ, a new nature, to birth, of a Maria Magdalene, perhaps, of
another Cybele, or of a witch.

> *It is the cunning of a reason which cannot be measured
> according to the system of reason alone. Hegel never fails to
> underline with some emphasis the feminine features which
> belong to cunning. 'It is through cunning that the will has
> become feminine', he writes in the* Jenaer Realphilosophie
> *(24: JR, 199). With its universality and lack of specificity,
> cunning turns against the particularized masculine drive
> and itself seduces, albeit unknowingly, the determinacy of
> knowledge into revealing its own weakness. Even as cun-
> ning itself unknowingly grasps the other, the ambivalence
> and ambiguity of this universality itself cannot be grasped
> by the other. Cunning – reading – is a cat. '[T]hese are*
> pattes de velour, *and what are velvet paws for the one are
> claws for the other; but whenever one tries to protect one-
> self, one is only clutching at flowing silk that will not be
> caught? (ibid., 195). In the battle of the sexes between the
> universal and the differentiated will it is the universal,
> ontologically inadequate, feminine will which proves by
> far superior, representing as it does nothing but pretence,
> with no further substantial interest of its own beyond that
> of seducing particular subjectivity and leading it to
> destruction. Masculine subjectivity 'is directed as a being
> against* beings, *and rationally speaking against being
> (against something); but it is not in earnest, like a cape
> offered to the bull who runs at it without striking but is*

> struck itself' (ibid., 200). Over and beyond the unity of
> reason in love, even the absolute offers itself the cloak of
> cunning, and striking nothing, find itself struck, and,
> stricken, falls.

Hegel – once more – reads. Reads what has been read, reads the
unreadable, the absolute differentiated into the particular forms of the
concept. But this his self-reading, the absolute process, only attains an
immediate unity after all, one which is opposed to itself as an abstract
other. A reading with claws in him, and when he defends himself
against it, he finds he is clutching at silk, soft and smooth, something
fluid he cannot contain. In advance of him precisely there where it follows and obeys him, this reading is an irrecuperable presupposition of
itself, of Hegel himself.

> Friedrich Schlegel, whose irony, according to Hegel, merely
> attains to self-knowledge of the absolute in a purely formal
> fashion (10: TWA, Enc., III, §571) and thus for him
> remains unpalatable, inedible, 'neither fish nor flesh' –
> and here we should remember Hegel's characterization of
> femininity as the 'internal enemy' of universal self-con-
> sciousness and the 'eternal irony of the community' (3:
> TWA, Phen., 352) – Schlegel writes from Paris on 20
> March 1804 to his brother August Wilhelm: 'Even more
> nauseating to me, however, are these Hegelian pronounce-
> ments. – I doubt if I shall ever bring myself to read any-
> thing by this man ever again; my time is more and more
> precious to me.' (65: Nicolin, 56).

An urgent matter. The time released by the absolute proves a vomitive for the concept which sucks it back inside again. And if the infinite
present repels itself from itself, retches and enriches itself, renders itself
finite once again, this is because it was always already both more and
less than itself, always already simply the form of its own impossible
simultaneity. The concept, the eternal return, is finite and it is only
because it is finite that it must repeat (itself). Thus if this text, like
every other, if this reading, like every other, proves a vomitive, an
organism which detaches itself from itself and causes (itself) retching,
precisely to be able to repeat itself through such distantiation, then

only because this text, and this reading, no more correspond to one another than they have ever done. And every repetition – which repeats the tear no less than it repeats this reading and this text – every 'once again' fails to be sufficient, even if this one, this once, this more, is accomplished, can never be enough and is always too much. Every repetition, including that of this reading of this text, proves to be a complement only by simultaneously affirming a diminution. No repetition repeats.

Hegel – once more, wants more –

Abbreviations

The following abbreviations are used in citations of texts in this book (the numbers in parentheses refer to the numbered entries in the Bibliography, where full details may be found).

Aesthetics	*Hegel's Aesthetics*, tr. Knox (15)
Ästhetik	Hegel, *Vorlesungen über die Ästhetik*, Vols I (13), II (14) and III (15)
CJ	Kant, *Kritik der Urteilskraft* (52)
CPR	Kant, *Kritik der reinen Vernunft* (54)
CPV	Kant, *Kritik der praktischen Vernunft* (53)
Dok.	Hoffmeister, *Dokumente zu Hegels Entwicklung* (44)
Enc.	Hegel, *Enzyklopädie der philosophischen Wissenschaften*, Vol. I, *Die Wissenschaft der Logik* (8), Vol. II, *Die Naturphilosophie* (9) and Vol. III, *Philosophie des Geistes* (10)
GW	Freud, *Gesammelte Werke* (34)
Hist. Philosophy	Hegel, *Vorlesungen über die Geschichte der Philosophie*, Vols I (18), II (19) and III (20)
J	Mendelssohn, *Jerusalem oder über religiöse Macht und Judentum* (63)
JR	*Hegels Jenaer Realphilosophie: Die Vorlesungen von 1805–6*, ed. Hoffmeister (24)
Knox	*Hegel's Early Theological Writings*, tr. Knox (21)
MEW	Marx and Engels, *Marx–Engels Werke* (60)
Nicolin	Nicolin, *Hegel in Berichten seiner Zeitgenossen* (65)
Nohl	*Hegels Theologische Jugendschriften*, ed. Nohl (21)
Phen.	Hegel, *Phänomenologie des Geistes* (3)
Phil. History	Hegel, *Vorlesungen über die Philosophie der Geschichte* (12)

Phil. Rel.	Hegel, *Vorlesungen über die Philosophie der Religion*, Vols I (16) and II (17)
Religion . . .	Kant, *Religion innerhalb der Grenzen der blossen Vernunft* (55)
Ros.	Rosenkranz, *G. W. F. Hegels Leben* (73)
TWA	Hegel, *Theorie-Werkausgabe*, ed. Moldenhauer and Michel (1–20)

Bibliography of Cited Works by Hegel

Hegel, G. W. F.: *Theorie-Werkausgabe*, Hg. Eva Moldenhauer/ Karl Markus Michel (Frankfurt a. M.: Suhrkamp, 1969–1972) [cited in text as TWA + vol.; + page number where relevant]:

1 *Frühe Schriften:*
'Über die neuesten inneren Verhältnisse Württembergs'; E. Tr.: 'On the recent domestic affairs of Wurtemberg', T. M. Knox, *Hegel's Political Writings* (Oxford: Oxford University Press, 1964).
'Verfassung Deutschlands'; E. Tr.: 'The German Constitution', ibid.

2 *Jenaer Schriften 1801–1807:*
'Differenz des Fichteschen und Schellingschen Systems der Philosophie' (Differenzschrift); E. Tr.: *The Difference between Fichte's and Schelling's Systems of Philosophy*, H. S. Harris/W. Cerf (Albany: State University of New York Press, 1977).
'Glauben und Wissen oder Reflexionsphilosophie der Subjektivität in der Vollständigkeit ihrer Formen als Kantische, Jacobische und Fichtesche Philosophie'; E. Tr.: *Faith and Knowledge*, H. S. Harris/W. Cerf (Albany: State University of New York Press, 1977).
'Über die wissenschaftlichen Behandlungsarten des Naturrechts, seine Stelle in der praktischen Philosophie und sein Verhältnis zu den Rechtswissenschaften'; E. Tr.: *Natural Law: The Scientific Ways of Treating Natural Law, Its Place in Moral Philosophy, and Its Relation to the Positive Sciences of law*, T. M. Knox (Philadelphia: University of Pennsylvania Press, 1975).

3 *Phänomenologie des Geistes* [cited as *Phen.*]; E. Tr.: *Hegel's Phenomenology of Spirit*, A. V. Miller (Oxford: Clarendon Press, 1977).

4 *Nürnberger und Heidelberger Schriften 1808–1817*
   'Beurteilung des Verhandlungen in der Versammlung der
   Landstände des Königreichs Würrtembergs im Jahre 1815 und
   1816; E. Tr.: 'Proceedings of the Estates Assembly in the Kingdom
   of Würtemberg 1815–16', in *Hegel's Political Writings* (see 1 above).
5 *Wissenschaft der Logik I.* E. Tr.: see 6.
6 *Wissenschaft der Logik II.* E. Tr. of nos. 5 and 6: *Hegel's Science of
   Logic,* A. V. Miller (London: Allen & Unwin, 1969).
7 *Grundlinien der Philosophie des Rechts;* E. Tr.: *Hegel's Philosophy of
   Right,* T. M. Knox (Oxford: Oxford University Press, 1967).
8 *Enzyklopädie der philosophischen Wissenschaften I: Die Wissenschaften der Logik* [cited as Enc., I]; E. Tr.: *Hegel's Logic,* W.
   Wallace (Oxford: Clarendon Press, 1975).
9 *Enzyklopädie der philosophischen Wissenschaften II: Die
   Naturphilosophie* [cited as Enc., II]; E. Tr.: *Hegel's Philosophy of
   Nature,* A. V. Miller (Oxford: Clarendon Press, 1970).
10 *Enzyklopädie der philosophischen Wissenschaften III: Philosophie des
   Geistes* [cited as Enc., III]; E. Tr.: *Hegel's Philosophy of Mind,* W.
   Wallace (Oxford: Clarendon Press, 1971).
11 *Berliner Schriften 1818–1831*
   'Über die englische Reformbill'; E. Tr.: 'The English Reform Bill',
   in *Hegel's Political Writings* (see 1 above).
12 *Vorlesungen über die Philosophie der Geschichte* [cited as *Phil.
   History*]; E. Tr.: *Hegel's Philosophy of History,* J. Sibree (New York:
   Dover, 1956).
13 *Vorlesungen über die Ästhetik I* [cited as *Ästhetik*]; E. Tr.: see 15.
14 *Vorlesungen über die Ästhetik II* [cited as *Ästhetik*]; E. Tr.: see 15.
15 *Vorlesungen über die Ästhetik I* [cited as *Ästhetik*]; E. Tr. of 13, 14
   and 15: *Hegel's Aesthetics,* 2 vols, T. M. Knox (Oxford: Clarendon,
   1975) [cited as *Aesthetics*].
16 *Vorlesungen über die Philosophie der Religion I* [cited as *Phil. Rel.*];
   E. Tr.: see 17.
17 *Vorlesungen über die Philosophie der Religion II* [cited as *Phil. Rel.*];
   E. Tr. of 16 and 17: *Hegel's Lectures on the Philosophy of Religion I,
   II* and *III,* E. B. Speirs/J. Burdon Sanderson (London: Routledge,
   1962).

18 *Vorlesungen über die Geschichte der Philosophie I* [cited as *Hist. Philosophy*]; E. Tr.: see 20.

19 *Vorlesungen über die Geschichte der Philosophie II* [cited as *Hist. Philosophy*]; E. Tr.: see 20.

20 *Vorlesungen über die Geschichte der Philosophie III* [cited as *Hist. Philosophy*]; E. Tr. of 18, 19 and 20: *Lectures on the History of Philosophy*, 3 vols, E. S. Haldane/F. H. Simpson (London: Paul,. Trench & Trubner, 1892–6).

Other Writings by Hegel not included in the above:

21a *Hegels Theologische Jugendschriften*, Hg. Hermann Nohl (Tübingen: Mohr, 1907) [cited as Nohl]; E. Tr. (partial): *Hegel's Early Theological Writings*, T. M. Knox (Philadelphia: University of Pennsylvania Press, 1971) [cited as Knox].
'Die Religion ist eine' (the Tübingen Essay); 'Unter objecktiver Religion' (the Berne Plan of 1794); 'Das früheste Systemprogamm des deutscheen Idealismus' (The System-programme); 'Glauben ist die Art' (Frankfurt Sketch on 'Faith and Being'); 'Über Urteil und Sein' (Hölderlin's fragment 'Judgement and Being'): all translated in H. S. Harris, *Hegel's Development: Toward the Sunlight 1770–1801*, pp. 479–516 (Oxford: Clarendon Press, 1972).
Hegel: Three Essays (contains 'The Tübingen Essay'; 'Berne Fragments' and 'The Life of Jesus', tr. J. Dobbins/P. Fuss (Notre Dame, IN: Indiana University Press, 1984).

21b Hegel. Der Geist des christentums (Schriften, 1796–1800), ed. Werner Hamacher (Frankfurt: Ullstein 1978).

22 *Hegels Jenenser Logik, Metaphysik und Naturphilosophie*, Hg. Georg Lasson (Leipzig: Meiner Verlag, 1923); E. Tr. (partial): *The Jena System 1804–5: Logic and Metaphysics*, John Burbidge (Montreal and Kingston: McGill/Queen's University Press, 1986).

23 *Hegels Jenaer Systementwürfe I: Das System der spekulativen Philosophie*, Hg. Klaus Düsing/Heinz Kimmerle (Hamburg: Felix Meiner Verlag, 1986); E. Tr.: in H. S. Harris, *Hegel's System of Ethical Life and First Philosophy of Spirit* (see 25 below).

24 *Hegels Jenaer Realphilosophie: Die Vorlesungen von 1805–6*, Hg.
   J. Hoffmeister (Leipzig: Meiner, 1967) [cited as *JR*]; E. Tr.: *Hegel
   and the Human Spirit: A Translation of the Jena Lectures on the
   Philosophy of Spirit 1805–6*, Leo Rauch (Detroit: Wayne State
   University Press, 1986).
25 *Hegels System der Sittlichkeit* (Hamburg: Felix Meiner, 1967); E.
   Tr.: *Hegel's System of Ethical Life and First Philosophy of Spirit*,
   H. S. Harris/T. M. Knox (Albany: State University of New York
   Press, 19??).

General Bibliography of Cited Texts

26 Adelung: *Grammatisch-kritisches Wörterbuch der hochdeutschen
   Mundart* (Leipzig: 1793).
27 Adorno, Theodor: *Drei Studien zu Hegel* (Frankfurt: Suhrkamp,
   1969); E. Tr.: *Hegel: Three Studies*, Shierry Weber Nicholsen
   (Cambridge, MA: MIT Press, 1993).
28 Aristotle: *Physica*; E. Tr.: *Aristotle's Physics: Books 1 and 2*,
   W. Charlton (Oxford: Clarendon, 1970).
29 Baumgarten, Alexander G.: *Metaphysica* (Halle: 1743).
30 Beck, Lewis White: *Early German Philosophy* (Cambridge, MA:
   1969).
31 *Corpus Christianorum*: series Latina XL (Turnhout: 1956).
32 Derrida, Jacques: *Glas* (Paris: Galilée, 1974); E. Tr.: *Glas*, J. P.
   Leavey/Richard Rand (Lincoln, NB: University of Nebraska Press,
   1987).
33 ——: *Marges de la philosophie* (Paris: Les Editions de Minuit,
   1972); E. Tr.: *Margins of Philosophy*, Alan Bass (Brighton:
   Harvester, 1982).
34 Freud, Sigmund: *Gesammelte Werke* [GW]; E. Tr.: *Complete
   Psychological Works of Sigmund Freud* (London: Hogarth Press and
   Institute of Psychoanalysis, 1951).
35 ——: *Bruchstück einer Hysterie-Analyse* (1905: GW V); E. Tr.: vol. 7
   of *Complete Psychological Works*).
36 ——: *Fetischismus* (1927: GW XIV); E. Tr.: 'Fetishism' in Freud,
   On Sexuality (Harmondsworth: Penguin, pp. 347–57. 1977).

37 ———: *Das Medusenhaupt* (1922: GW XVII).

38 Freud, Sigmund: *Totem und Tabu* (1912: GW IX); E. Tr.: 'Totem and Tabu' in Freud, *The Origins of Religion* (Harmondsworth: Penguin, 1985).

39 Harris, H. S.: *Hegel's Development: Towards the Sunlight 1770–1801* (Oxford: Clarendon Press, 1972).

40 Haym, Rudolf: *Hegel und seine Zeit* (Berlin: Rudolph Gaertner, 1857).

41 Heidegger, Martin: *Unterwegs zur Sprache* (Pfullingen: Neske, 1959); E. Tr.: *On the Way to Language*, P. D. Gertz/Joan Stambaugh (New York: Harper & Row, 1966).

42 Heine, Heinrich: *Zur Geschichte der Religion und Philosophie in Deutschland* [1835] (Leipzig: 1970); E. Tr.: *Religion and Philosophy in Germany*, J. Snodgrass (London: 1882).

43 Henrich, Dieter: *Hegel im Kontext* (Frankfurt: Suhrkamp Verlag, 1971).

44 Hoffmeister, Johannes: *Dokumente zu Hegels Entwicklung* (Stuttgart: Fromann Verlag, 1936) [cited as *Dok.*].

45 Hölderlin, Friedrigh: *Sämtliche Werke* (Grosse Stuttgarter Ausgabe), Hg. Friedrich Beissner/Adolf Beck, 8 Bände (Stuttgart: Kohlhammer, 1946–85).

46 ———: *Friedrich Hölderlin: Essays and Letters on Theory*, ed. and tr. Thomas Pfau (Albany: State University of New York Press, 1988).

47 ———: *Friedrich Hölderlin: Poems and Fragments*, tr. Michael Hamburger (London: Anvil Press Poetry, 1994).

48 Irenaeus: *Adversus Haereses* (Kempten: 1912).

49 Jonas, Hans: *Gnosis und spätantiker Geist* (Göttingen: 1964).

50 Kant, Immanuel: *Kants Gesammelte Schriften*, 22 Bände (Akademie Ausgabe), (Berlin: Georg Reimer/Walter de Gruyter, 1910 ff.).

51 ———: *Anthropologie in pragmatischer Hinsicht*, E. Tr.: *Anthropology from a Pragmatic Point of View*, M. J. Gregor (The Hague: Marinus Nijhoff, 1974).

52 ———: *Kritik der Urteilskraft* [cited as *CJ*]; E. Tr.: *Critique of Judgement: Including the first Introduction*, W. S. Pluhar (Indianapolis: Hackett, 1987).

53 Kant, Immanuel: *Kritik der praktischen Vernunft* [cited as *CPrR*]; E. Tr.: *Critique of Practical Reason*, Lewis White Beck (Indianapolis: Bobbs-Merrill, 1956).

54 ——: *Kritik der reinen Vernunft* [cited as *CPR*]; E. Tr.: *Critique of Pure Reason*, Norman Kemp Smith (2nd edn, London: Macmillan, 1933).

55 ——: *Religion innerhalb der Grenzen der blossen Vernunft* [cited as *Religion . . .*]; E. Tr.: *Religion within the Limits of Reason Alone*, T. M. Greene/H. H. Hudson (New York: Harper & Row, 1960).

56 Kierkgaard, S.: *Concluding Unscientific Postscript to the Philosophical Fragments*, tr. David F. Swenson/Walter Lowrie (Princeton: Princeton University Press, 1941).

57 Lacan, Jacques: *Écrits* (Paris: Editions de Seuil, 1966), E. Tr.: *Écrits: a Selection*, Alan Sheridan (London: Tavistock, 1977).

58 Lessing, Gotthold Ephraim: *Sämtliche Schriften*, Hg. K. Lachmann, 3rd edn, Rev. F. Muncker, 23 vols (Berlin: de Gruyter, 1886–1924).

59 ——: *Laocoon, Nathan the Wise, Minna von Barnhelm*, tr. W. A. Steel/A. Dent (London: Everyman, 1930).

60 Marx, Karl/Engels, Friedrich: *Marx–Engels Werke* [cited as *MEW*] (Berlin: Dietz Verlag, 1956–68).

61 ——: *On the Jewish Question* (MEW I), in Karl Marx, *Early Writings*, tr. Rodney Livingstone/Gregor Benton (Harmondsworth: Penguin, 1975).

62 ——: *Capital*, vols 1 and 2, tr. Ben Fowkes and David Fernbach (Harmondsworth: Penguin, 1976 and 1978).

63 Mendelssohn, Moses: *Jerusalem oder über religiöse Macht und Judentum* (Berlin: 1783) [cited as *J*]. E. Tr.: Jerusalem, and other writings on Judaism, Alfred Jospe (New York: Schocken 1969).

64 *Missale Romanum*: 'De defectibus in celebratione Missarum occurrentibus' (Ratisbon: 1953).

65 Nicolin, Günther, Hg.: *Hegel in Berichten seiner Zeitgenossen* (Hamburg: Meiner Verlag, 1970) [cited as Nicolin].

66 Nietzsche, Friedrich: *Werke in drei Bänden*, Hg. Karl Schlechta (Munich: 1966).

67 ——: *Der Antichrist*; E. Tr.: *The Antichrist*, Walter Kaufmann, in *The Portable Nietzsche* (New York: Viking Press, 1954).

68 Nietzsche, Friedrich: *Ecce Homo*; E. Tr.: *Ecce Homo*, Walter Kaufmann (New York: Vintage Press, 1968).

69 ——: *Die fröhliche Wissenschaft*; E. Tr.: *The Gay Science*, Walter Kaufmann (New York: Vintage Press, 1974).

70 ——: *Thus Spoke Zarathustra*, Walter Kaufmann in *The Portable Nietzsche* (New York: Viking Press, 1954).

71 ——: *Zur Genealogie der Moral*; E. Tr.: *On the Genealogy of Morals*, Walter Kaufmann/R. J. Hollingdale (New York: Vintage Press, 1968).

72 Novalis (Friedrich von Hardenberg): *Schriften*, Hg. Richard Samuel (Stuttgart: Kohlhammer, 1968).

73 Rosenkranz, Karl: *G. W. F. Hegels Leben* (Berlin: 1844; reprinted, Darmstadt; Wissenschaftliche Buchgesellschaft, 1977) [cited as Ros.].

74 Rousseau, Jean-Jacques: *Oeuvres* (Paris: 1820).

75 Sartre, Jean-Paul: *L'Etre et le Néant* (Paris: Gallimard, 1943); E. Tr.: *Being and Northingness: An Essay on Phenomenological Ontology*, Hazel Barnes (London: Methuen, 1969).

76 Schelling, Friedrich Wilhelm Joseph von: *Sämtliche Werke*, Hg. K. F. A. Schelling, 14 Bände (Stuttgart/Augsburg: 1856 ff.).

77 ——: *Werke*, Hg. Manfred Schröter, 6 Bände (Munich, 1927–8; 2 supplementary volumes, 1943 and 1956).

78 Schlegel, Friedrich: *Kritische Ausgabe*, Hg. E. Behler (Paderborn: 1962).

79 Schmidt, J. C. von: *Schwäbisches Wörterbuch mit etymologischen und historischen Anmerkungen* (Stuttgart: 1831).

80 Scholem, Gerschom: *Ursprung und Anfänge der Kabbala* (Berlin: 1962).

81 Spitz, H.-J.: *Die Metaphorik des geistigen Schriftsinns* (Munich: 1972).

82 Strachey, James: 'Some unconscious factors in reading', in the *International Journal of Psychoanalysis*, vol. XI (London: 1930).

83 Wolff, Christian: *Philosophia Prima sive Ontologia* (1730).

84 ——: *Philosophia rationalis sive Logica* (1728).